The Fall of Interpretation

Philosophical Foundations for a Creational Hermeneutic

James K. A. Smith

InterVarsity Press
Downers Grove, Illinois

InterVarsity Press
P.O. Box 1400, Downers Grove, IL 60515
World Wide Web: www.ivpress.com
E-mail: mail@ivpress.com

InterVarsity Press® is the book-publishing division of InterVarsity Christian Fellowship/USA®, a student movement active on campus at hundreds of universities, colleges and schools of nursing in the United States of America, and a member movement of the International Fellowship of Evangelical Students. For information about local and regional activities, write Public Relations Dept., InterVarsity Christian Fellowship/USA, 6400 Schroeder Rd., P.O. Box 7895, Madison, WI 53707-7895.

Scripture quotations, unless otherwise noted, are from the New Revised Standard Version of the Bible, copyright 1989 by the Division of Christian Education of the National Council of the Churches of Christ in the USA. Used by permission. All rights reserved.

Cover photograph: Scala/Art Resource, N.Y.

ISBN 0-8308-1574-0

Printed in the United States of America ∞

Library of Congress Cataloging-in-Publication Data

Smith, James K. A., 1970-
    The fall of interpretation : philosophical foundations for a creational hermeneutic /
James K. A. Smith
    p. cm.
    Includes bibliographical references and index.
    ISBN 0-8308-1574-0 (alk. paper)
    1. Hermeneutics. 2. Hermeneutics—Religious aspects—Christianity. I. Title.
BD241.S595 2000
121'.686—dc21
                                                                    00-024893

15 14 13 12 11 10 9 8 7 6 5 4 3 2 1

10 09 08 07 06 05 04 03 02 01 00

For Deanna,
who has made all the difference

CONTENTS

Preface

In many respects the *telos* of this book lies beyond its scope, outside the margins, just as its *archē*. In good Pentecostal fashion, and following the model of Augustine, the project of this book is born out of my own *experience* of interpretive difference, or more specifically, the experience of having interpretations that differed from the interpretations of those who thought themselves to be in possession of the one true interpretation—which was not an interpretation at all but simply what God said. (Augustine has something to say about them in his *Confessions* 12.) While it may not be immediately evident, this book has an ecclesial destination grounded in its ecclesial genesis. As those closest to me would know, it reads as something of an *apologia* on behalf of difference within the community. And, as has become increasingly evident to myself, it is a book that has been penned with wounds. Having been at times excluded from my own tradition for being *too* different, the project of this book is to make space for difference within our communities.

But while the book's impetus is found in this experience of exclusion, its writing has been made possible by the welcoming and healing communities that we have since been a part of, one during its conception and gestation, the other during its labor and birth. I would like to here say a special thank you to Rev. Charles Swartwood, Patrick and Dorothy St. Pierre and the saints at Bethel Pentecostal Tabernacle, who embraced us as we made our way up to Pentecost. Thanks also to Rev. Ron Billings, Rev. Al Wise, David and Stephanie Burton, and our brothers and sisters at Horsham Christian Fellowship and Del Aire Assembly of God, who have encouraged us to keep the feast. It will be a surprise to many, but not to us, that these Pentecostal communities have been a source of unflagging support for my academic endeavors.

The production of this book has also spanned several academic communities. Its deepest roots lie in the tradition of the first, the Institute for Christian Studies, where I learned to think as a Christian. In particular, I would like to thank Jim Olthuis, who was truly a mentor, granting me the freedom to be creative and guiding me through a period of academic growth with deep existential roots. Thanks also to Richard Middleton for his constant encouragement and model of Christian scholarship, and to Shane Cudney, who is not only a colleague but a cotraveler with me on this journey. I count it a blessing to call him my friend. For several years I was nourished by my colleagues in the department of philosophy at Villanova University. In particular, I want to thank Dr. James McCartney, O.S.A., for his encouragement and interest in my work and for permitting me the opportunity to explore these matters in courses on Augustine. One of the wonderful privileges of moving from ICS to Villanova was the fact that John Caputo, whose writing has had significant impact on my thought, has now become a personal mentor. I deeply appreciate his openness and encouragement and continue to value his work, but most of all I am grateful for his friendship. Finally, my colleagues at Loyola Marymount University have welcomed me and provided encouragement during the final stages, and my assisant Bil Van Otterloo provided much help with the proofs and index.

Without my family this work would never have been accomplished. Thanks to my parents, Pat and Dale, for their interest and encouragement, and to my wife's parents, Gary and Gerry, for their support and understanding. Jennifer and Jessica have been there for us whenever we needed them; I hope they know how much we love and appreciate them. It is also a special treasure to call my brother, Scott, my best friend. And I would be amiss not to mention the steady prayers and support of my wife's grandmother Doris Currie, who exemplifies for us Christian devotion and love for her family. She has helped us in more ways than one.

Finally, I owe a special debt to my wife and children. Often when my colleagues learn that we have four young children at home, they ask, "How do you ever get anything done?" The fact is, I could never have done it without them. Deanna, your love and support is nothing short of astonishing. When I think of all that you give for me, I stand as Gomer stood before Hosea, awed and wondering how someone could give so generously and selflessly. Grayson, Coleson, Madison and Jackson—you are everything to me: it is in your smiles that I find God every single day. It was a hard lesson to learn, hardest for you, but I would drop everything for those smiles.

Acknowledgments

Portions of chapter one have been adapted from my earlier essay "How to Avoid Not Speaking: Attestations" (in *Knowing Other-wise: Philosophy on the Threshold of Spirituality*, Perspectives in Continental Philosophy, ed. James H. Olthuis [Bronx, N.Y.: Fordham University Press, 1997], pp. 217-34) and are included here by permission. An earlier version of chapter four was published as "Originary Violence: The Fallenness of Interpretation in Derrida" (*Concept* 19 [1996]: 27-41) and is included here by permission of the editors. Finally, selected sections of chapter five are developed from "The Time of Language: The Fall to Interpretation in Early Augustine" (in *The Proceedings of the ACPA*, ACPQ 72 [1998]: 185-99) and are used here by permission. Thanks to all of the editors and publishers for their permission to use these materials here.

Part of the research and writing of this book was made possible by a generous fellowship from the Social Sciences and Humanities Research Council of Canada, whose support is gratefully acknowledged.

Abbreviations

BT   Heidegger, Martin. *Being and Time.* Translated by John Macquarrie and Edward Robinson. New York: Harper & Row, 1962.

CSA   Augustine. *Confessions.* Translated by Henry Chadwick. Oxford: Oxford University Press, 1991.

FL   Derrida, Jacques. "Force of Law: The 'Mystical Foundation of Authority.'" Translated by Mary Quaintance. In *Deconstruction and the Possibility of Justice.* Edited by Drucilla Cornell et al. New York: Routledge, 1992, pp. 3-67.

FT   Lints, Richard. *The Fabric of Theology: A Prolegomenon to Evangelical Theology.* Grand Rapids, Mich.: Eerdmans, 1993.

HCU   Habermas, Jürgen. "On Hermeneutics' Claim to Universality." In *The Hermeneutics Reader.* Edited by Kurt Mueller-Vollmer. New York: Continuum, 1985, pp. 294-319.

JG   Lyotard, Jean-François, and Jean-Loup Thébaud. *Just Gaming.* Translated by Wlad Godzich. Minneapolis: University of Minnesota Press, 1985.

MB   Derrida, Jacques. *Memoirs of the Blind: The Self Portrait and Other Ruins.* Translated by Pascale-Anne Brault and Michel Naas. Chicago: University of Chicago Press, 1993.

MIG   Pannenberg, Wolfhart. *Metaphysics and the Idea of God.* Translated by Philip Clayton. Grand Rapids, Mich.: Eerdmans, 1990.

OBBE Levinas, Emmanuel. *Otherwise Than Being or Beyond Essence.* Translated by Alphonso Lingis. The Hague: Martinus Nijhoff, 1981.

14 THE FALL OF INTERPRETATION

OG   Derrida, Jacques. *Of Grammatology*. Translated by Gayatri Chakra-
      vorty Spivak. Baltimore: Johns Hopkins University Press, 1976.

OHF   Heidegger, Martin. *Ontologie (Hermeneutik der Faktizität)*. Edited by
      Kate Bröcker-Oltmanns. Vol. 63 of Gesamtausgabe. Frankfurt: Vit-
      torio Klostermann, 1988.

OLOF Koivisto, Rex A. *One Lord, One Faith: A Theology for Cross-Denomi-
      national Renewal*. Wheaton, Ill.: Bridgepoint/Victor, 1993.

OS   Derrida, Jacques. *Of Spirit: Heidegger and the Question*. Translated
      by Geoffrey Bennington and Rachel Bowlby. Chicago: University
      of Chicago Press, 1989.

PC   Derrida, Jacques. *The Post Card: From Socrates to Freud and Beyond*.
      Translated by Alan Bass. Chicago: University of Chicago Press, 1987.

PIA   Heidegger, Martin. *Phänomenologische Interpretationen zu Aristote-
      les: Einführung in die Phänomenologische Forschung*. Edited by
      Walter Bröcker and Kate Bröcker-Oltmanns. Vol. 61 of Gesamtaus-
      gabe. Frankfurt: Vittorio Klostermann, 1985.

PIRA Heidegger, Martin. "Phenomenological Interpretations with
      Respect to Aristotle: Indication of the Hermeneutical Situation."
      In *Man and World* 25 (1992): 355-93. Translated by Michael Baur.

PMC   Lyotard, Jean-François. *The Postmodern Condition: A Report on
      Knowledge*. Translated by Geoff Bennington and Brian Massumi.
      Minneapolis: University of Minnesota Press, 1984.

ST   Pannenberg, Wolfhart. *Systematic Theology*, vols. 1 and 2. Translated
      by Geoffrey W. Bromiley. Grand Rapidsm, Mich.: Eerdmans, 1991,
      1994.

TB   Derrida, Jacques. "Des Tours de Babel." In *A Derrida Reader:
      Between the Blinds*. Translated by Joseph F. Graham. Edited by
      Peggy Kamuf. New York: Columbia University Press, 1991, pp.
      244-53.

TI   Levinas, Emmanuel. *Totality and Infinity.* Translated by Alphonso Lingis. Pittsburgh: Duquesne University Press, 1969.

TM   Gadamer, Hans-Georg. *Truth and Method.* Translated by Joel Weinsheimer and Donald G. Marshall. Rev. ed. New York: Continuum, 1989.

Introduction

Interpretation
& the Fall

However one wants to characterize it—
whether as finitude, limit, mortality, opinion, partiality,
mutability, or immanence—
the first topic of philosophy has generally been taken
to be something to be overcome.

DENNIS J. SCHMIDT
The Ubiquity of the Finite: Hegel,
Heidegger and the Entitlements of Philosophy

Interpretation has long been a sin. Understood as a postlapsarian phenomenon from which humanity must be redeemed, hermeneutics has traditionally been linked with the curse and banishment from the Garden. Interpretation, in short, is a result of the Fall, is itself a fall—from the intelligible to the sensible, from immediacy to mediation, from reading to hermeneutics. As the medieval poet Dante tells the story, the nature of the Fall itself was the transgression of the sign *(il trapassar del segno)*,[1] a lawless semiotic act that initiated the tragic history of interpretation and corrupted the previous immediacy Adam enjoyed in Eden. Hermeneutics is something to be overcome by redemption, whereby the curse of interpretation will be removed in a hermeneutical paradise where interpretation is absent.

Having been banished from the Garden, Adam and his progeny were plagued by the curse of interpretation and the interpolation of a hermeneutical space, but when paradise is regained, it is hermeneutics itself that is banished. Thus Adam in *Paradise* can proclaim to Dante, "Even if thou tell it not to me, I can discern thy wish, with greater ease than thou canst know what seems to be most sure. For I can see it in the Glass[2] of Truth, which is Itself reflector of all things, but which itself can never be reflected."[3] The redeemed Adam stands as the towering master hermeneut who is in fact no hermeneut at all precisely because his knowledge is not vexed by the mediation of interpretation but is rather an immediate access.[4]

Or so the story goes. It should be noted, however, that this comedic tale does not unfold only in medieval philosophers and poets. In many ways it is as ancient as the origins of Western philosophy. Further, it continues to be told in our own era, by traditions as diverse as Christian theology and contemporary continental philosophy.[5] In sectors of both of these traditions, I will argue, interpretation remains inextricably linked to the Fall and fallenness: interpretation arrives upon the scene *after Eden* as a curse, a postlapsarian disease (or perhaps an originary lapse). The task of this book is to explore various understandings of interpretation in light of these common categories of "creation" and "fall."

As such, the book is characterized by two movements: the first movement is a critical analysis of the way in which interpretation has been linked to the Fall in the theological and philosophical tradition. Throughout this critical exposition I will argue that such a link between hermeneutics and fallenness contradicts an integral Christian understanding of human finitude and language. Drawing on alternative aspects within evangelical theology and continental philosophy, the second, constructive movement (in part three) involves sketching the contours of a philosophical hermeneutic that considers language and finitude on the basis of

an affirmation of the goodness of creation. Two initial points in
this regard should be noted.

Models of Interpretations of Interpretation

First of all, I must emphasize that my task is not to examine how
various authors or traditions interpret; that is, I am not interested
primarily in their hermeneutics. My focus is how these authors
and traditions understand interpretation itself: What status do they
accord to the "act" of interpretation? What does an author understand to be happening in the process of reading? What valuation is
accorded to interpretation? In brief, my question is *not,* how does a
philosophical and theological tradition interpret this text? but
rather, how does the tradition interpret *interpretation* itself? As
such, my goal is to disclose not the hermeneutical processes of the
authors below but rather their construal of interpretation as a
human activity—their "interpretations of interpretation."[6] The
project of this book is, then (if I may use such a prodigious prefix),
meta-hermeneutical—which, of course, remains hermeneutical.

   In a sense my aim is to expound each author or tradition (corresponding to chapters below) as *models* of how interpretation is
understood. This employment of "models" is now commonplace,
particularly in theology[7] and specifically in discussions regarding
hermeneutics. A now-classic work is David Kelsey's *The Use of
Scripture in Recent Theology,*[8] which describes how the Bible is read
or functions in various authors by encapsulating them in seven
models. In a similar vein John Goldingay proposed four models for
Scripture[9] and more recently has attempted to outline similar models for the interpretation of Scripture.[10] The work of Kelsey and
Goldingay, however, remains at the level of hermeneutical principles, constructing models of how various traditions and theologians interpret and employ Scripture in theology. Neither of these
authors really addresses how interpretation itself is construed in
these contexts.

   My goal, then, is to take one further step back and analyze (1) how various philosophers and theologians understand the role of interpretation in "knowing," (2) what status they accord to the result of interpretation, and (3) how they conceive of the relationship between hermeneutics and human "be-ing."[11] These matters will be uncovered, for instance, in considering the scope that each author attributes to interpretation, or how someone understands the relationship between reading and interpretation, or the way in which "interpretation" is contrasted with or related to "knowledge."[12] What I am attempting to uncover remains largely un-thought in most theologians and, I will contend, a number of philosophers. To construct models of such interpretations of interpretation, one must work at a level of indirectly unveiled assumptions and commitments. This method should become clearer in later chapters.

Let me say another word about my use of *models*. Each chapter considers one or two theologians and philosophers and attempts to piece together how they understand the role and status of interpretation. I have chosen to focus on representative works that flesh out several models that I see operating in much of traditional and contemporary thought. In this book, then, each *part* represents a model, and each *chapter* depicts a variation of that model—a model within a model, if you will.

Chapter one considers Rex Koivisto and Richard Lints as representatives of certain aspects (but not the entirety) of contemporary evangelical theology where hermeneutics is understood as originating in the Fall. Interpretation, from this perspective, is a mediation that is to be overcome, restoring a prelapsarian immediacy. Eden, which was lost (but is now regained), was a paradise of perpetual connection: a hermeneutical paradise because of the *absence* of hermeneutics. Koivisto and Lints, then, represent what I will call a *present immediacy model*, which is something of a realized eschatology: the curse of interpretation is lifted here and now (for the evangelical Christian, that is). Though I focus on Koivisto and Lints, many others could be located in this model; these others will often be referred to in endnotes, but they will not be discussed extensively.

In chapter two I focus on the work of German theologian Wolfhart Pannenberg as a representative of a "dim-mirror hermeneutic," or an *eschatological immediacy model*. For Pannenberg also, interpretation is a state of affairs from which humanity must be redeemed. However, this overcoming does not occur until the eschaton, until the end of time, at which time immediacy will be restored. In this model I will also refer to Hans-Georg Gadamer's philosophical hermeneutics and Jürgen Habermas's critical theory as further examples.

In both of these chapters (which compose part one) we see theologians and philosophers who consider hermeneutics to be a result of the Fall and who understand interpretation as somehow fallen. In addition, both models posit a time when this state of affairs is overcome. These thinkers express the confident hope of overcoming and escaping human finitude, and they represent yet another chapter in a long philosophical story of ascent to the Absolute and Unconditioned.

In part two, however, we will engage two philosophers who also understand hermeneutics as fallen but who have no desire or dream of overcoming or escaping this condition. They have no memories of a prelapsarian paradise nor any expectations for an eschatological heavenly city. Thus for Martin Heidegger (chapter three), hermeneutics is always violent because it constantly struggles against the pull to everydayness—the everyday temptation of being-in-the-world. Further, human being-in-the-world is "essentially" fallen for Heidegger, and it is characterized by a structural "concern" that St. Paul (whom Heidegger is drawing on) connects with absorption in the world (1 Cor 7). However, Heidegger effects an essentialization of this absorption in the world, understanding it as a structural aspect of finite, human existence.

Jacques Derrida, I will contend in chapter four, operates within a similar model. According to him interpretation is always a violent act, an incision, a cut, which necessarily excludes and amputates.

The fall is not *from* presence but always already *within* presence.[13] Misunderstanding and misinterpretation are built into the structure of the sign and system of signifiers. Every interpretation is a decision; every decision is "structurally finite" and, as such, "structurally violent." Hermeneutics, which is constitutive of human be-ing, is always already violent and a violation; thus to be human is to do violence.

Both Heidegger and Derrida represent a model that I may describe as a *violent mediation model.* Again, many others could be situated in this description, particularly Emmanuel Levinas, whom I will discuss only briefly.

In part three I will propose a *creational model* of interpretation— in contrast to the models described above—drawing on resources found in (a non-Platonic) Augustine.[14] Briefly intimated, this model understands interpretation and hermeneutical mediation as constitutive aspects of human being-in-the-world. As such it contrasts with the immediacy models above, which contend that the space of interpretation can be closed. I will argue that this is a vain hope that attempts to overcome fundamental aspects of being human (and being a creature), aspects such as the finitude and locality of human existence.

But further, in contrast to Heidegger and Derrida, a creational-pneumatic hermeneutic does not understand this necessity and inescapability of interpretation as a violent state of affairs but rather as an aspect of a good, peaceful creation. Hermeneutics is not a postlapsarian phenomenon, coming upon the scene "after Eden." Instead interpretation is found "in Eden" and is thus included in the pronouncement of goodness (Gen 1:31). Hermeneutics, then, is not an evil to be overcome (or in the case of Derrida, an inescapable, violent state of affairs) but rather an aspect of creation and human life that ought to be affirmed as "good."

Such a (demythologized)[15] Augustinian[16] hermeneutic would link Augustine's insights on the temporality of human be-ing and language with his affirmation of the fundamental goodness of creation; the result is an understanding of the *status* of interpretation as a "creational" task, a task that is constitutive of finitude and thus not a "labor" to be escaped or overcome. Such an "interpretation of interpretation" *re*-values embodiment and ultimately ends in an ethical respect for difference as the gift of a creating God who loves difference and who loves differently. The heart of a creational hermeneutic is also rather "Pentecostal," creating a space where there is room for a plurality of God's creatures to speak, sing and dance in a multivalent chorus of tongues.

Model	Creation/ Fall	Im/Mediacy	Proponents
Present Immediacy	Hermeneutics as result of Fall	Mediation overcome in the present	Lints, Koivisto
Eschatological Immediacy ("dim-mirror" model)	Hermeneutics as result of Fall	Mediation overcome in the future *(chronos* or *kairos)*	Pannenberg, Gadamer, Habermas
Violent Mediation	Hermeneutics is constitutive of human be-ing but is also structurally violent	Mediation cannot be overcome, and thus neither can violence.	Heidegger, Derrida
Creational Hermeneutic	Hermeneutics is constitutive of creaturehood but also, as created, is structurally good.	Mediation cannot be overcome but is an aspect of creaturehood; violence is possible and real but not necessary.	[Augustine]

Figure 1. Models of interpretations of interpretation

I have outlined the four models explored in this book not only to indicate my direction but also to demonstrate how I understand

these models to function. They must not be understood as definitive, airtight boxes that encapsulate and enframe each thinker, let
alone a "tradition."[17] They are intended to function as *heuristic
devices* that are not definitive but are nevertheless helpful in ascer-
taining differences and contrasts.[18] These models are necessarily
constructions: they are fictions, but they are useful fictions that
attempt to describe how interpretation is understood by several different thinkers and traditions. They also provide us with the opportunity to uncover similarities that throughout this book will also be
a fundamental point of critique: namely, the connection between
interpretation and the violence of fallenness. Finally, I think these
models will prove useful inasmuch as they help to situate other
philosophers and theologians in the spectrum (which I will
attempt to some extent, largely in endnotes).[19] In this respect this
book is a kind of workshop, one that tries to give the reader a
framework or constellation in which to critically think about these
matters and to then apply them to other contexts—and all of this
toward the goal of developing an understanding of philosophical
hermeneutics in Christian perspective.

When I emphasize that these models are simply heuristic
devices, then it is not expected that individuals will "fit" into these
descriptions. My use of models is in fact an exercise in what I am
theoretically arguing for in this book: that description and interpretation are violent only if they operate against an expectation of full
presence—an expectation of perfect representation unconditioned
by finitude. Because I have no pretensions of "categorization," I
have no difficulty in employing these descriptive devices. Contemporary continental philosophy would insist that these models "fail"
to define each thinker and thereby do violence to her or him. But I
will contend that this fails and is violent only if we remain haunted
by a ghost of full presence.[20] As will be discussed much more fully
below, what is at stake here are the way in which we *use* concepts
and the *status* we grant to our interpretations. These models are
not violent, I contend, because they do not *claim* to be encompass-

ing, to "grasp" or "seize" a thinker's idea by a label or concept *(con-capere)*.[21]

On the Categories "Creation" and "Fall"

I stated above that the task of this book is to explore various understandings of interpretation in light of the common categories of "creation" and "Fall." So far I have addressed the issue of models as an attempt to uncover the status and role of interpretation in the philosophers and theologians that will be considered.

A second issue that must be addressed is the usefulness or legitimacy of the categories of creation and Fall. This is an issue only because this project spills over the disciplinary boundaries of theology and philosophy.[22] The terms *creation* and *Fall* are common parlance in theology, but can this terminology be transported into philosophical discourse? Is this not faith language and therefore inadmissible in philosophy? If this is the case, Heidegger and Derrida are not aware of it. Notions of the Fall and fallenness occupy important theoretical places in the early work of Heidegger and Derrida, although both are insistent and persistent in denying that these notions have any connection with theology. Heidegger contends that the analysis of fallenness in his early period "has nothing to do with any doctrine of the corruption of human nature or any theory of original sin."[23] Nevertheless, the Fall remains a live category for both of these philosophers and others, even if creation does not. My object is to take up this discourse and to understand why Heidegger, Derrida and others retain such terminology, particularly given its theological roots.

The categories of creation and Fall, then, lend themselves as helpful tools or points of contact in the ensuing discussion. They function, despite all of Heidegger's protests to the contrary, as "evaluative indicators" with regard to interpretation and hermeneutics—and more generally, with regard to human existence in general. My constructive proposal in part three attempts to make creation a live philosophical category for understanding the nature of hermeneutics as constitutive of human be-ing. Interpretation, as I will argue, is *creational;* it is an inescapable state of affairs that accompanies the finitude of creaturehood and, since it is an aspect of creation, is "good." While this will be unfolded in more detail in chapters five and six, I would like to open a space here for these categories to be heard and not dismissed out of hand as simply another naive appropriation of a very old metaphysic.

In some respects, any attempt to translate the categories of creation and Fall into philosophical language ends up implicating them in a side of the Western tradition that I am attempting to avoid. However, I am willing to briefly take that risk in order to indicate my understanding of these terms. When I speak of interpretation as "creational," I mean that the need to interpret is "essential" to human be-ing; hermeneutics is "by nature" part of human existence. I am, in a certain sense, saying that interpretation is a "normative" state of affairs, "constitutive" of human life—what Heidegger would describe as an "existentiale." This would be in contrast to Lints and Pannenberg who, when they link interpretation to the Fall, are basically saying that hermeneutics is "accidental" or "anormative" and not a constitutive aspect of human experience. That is very different from Heidegger and Derrida, who by no means understand interpretation as something that can be eradicated; that is, Heidegger, Derrida and I agree about the inescapability of interpretation for human beings. However, we diverge when they relate this to fallenness—albeit a fallenness without creation (a fall *within,* not a fall *from*)—as "essentially fallen" (*BT* 264-65).

For Heidegger and Derrida, fallenness does not describe the anormativity of interpretation but rather the *violence* of interpretation. In contrast, my creational hermeneutic contends that if interpretation is constitutive of human be-ing and creaturehood, then it must be "good" and not necessarily or essentially violent (though it is nevertheless distorted and corrupted by the Fall). If to interpret is *ipso facto* violent and if interpretation is constitutive of human existence or creaturehood, then being human would mean being necessarily violent. But if human life as created is "good," then this cannot be the case—though again we emphasize that understanding hermeneutics as "creational" does not deny that we now inhabit a broken, fallen creation. But the effect of the Fall is not the appearance of interpretation but rather the distortion or corruption of interpretation.[24]

My proposal, then, is "simultaneously very far from and very near to Heidegger's [and Derrida's]" (*PC* 66). The state of affairs that Heidegger and Derrida are describing as fallen and violent, I am portraying as creational and good. We all agree, however, that this state of affairs is a necessary aspect of human experience, in contrast to Lints and Pannenberg. On the other hand, along with Lints and other evangelicals I believe in the goodness of creation and the hope for restoration. But again, in contrast with certain aspects of this theological tradition, I do not identify this with immediacy or full presence; instead hermeneutical mediation is the necessary accompaniment of the finitude of human life.

I have not yet addressed a significant issue: my belief in the goodness of creation and the question of "hermeneutic violence." I will leave an explication of this until chapter six. Let me note here, however, that I am not unaware of the problems associated with this assumption, particularly for those who do not share it. It is precisely this point that lies at the heart of my disagreement with Derrida. I am opting, it may be said, for what John D. Caputo describes as the "religious" construal of the world (as exemplified in Søren Kierkegaard) over against the "tragic" understanding of Nietzsche.[25] Both stare into the "abyss" of a broken world and see something very different: Kierkegaard, looking through the eyes of faith, sees a world broken by sin but also sees an Incarnate God who comes to restore.

I must remind myself, however, that Zarathustra's laughter echoes in Abraham's ears, haunting Abraham's decision. Nevertheless (and I must leave a more extended discussion of this until chapter six), I would also remind Caputo and Derrida that, given the "fact" of undecidability, Zarathustra must sometimes lie awake at night wondering whether Abraham is right; that is, if my faith in the goodness of creation is a "construal," Heidegger's and Derrida's (and Nietzsche's) "belief" in the violence of human existence is no less a construal.

It is my hope that the usefulness of these categories will demonstrate itself in the following chapters. My goal in this brief introduction was to open a space for these categories to be used without being initially dismissed as simple neoscholastic retrievals.

A Note on a Note from Caputo's *Against Ethics*

But isn't it a little late for creation? Have we not arrived on the scene long after such an idea (let alone an event) has been relegated to a history that is better forgotten—a history of "violence and metaphysics"? Is not this proposal for speaking of interpretation "in" or "after" Eden rather quaint, and perhaps even a little humorous? And is it not also horrifying or at least horrifyingly irresponsible? For who could responsibly speak of Eden after Auschwitz? Are we not everywhere encompassed only by the tragedy of fallenness and a ruptured world? Creation, at this time (in history)—or at least talk of creation—would seem both philosophically and ethically problematic. If I am going to be able to speak of a "creational" hermeneutic, it will be important to first respond to these challenges.

The first (philosophical) kind of criticism locates creation in a metaphysical tradition tied to the Infinite and thereby implicated in a story that purportedly ended with Hegel. To speak, as I will, of creation and finitude in this "postmetaphysical" age is to lapse into a naive epoch of ontotheology. As Caputo notes:

> The language of limit and finitude—like the word "creature"—
> belongs to the most traditional metaphysics of infinity; it suggests
> that it is to be followed up by a philosophy of the unlimited. (The old
> Jesuit curriculum used to have two courses: metaphysics of finite
> being [creatures]; metaphysics of infinite being [God].) . . . That is

why Derrida writes that "the return to finitude" does not take "a single step outside of metaphysics."[26]

If this is the case, then to speak of finitude and creation is to
once again succumb to the "erotic pull" of the unconditioned, a
love affair played out in the history of Western philosophy since
Plato.[27] And here I agree with Caputo and Derrida that this quest
for the unconditioned, unmediated, absolute Infinite is a dangerous and impossible dream—a vision given to metaphysical violence. But *must* language of creation and finitude necessarily be
followed by talk of the Infinite and Absolute Knowledge? Traditionally such discourse has certainly taken that route; and inasmuch as
the categories are inherited from that tradition, there is certainly a
sense in which terms like *creation* and *finitude* "suggest" a discourse
on the Infinite, that is, a metaphysical discourse. But is it necessarily the case?

By employing the notion of finitude, I run the risk of being identified, on the one hand, with a "Gadamerian conservatism"[28] or, on
the other, with the Habermasian tradition of critical theory.[29] In
the end, it seems to me that both of these traditions deny the very
finitude that they purport to honor. In fact, despite his protests to
the contrary, I do think that Derrida is a philosopher of finitude
par excellence.[30] As Caputo mentions, however, Derrida avoids such
categories as neo-ontotheological:

> It would not mean a single step outside of metaphysics if nothing
> more than a new motif of "return to finitude," of "God's death," etc.,
> were the result of this move. It is that conceptuality and that problem-
> atics that must be deconstructed. They belong to the onto-theology
> they fight against. Differance is also something other than finitude.
> (*OG* 68)

Does this mean that Derrida has a language and a set of concep-
tual categories up his sleeve that are *not* part of the ontotheological
tradition? *Can* we step outside of metaphysics? Are conceptuali-
ties deconstructed from outside? I ask these questions as one

intent not upon neoscholastically rehabilitating metaphysics but rather upon Derrida's suggestion. For is not the "task" of deconstruction precisely to inhabit that which is insufficient despite the risk— gladly facing the challenge as *un beau risque?* Before the passage above, Derrida is insistent that "one must *accentuate* the 'naiveté' of a breakthrough which cannot attempt a step outside of metaphysics, which cannot *criticize* metaphysics radically without still utilizing in a certain way, in a certain type or a certain style of *text*, propositions that . . . have always been and will always be 'naivetés,' incoherent signs of an absolute appurtenance" (*OG* 19). It is difficult to see, then, how Derrida and Caputo can critique every discourse concerning finitude as ontotheological if it is impossible to step outside of that tradition.

That is not to say that the language of creation and finitude is always postmetaphysically aware and vigilant (which is precisely the problem I have with P. Christopher Smith's "Gadamerian conservatism" and Habermas's "embodied rationality"). It does mean, however, that it is possible to inhabit this discourse differently, "in a certain way," so as to deconstruct the tradition from within while at the same time describing a state of affairs in a new manner. In a sense, to speak of finitude is "good deconstruction" and an instance where Derrida's text deconstructs itself, for my project is precisely what Derrida outlines as the project of deconstruction.

> The movements of deconstruction do not destroy structures from the outside. They are not possible and effective, nor can they take accurate aim, except by inhabiting those structures. Inhabiting them *in a certain way*, because one always inhabits, and all the more when one does not suspect it. Operating necessarily from the inside, borrowing all the strategic and economic resources of subversion from the old structure, borrowing them structurally, that is to say without being able to isolate their elements and atoms, the enterprise of deconstruction always in a certain way falls prey to its own work. (*OG* 24)

I maintain the use of a word such as *finite* inasmuch as I am forced to inhabit a discourse and sociolinguistic tradition. However, by doing so I constantly risk "falling back within what is being deconstructed." Therefore:

it is necessary to surround the critical concepts with a careful and thorough discourse—to mark the conditions, the medium, and the limits of their effectiveness and to designate rigorously their intimate relationship to the machine whose deconstruction they permit; and, in the same process, designate the crevice through which the yet unnameable glimmer beyond the closure can be glimpsed. (*OG* 14)

My use of *finitude* would be an example. When I speak of finitude, I am not thinking of the finite as *limited* against the Infinite; I am thinking of situationality—being human, being here. *Finite*, unfortunately, seems to describe something in terms of lack or deficiency—precisely the paradigm that I am attempting to critique. It will be evident then that mine is a finitude without the Infinite; for me, finitude is differance without the ghost of full presence continuing to haunt it.

Two other terms that I will employ need to be marked and surrounded with a discourse to designate their conditions simply in order to signal that my use of them is not oblivious to difficulties and risks (and that all of these notions will be further explored in the following chapters). The first term is *mediation:* the state of affairs that I am denoting by the term is described as mediation only against a horizon of immediacy—again, precisely what I am attempting to avoid. To naively employ the notion would be to remain enclosed by the dialectical poles of identity and difference, same and other. I am attempting to describe this state of affairs with existing vocabulary, and so I use the term *mediation* "in a certain way" to indicate that human experience of other people and things is fundamentally interconnected but is nevertheless always experienced "as" something, always experienced hermeneutically.

A second term is *traditionality*, which would seem to initially connect me with a more Gadamerian train of thought—the Great Train of Being. While my use is not completely divorced from Gadamer's philosophical hermeneutics, I am not interested in rehabilitating *the* Tradition; further, my sense is (and here I agree with Habermas) that, for Gadamer, I am delivered over to the tradition without any recourse for critique of its violence. In contrast, when I speak of traditionality or "traditionedness," I am emphasizing that we belong to a host of traditions and that such a state of affairs is constitutive of human existence, of finitude. In fact, *finitude* and *traditionality* will be seen to be almost interchangeable in what follows.

In the Beginning

At this juncture I should say a brief word about the idea of creation, which again will be further developed in chapter five. First, no connection should be drawn between my use of the term *creation* as a philosophical category and "creationism" or "creation science."[31] Nor am I once again attempting to revive the metaphysics that construes being as *ens creatum*.[32] (As a Pentecostal, I'm all for revivals—but not under the tent of Being.) I am not proposing creation as an ontological theory of origins, nor even as an-archic or pre-originary; mine is, if you will, a present creation. It is creation as a metaphor[33] for what phenomenology describes as the given or the gift—the *es gibt*. Creation is a way of construing the state of affairs that is described in phenomenology as "world," and as a construal, its status is undecidable but also on par with every other construal.

Further, in response to the "ethical" criticism noted above, a discourse on creation ought not be understood as inherently conservative or as legitimating the status quo. As Richard Middleton has argued, rather than serving as a legitimating framework, creation provides the sources for critique and liberation in the midst of the tradition. It is a postexilic myth told not by those in power but rather by those deprived of power, crushed by the dominant power and exiled to the margins.[34] To speak of the goodness of creation is not to invoke *the* Good, which gives birth to its own fundamentalism. Creation is, as Caputo argues, a pluralist idea.[35]

The hermeneutical structure of creation is good; it produces goods: a plurality of interpretations and a diversity of readings. The sin of Babel was its quest for unity—one interpretation, one reading, one people—which was an abandonment of creational diversity and plurality in favor of exclusion and violence; and "the ravages of hatred have an ominous sameness."[36] Plurality in interpretation is not the original sin; it is, on the contrary, the original goodness of creation:[37] a creation where many flowers bloom and many voices are heard, where God is praised by a multitude from "every tribe and language and people and nation" (Rev 5:9), singing songs in a diversity of tongues, even worshiping through a diversity of theologies.[38] So once again, as with the terms *finitude, mediation* and *traditionality,* the term *creation* is utilized "in a certain way," as a way of inhabiting a discourse and attempting to uncover and describe a state of affairs that might also be portrayed as "the human condition."

My goal in this introduction has been twofold: to indicate the direction of the book and to mark some key terms and categories that will be used herein. I have focused largely on the second aspect precisely because I recognize I will be implementing nomenclature that could be easily dismissed as part of an uncritical and naive tradition of metaphysics. In this introduction I have only made brief remarks about this terminology and have done so to create an initial opening for them to be heard. They will be unfolded in the critique and proposals that follow.

Part I

The Fallenness of Hermeneutics

One

Paradise
Regained

F or a certain "traditional" evangelical theology,[1] the Fall was a fall
from immediacy to mediation, from understanding to distortion,
from reading to interpretation. Eden, for such theologians, was a
paradise of perpetual connection: a hermeneutical paradise precisely because of the absence of hermeneutics. As Richard Lints
tells the story:

> In the beginning, Adam and Eve enjoyed *perfect clarity* in their com-
> prehension of the purposes and presence of God. The creatures and
> the Creator understood each other. But the fall destroyed this clarity
> and Adam and Eve immediately sought to cover their nakedness, to
> find shelter from God, to hide from him. (*FT* 71, emphasis added)

The Fall, then, destroyed the pristine perspicuity of Edenic
immediacy, where "knowing" was not hindered by the space of
interpretation.[2] Of course, the story doesn't end there: redemption
is a restoration of this interpretive paradise (at least for these evan-

gelical readers)[3] by the illumination of the Spirit coupled with the
perspicuity of Scripture. Hermeneutics is a curse, but it is one from
which we can be redeemed in the here and now; we can return
from mediation to immediacy, from distortion to "perfect clarity"
and from interpretation to "pure reading."

Permit me one illustration of this kind of evangelical "interpretation of interpretation": part of the Friday ritual in our home is to
pack up the kids, drag the playpen and pajamas for everyone out to
the car and head to one of our friends' homes to enjoy a potluck
dinner and then a weekly home Bible study discussion. After
enjoying a time of "fellowship" (evangelical code word for food),
we put the children to sleep in various rooms and closets in the
house and then open our Bibles for discussion.

Leadership for the study is shared by all in a rotating fashion,
and each leader is free to choose a passage or narrative to consider
and reflect upon. We devote our time to discussion and participation, welcoming the input of all involved. The group is rather
eclectic; the people who gather represent a plurality of traditions
and denominations such as Plymouth Brethren, Presbyterian, Bap-
tist and Pentecostal, and a few are from nondenominational
churches. Each person has a unique narrative and testimony that
makes every individual's contribution different. In sum, this is a
wonderful site to see the role of hermeneutics at work and to see
how people understand interpretation within the evangelical tradition.

Of course, not every interpretation is a good interpretation.[4] My
favorite, offered by one of the more, let's say, "traditional" men in
the group, suggested that Jesus first appeared to women after the
resurrection in order to guarantee that word would spread quickly.
After all, he concluded (citing specific data), we all know women
say an average of twelve thousand words per day and men only
five thousand; his "gossip theory" suggested that Jesus had this in
mind when appearing to the women at the tomb.

Now, apart from my wife's rather ferocious response to such an interpretation, the general dynamics of such a reading, and such a group in general, illustrate an interesting point. While a myriad of groups such as this meet every night across the country—and while just as many "readings" or "interpretations" are offered—in the end all of these Bible students tend to think that interpretation is an inconvenience, that interpretation is somehow "our fault" and that God helps us to overcome it. When, for instance, I offer an interpretation that might suggest something contrary to a traditional reading, I am often met with the response, "Well, that might be your interpretation, but *my* Bible *clearly* says women are to be silent in church!" I am complicating matters *by interpretation*, my interlocutor suggests (another product of my academic corruption, I'm usually told); he, on the other hand, is simply reading what God's Word clearly says in black and white.

This general "interpretation of interpretation" was captured very well by a recent advertisement in a leading evangelical periodical: "God's Word. Today's Bible translation that says what it means," the dust cover boldly proclaimed. Underneath the photograph, in large bold letters the publishers heralded "NO INTERPRETATION NEEDED."[5]

Issues of a general hermeneutical nature have finally come to the fore in recent evangelical discussions, as have a number of new contributions on theological method.[6] In their attempts to engage recent philosophical and theological developments such as existentialism, philosophical hermeneutics and deconstruction, evangelicals are increasingly attentive to questions of tradition, historicality, contextuality and cultural conditioning. However, all of these elements and conditions are construed as inextricably linked with hermeneutics and, further, as conditions that must somehow be overcome. While many pay heed to the influence of sociolinguistic and historical conditioning, in the end much recent work in evangelical theology continues to assert that it is somehow possible to surmount these conditions and attain a pure reading that delivers the "explicit teaching of Scripture."

In looking at two of these proposals in this chapter, I will attempt to demonstrate that this penchant for overcoming historical and linguistic conditioning unwittingly ends up being an attempt to overcome our humanity and that, as such, it is a devaluing of creation, which evangelicals seek to honor. I am suspicious that underlying this claim to immediacy and "objectivity," there is an unconscious (and likely, unintended) drive to escape interpretation and to overcome creaturehood, a drive that is itself reminiscent of the Edenic Fall and the trespass of the sign, for it is fundamentally a striving to be like God (Gen 3:5).

It seems to be but another ("Christian") chapter in a long history of metaphysics, in which we are seduced by the erotic pull of the Infinite and determined to ascend to such pristine heights. In much the same way that Dennis Schmidt describes the history of philosophy, this stream of evangelical theology is resolute in its quest "to see beyond the captivity of finite perspectives and prejudices of every sort—national, historical, egoistic, linguistic, physical—to a perceived or simply promised metaphysical region of free and abstract generality which is said to first grant thought its mandate to speak intelligibly about the world in which we find ourselves."[7] (As such, modern philosophers such as René Descartes and John Locke could be included in the immediacy model explored in this chapter, inasmuch as both posit a model of knowing that claims to deliver the world as it "really" is in a correspondence theory of truth.)[8]

I have chosen to consider two recent evangelical proposals from Rex Koivisto and Richard Lints as paradigmatic examples of this "interpretation of interpretation" because they provide very explicit examples of my thesis; further, they range across the evangelical spectrum: Koivisto representing a low-ecclesiology, Baptist-revivalist tradition and Lints coming from a Presbyterian, classical-Reformed paradigm. My project is to show the continuity of their proposals and critique their base assumption regarding the fallenness of hermeneutics.

Reading with Dante's Adam: Koivisto

Koivisto's interpretation of interpretation is uncovered in his recent book *One Lord, One Faith,* which is a sustained call for restoration of Christian unity in a manner rarely heard from evangelicals. In many ways, I appreciate his attempt to forge a "theology for cross-denominational renewal" (the subtitle of the book). However, I think this project is marred by a hermeneutical framework that centers around immediacy. To demonstrate this, I must first outline his proposal for renewed "catholicity."

Koivisto takes denominational distinctives that are understood as divine imperatives to be the main barrier to Christian unity. To overcome this situation, Christians must be able to distinguish between "the core orthodoxy which they warmly share with other believers and their own peculiar distinctives" (*OLOF* 123); these denominational distinctives are what Koivisto describes as "tradition," or more specifically, "micro-tradition." By making this distinction, he is trying to point out to evangelicals that much of what they consider to be "explicit biblical teaching" is only "tradition," that is (for Koivisto), *interpretation,* a kind of "style" (*OLOF* 135). Much of what evangelicals of differing stripes consider to be a divine imperative is actually a highly mediated interpretation.

On one level, Koivisto is exposing the myth of unbiased interpretation: "None of us," he argues, "interprets the Bible in a vacuum. We interpret *out of* a cultural, historical context, *through* an ecclesiastical context, *looking for* the Bible's relevance to cultural problems" (*OLOF* 136). He explicitly rejects any "leapfrog" model of interpretation that claims to go directly to the Bible, uninfluenced by tradition; instead, interpretive traditions are unavoidable.

However, Koivisto's text deconstructs itself[9] in the next paragraph where he restores just such a model of bias-free interpretation on another level by asserting that we must distinguish our (micro)traditions from *"the clear teachings of Scripture."* Our denominational distinctives are interpretations (microtradition) and as such must be stated with a "hermeneutical humility." In order for

Christians to be united (which is Koivisto's overall project), micro-tradition must be relativized, which is to say that these distinctives must be seen as interpretations and therefore fallible. But the constructive part of Koivisto's proposal is found in his notion of "core orthodoxy," which is what all (true) Christians share in common. It is this core orthodoxy that is the "explicit teaching of Scripture"—explicit because it is not *interpreted* but simply *read*.

Thus microtradition is composed of "those traditions which make up the unique interpretive distinctives of a congregation, denomination or stream within the whole church" (*OLOF* 342 n. 6). It can further be classified as "interpretive" or "external": as external, tradition involves practices and doctrines that are based not on "explicit biblical support" but rather on ancient or denominational founding practice (*OLOF* 146-47). Macrotradition, on the other hand, "is the interpretive tradition of the church *as a whole*" (*OLOF* 342 n. 6) and is to be identified with the core orthodoxy shared by the entire church (*OLOF* 182).

In order to construct a cross-denominational theology, Koivisto argues, it is imperative that these two levels be distinguished: those beliefs that are explicit biblical teaching (macrotradition) and those beliefs that are the result of interpretation (microtradition). "Only when we have separated out what is traditional," he continues, "can we be allowed to hear the crisp, unadorned voice of God ringing out from Scripture alone" (*OLOF* 140).

But here we stumble upon an interesting *aporia* in Koivisto's text: denominational distinctives are interpretations influenced by tradition; thus Koivisto categorizes them as microtradition. Core orthodoxy, or macrotradition, however, represents the "clear teaching of Scripture." May we not legitimately ask, at this juncture, whether Koivisto's core orthodoxy—the clear teachings of Scripture—is not also influenced by tradition? Does not Koivisto himself concede such when he describes this core orthodoxy as macro*tradition?* As macrotradition, can it ever deliver the crisp, unadorned voice of God?

In this framework, interpretation is relegated to the level of denominational distinctives and secondary matters. Too many Christians have proclaimed their denominational practices as the "clear teaching of Scripture," whereas Koivisto is unveiling the fact that these matters are "clear" only because of the colored glasses of one's interpretive tradition. But Koivisto fails to recognize that interpretive glasses are "cemented to our face" (Abraham Kuyper). That is, he is still holding out a group of teachings that *are* "clear teachings of Scripture"—not the product of interpretation but rather delivered immediately, unhampered by the space of hermeneutics. But do we ever possess the "crisp, unadorned voice of God"? If, as Koivisto asserts, we never interpret the Bible in a vacuum but always through the lens of a cultural, historical and linguistic context (*OLOF* 136), can there be any such thing as "explicit biblical teaching"?[10]

In a conservative critique of Koivisto's proposal, John Fish hits upon precisely this point (though he takes a different direction than I will). Fish, offering criticism of Koivisto from a Brethren standpoint, correctly perceives the implications of the relativization of microtradition. But it is precisely for this reason that Fish rejects the interpreted status of these denominational distinctives. What Koivisto describes as matters of interpretation and tradition, Fish understands to be "New Testament Church Truth"—as though uninterpreted, simply uncovered by reading.

When Koivisto concludes that these distinctives are "tradition," he means to say that they are without "clear Scriptural mandate"— which for him means that they are matters of interpretation. But such a distinction cuts at the very heart of Brethren theology, as Fish realizes: "For those in the assemblies of Christian Brethren (sometimes called Plymouth Brethren) the subject of church truth has always meant those truths concerning the church which are taught and practised in the New Testament and are normative for today."[11] Fish's project is to demonstrate that these distinctives are not matters of "preference, practicality or expediency"—that is, they are not matters of interpretation—but rather are "essentials" from Scripture.[12]

Commenting on Koivisto's notion of interpretive tradition, Fish rightly perceives (while Koivisto does not) that "we now shift the neutral attitude toward tradition in the earlier sense [of external tradition] toward anything which is a matter of interpretation." But Fish continues:

> are we not in danger here of nullifying the Word of God by what we are calling tradition? Once everything which is disputed becomes a matter of interpretive tradition, then the Bible is *unclear* in every area because every teaching of the Bible has been disputed. Everything is a matter of tradition and therefore may not be held as intrinsically biblical. Everything is simply a matter of "perspective" or "preference." In fact, we will not even be able to protect what Koivisto calls our core orthodoxy.[13]

Indeed! Fish has perhaps appreciated the implications of Koivisto's project better than Koivisto has himself. Koivisto affirms the tradition-influenced nature of interpretation in the realm of microtradition; but macrotradition, or core orthodoxy, somehow escapes this historicity and falls pure from the mind of God. Fish indicates this is the problem with Koivisto's work, which is correct; Fish's response, however, is to therefore reject the conditioning of tradition and context in interpretation and affirm reading over interpretation.[14]

In contrast to both, I am arguing that everything is a matter of interpretation, including those interpretations described as core orthodoxy.[15] We never have the "crisp, unadorned voice of God" because it is always heard and read through the lens of our finitude and situationality. Even when someone purports to deliver to us the unadorned voice of God, or "what *God* meant" (*OLOF* 162), we always receive only someone's interpretation, which is wearing the badge of divinity.

This is seen very clearly in Koivisto's ensuing discussion of just what constitutes core orthodoxy. After rejecting earlier options such as the *Fundamentals* of the early twenties, the creeds of the undivided church and the Vincentian view ("what all men have at all times believed"), Koivisto finally delivers to us that which unites all Christians—*the gospel message,* which he then specifies: *"God sent His Son into the world to die as an atonement for sin, and God raised Him from the dead, so that anyone who places faith in Him receives the free gift of salvation"* (*OLOF* 197). But that, I would contend, is only one interpretation of the gospel and cannot claim divine status. For instance, his interpretation of the atonement already excludes the Wesleyan interpretation, which rejects the penal substitutionary doctrine of the atonement "as a forensic and unreal 'credit card' theology."[16] As he expounds his definition, it becomes clear that what is delivered to us as the gospel is in fact heavily indebted to a traditional (Princetonian) evangelical interpretation of the gospel (*OLOF* 193), with little or no acknowledgment (perhaps even exclusion) of Catholic, Eastern Orthodox, Pentecostal and mainline Protestant interpretations. This interpretation of the gospel is sent to us as God's interpretation; in fact, it is not an interpretation at all, but only a reading of the crisp, unadorned voice of God. By proposing to deliver the gospel and the "crisp, unadorned voice of God," it seems that Koivisto claims to be a veritable *facteur de la vérité* (*PC* 413-96).[17]

A Post Card from the Edge: Koivisto Meets Derrida

This claim to hear God's unadulterated and unmediated Word appears to be a contemporary instantiation of the traditional Protestant doctrine of the perspicuity of Scripture, which is really a claim to immediacy, to an absence of (subjective) interpretation and to a pure reading and unalloyed reception of truth (*OLOF* 154-55). This tradition within evangelical theology, thoroughly shaped by modern notions of science and epistemology, reduces faith as trust to faith as belief in propositions. As such, the Bible is reduced to Charles Hodge's notorious "storehouse of facts," and its contents—propositions—yield themselves immediately to the mind.[18] Thus what the

Reformers described as perspicuity is reduced to a lingual-analytic clarity accessible to reason. This is part of what Jacques Derrida describes as a postal desire, the claim to hear God's Word "without *courrier*" (*PC* 23). But I would agree with Derrida that this is a myth, a postal story of the sort that Cliff Claven would tell—a tall tale about Being's love notes that never get lost in the mail.

In Derrida's *The Post Card* we find a collection of "love letters" and post cards entitled "Envois," the goal of which is to point out the mythology of immediacy in Being's epistles. There Derrida suggests in a letter that the space of interpretation he describes as the "postal system" is rather unreliable:

> If the post (technology, position, "metaphysics") is announced at the "first" *envoi*, then there is no longer A metaphysics, etc., . . . nor even AN *envoi*, but *envois* without destination. For to coordinate the different epochs, halts, determinations, in a word the entire history of Being with a destination of Being is perhaps the most outlandish postal lure. There is not even the post or the *envoi*. . . . In a word, . . . as soon as there is, there is differance . . . and there is postal maneuvering, relays, delay, anticipation, destination, telecommunicating, network, the possibility, and therefore the fatal necessity of going astray, etc. (*PC* 66)

Communication between lovers is left in the hands of an unreliable postal system. As soon as I drop the letter in the box (as soon as I seal the envelope!), my expression of love is subject to the whim of the postal gods, of whom Hermes is in charge. But this is true for more than love letters or post cards or even junk mail; it is the case of language and communication itself. Derrida's point is that "within every sign already, every mark or every trait, there is distancing, the post, what there has to be so that it is legible for another, another other than you or me" (*PC* 29). The very "space" or distance that makes communication possible is also the site of miscommunication and even alienation.

But the post "has to be": we cannot escape the postal system, the hermeneutical space of interpretation. This distancing, creating a space of dif-ference and de-ferral, is necessary for enabling others to read the envelope and direct the correspondence to the proper destination. We are always already posted and postal: we can never destroy or "overcome" the postal system. But the inescapable interpolation of the postal system means there is a possibility that letters can be lost.[19]

For Western metaphysics and for much of evangelical theology (which is, ironically, very modern), the letter is not able not to arrive; that is, the letter *always* arrives. Metaphysics and fundamentalism have an extremely reliable—I should say "infallible"—postal system. It is a telecommunications network equipped with unbreakable lines, virus-proof computers and the latest technological advances. Acquiring this inerrant technology means always receiving God's Word unmediated and unaffected by the postal or telecommunications system. God's Word and the reading of that text receive a privileged place outside the tangled chain of signifiers; and evangelical theology—which speaks for God—communicates this God to us, itself immune to linguistic and historical conditioning. The letter always arrives "without *courrier*": right on time, perfectly intact, never torn or lost or delayed by postal strikes.

It is this impeccable postal service that frightens Derrida, for such a theological system built on a flawless telecommunications network knows God and speaks for God *without mediation*. But this, I would contend with Derrida, is impossible because there is nothing outside of the text (*OG* 158). As John Caputo has clearly pointed out, this should not be understood as "a sort of linguistic Berkeleyianism," as if "Derrida thinks there *is* nothing other than words and texts."[20] Instead, Derrida is insisting "that there is no reference without difference, no reference *(il n'y a pas)* outside of a textual chain *(hors-texte)*."[21] This is not to say, then, that texts lack reference but only that no reference can escape the influence of textuality; no reading bypasses the hermeneutical space of interpretation.

Thus when Koivisto "delivers" us "the gospel," it has already traversed this postal space and has been appropriated by one reading from within a certain tradition, or rather from within a plurality of traditions: a linguistic tradition, a theological tradition, a sociological and cultural context and so on. Koivisto's analysis of interpretation with regards to microtradition emphasizes precisely this point; what he misses, however, is the *ubiquity* of interpretation.

Such a desire for immediacy is not only impossible, it can be dangerous (just ask Salman Rushdie), because those who have such privileged access speak *for* God and consider themselves God's private police force (and postal crimes are always a federal offense, like original sin). The rest of us should cringe in terror, Caputo warns, whenever someone claims to have an unconditioned revelation or reading:

> for what we always get—it never fails—in the name of the Unmediated is someone's highly mediated Absolute: their Jealous Jahweh, their righteous Allah, their infallible church, their absolute Geist that inevitably speaks German. In the name of the Unmediated we are buried in an avalanche of mediations, and sometimes just buried, period. Somehow this absolutely absolute always ends up with a particular attachment to some historical, natural language, a particular nation, a particular religion. To disagree with someone who speaks in the name of God always means disagreeing with God. Be prepared to beat a hasty retreat. The unmediated is never delivered without massive mediation.[22]

Koivisto's gospel, or "saving orthodoxy" (*OLOF* 197), excludes many from the kingdom or at least rules out other interpretations of "saving orthodoxy," which is the danger that, ironically, he alludes to: "there is the ever-present danger . . . to confuse the authority of Scripture with a given line of interpretation" (*OLOF* 201). Is that not precisely what Koivisto has done? Has he not conflated his particular, situated, evangelical interpretation with gospel, with God's meaning? Is not his delivery of Scripture "unalloyed" (*OLOF* 193) in fact a remarkable piece of metallurgy and the production of a highly alloyed gospel? Does not his "unadorned voice of God" have a distinctively American fundamentalist accent? And would this not indicate that even what he describes as macrotradition is also the product of interpretation?

Overcoming (the) Tradition: Lints

While Koivisto laments the disunity of the Christian church, Lints offers a jeremiad lamenting the state of evangelical theology, particularly its contamination by American culture and popular religion.[23] This brings to the fore the relationship between theology and culture, and as such it provides a helpful arena to uncover Lints's interpretation of interpretation. Lints, unlike many classical evangelical theologians, argues that the impact of culture on theologizing must be recognized. As he summarizes the problem:

> ours is not a simple distillation of the pure gospel. Nor can we lay claim to a Christian America as much as we can to an Americanized Christianity. As evangelical theology approaches the twenty-first century, it must take these trends seriously. It is not feasible any longer to argue that only our opponents are biased in their theologizing. Evangelical theology must not only engage a culture that is largely resistant to claims of absolute truth but must also recognize the influence which that culture has exercised upon it. Evangelicals must acknowledge the reality of cultural influence and cultural bias in their own community. (*FT* 25-26)

Such an evaluation would seem to place Lints closer to Hans-Georg Gadamer than to Koivisto and other elements of the evangelical tradition; that is, he would appear to appreciate the situationality of all interpretation and the conditions of hermeneutics described by Gadamer as "historically effected consciousness." But in the end, he urges evangelicals to recognize the influence of culture only so that they can *overcome* it. He is critical of evangelical theology for its thinking it was culturally neutral when it was really Americanized, but he does so only to then deliver us a "biblical," un-American, ahistorical theology—which in the end is really God's theology, "his interpretation" (*FT* 79).

Thus "a *genuine biblical* theology will strongly affirm that humans (Christian and non-Christian) are inevitably influenced by their own culture, tradition, experience. Until and unless the evangelical community wrestles more seriously with this fact, they will not *overcome* the unreflective biases that characterize the evangelical appropriation of the Bible" (*FT* 27, emphasis added). What he describes as the "bias principle" is eventually overcome by the "realism principle," whereby the influences of culture, tradition and experience—which distort and interfere—are purged from our interpretations so that we can hear the "speech of God . . . His very voice" (*FT* 58-59). Though we ourselves cannot "jump out of our skins and become bias-free" by mental effort, "God breaks through to us" (*FT* 281). Either way, Lints sees our skin, our humanity, our being-here, as a distorting limitation that prevents us from really hearing God.

The goal of this chapter is to demonstrate the link made by evangelical thought between interpretation and the Fall, and Lints's proposal provides ample opportunity to do so. As a loyal disciple of biblical theologian Geerhardus Vos, Lints loves to tell a story about the "history of redemption": "In the beginning," he recounts, "Adam and Eve enjoyed perfect clarity in their comprehension of the purposes and presence of God. The creatures and the Creator understood each other. But the fall destroyed this clarity and Adam and Eve immediately sought to cover their nakedness, to find shelter from God, to hide from him" (*FT* 71). (It seems that I have heard something like this before, in Italian perhaps?)

Nevertheless, it will be recognized that the Fall, for Lints (as for Dante), resulted in a loss of "perfect clarity" and the interruption of understanding. In this postlapsarian world we are plagued by mediation and misunderstandings that result in distortion. More specifically, after the Fall humanity becomes plagued by "expectations" and presuppositions that act as "filters" and condition how we hear and read, especially God's voice and Word. God's speech is "often misunderstood and misinterpreted, because those who listen to the speech come with expectations about it. . . . Do we all do this to some degree?" Lints asks. "Yes. Must it happen all the time? No. *We all participate in the fallenness of creation.* If we want to be able to listen to the conversation with God, we have to be able to see how our own expectations color our understanding of the conversation" (*FT* 60, emphasis added).

My difficulty is not with Lints's discussion of fallenness but rather with what he links to fallenness: namely, presuppositions and horizons of expectation. That my hearing the voice of God and reading the word of God are conditioned by historical horizons of expectation, Lints takes to be indicative of the fallenness of creation. As he later notes, "we hear the divine conversation only after it has passed through several filters—our culture, our religious tradition, our personal history, and so on. If we take these filters seriously, we may be able to decrease the distortion with which we hear the conversation" (*FT* 61).

But are not culture, traditionality and personal history constitutive aspects of simply being human, of being a creature? Is not the finitude of creaturehood inextricably linked to conditionality and situationality? Am I not, as a human being, limited to this space where I stand, with these horizons, which move with me but nevertheless remain *my* horizons? Are not the "filters" or "presuppositions" that I inherit from a multitude of traditions (religious, sociolinguistic, familial) an inescapable aspect of human experience as created by God? And if so, is not Lints in fact devaluing creation by linking such conditions of finitude to the Fall and sin? If being human necessarily entails our having expectations and presuppositions and if being human means being God's creatures, then why should such expectations and filters be described as "distortions" that "color" our understanding? Is that not to make being human a sin?

Lints takes up a more extended discussion of the filters of tradition, culture and reason in "The Trajectory of Theology," chapter four of *The Fabric of Theology*. Evangelical theology, he urges, needs to take into account how these filters influence interpretation and the reception of an authority. "The goal of theology," then, "is to bring the biblical revelation into a position of judgment on all of life, *including the filters,* and thereby bring the cleansing power of God's redemption into all of life" (*FT* 82, emphasis added). We stand in need of redemption—from history, tradition and culture; we must be cleansed of these filters. And God's redemption accomplishes that restoration of immediacy in the here and now.[24]

Our problem is that "we concede a disproportionate influence to our filters in our efforts to understand the biblical revelation. We force the message of redemption into a cultural package that distorts its actual intentions" (*FT* 82). Lints points to the example of Nicodemus, who misunderstood Jesus' discussion of the new birth as speaking of a second physical birth (Jn 3):

> Nicodemus and the Pharisees stood in a tradition, were conditioned by a culture, and applied certain principles of rationality to their conversations with Jesus. We do the same today. It is part of the theologian's task to bring the people of God to an awareness of their historical, cultural, and rational filters so that they will not be ruled by them. (*FT* 83)

Nicodemus's sinful misunderstanding is to be blamed on the fact that he stood in a tradition and was part of a culture—in short, I would argue, because he was a human being. Apparently Lints, as a theologian and evangelical, is not part of a tradition or a culture, or he can somehow step outside of such distorting influences to hear the "crisp, unadorned voice of God." But does he? As with Koivisto's God, doesn't Lints's God speak a rather traditional language? Like Koivisto, Lints seems to miss the ubiquity of interpretation: the inescapability of conditions of knowing that are described as "distortions" or "colorings" only against the mythical horizon of "perfect clarity." Lints has a dream—a dream of immediacy and pure reading and listening. But his dream may quickly turn to a nightmare for any who lie outside the parameters of *his* "people of God," people on the margins like Pentecostals or even Catholics.[25]

Despite all of his talk of filters, presuppositions and expectations, in the end Lints believes these are all necessarily distortions that must be overcome in order to hear God's unadorned voice. He operates with a peculiar *volitional model*[26] with regard to tradition, history and culture; that is, he thinks that humanity *chooses* to be influenced by tradition and history and therefore can also choose *not* to be, can choose to read without these lenses. Thus "the validity of any particular theological conviction ought finally and ultimately to be judged by its fidelity to the Scriptures rather than its fidelity to any given tradition" (*FT* 86).[27] But Lints fails to realize we never have simply "the Scriptures" pure and uninterpreted; every appeal to "what the Bible says" is an appeal to an *interpretation* of the Bible. Whenever someone promises to deliver "the Scriptures alone," he or she has always already delivered an interpretation that is carried out within an interpretive tradition.[28] Fidelity to the Scriptures is always fidelity to an interpretation of the Scriptures and thus operates only within an interpretive tradition, a way of reading one cannot step outside of (though one may participate in a different interpretive tradition).

Further, the New Testament writings are themselves interpretations of a person and an event.[29] As a result we never have "the Scriptures themselves" (*FT* 291) in any pure, unadorned sense; rather, every appeal to Scripture is always already an appeal to an interpretation of Scripture. Thus though the Reformational principle of *sola Scriptura* is a salutary emphasis on the intertextual and canonical nature of Scripture, we must concede that the principle "scripture interprets scripture" does not allow us to appeal to uninterpreted Scriptures to clarify matters of interpretation elsewhere.[30] It will always be interpretations of interpretations.

What Lints describes as the "cultural lens" is said to operate in a similar manner; that is, Lints can ask to what degree culture "ought" to influence theology. But such language again betrays his notion of the accidental relationship between theology and culture and that one can separate the two, in order to then later "contextualize" it.[31] God can "break through our cultural blinders and thereby enable us to see ourselves more clearly by the radiance of his glory" (*FT* 106). This happens when the biblical revelation challenges and transforms our "culture-bound experience," disclosing its "meaning" (*FT* 115). Because culture is opposed to truth (*FT* 114, 116), the influence of culture must be overcome; after all, "it is truth we are after" (*FT* 95). (Unfortunately and all too often, it is someone's truth who is after us, ready to pounce on us at any moment.)

As we interpret the Bible, Lints argues, we need to become aware of these cultural predispositions, otherwise our theology will be distorted by these parameters. The only way that we can really read the Bible is if we are delivered (by God) from culture, are cleansed of the distorting influence of being human. Thus Lints remarks, "It is my contention that the horizons ought not to be fused [pace Gadamer] but rather that the horizon of the historical situation ought to be transformed by the horizon of the text" (*FT* 115 n. 33). But this is to miss the fact that the text is itself the product of another historical situation.[32]

It is important to reiterate one point with regard to Lints's framework and his interpretation of interpretation: throughout the book, he insists that the final interpretive lens must be "the Scriptures themselves." The Bible is the final authority for our interpretations, and it stands over against our hermeneutical ventures. In discussing the movement from text to theology, he describes the criteria for interpretation:

> Protestantism has managed to preserve a sense that Scripture is the final authority for the life of the believer; it has simply failed to affirm the hermeneutical parameters that are properly implicit in the principle of *sola Scriptura*. If Scripture is the final authority, then in some important sense Scripture must be allowed to interpret Scripture—which entails another fundamental principle of the Reformers, the *analogia fidei* (the analogy of faith). The faith defined in any given scriptural passage is to be interpreted by the faith defined in the whole of the Scriptures. The authority of the Scriptures is integrally connected with a proper understanding of those Scriptures, and the final court of appeals in interpretive matters must be the Scriptures themselves. (*FT* 291)

First, we must affirm the canonical horizon of interpretation and in this sense affirm the principle of *sola Scriptura* in terms of the *analogia fidei*. It seems that recently canonical criticism and the work of figures such as Hans Frei (and even Walter Brueggemann), have sought to retrieve this principle such that Scripture is taken "on its own terms." As suggested above, this highlights the intertextuality of Scripture and works as a counterweight to the neoscholasticism of Protestant fundamentalism as well as to the imposition of modern criteria of interpretation as practiced in Enlightenment historical-critical approaches. Further, it properly situates the site of interpretation within the believing community, the church.[33] Again, here must be noted the contributions of postliberal discussions that have renewed our appreciation for biblical interpretation as an ecclesial task.[34]

But for Lints and certain other evangelicals, the principle of "Scripture interprets Scripture" also means that "our interpretive matrix should be the interpretive matrix of the Scriptures" (*FT* 269) that mediate to us "the divine and apostolic interpretation" (*FT* 279); on the pages of Scripture we find "divine interpretations" (*FT* 264). As such, the interpretive matrix of the Scriptures turns out to be God's interpretive matrix (which, it seems is the same as the apostles' interpretation which is the same as Luther's interpretation) that has fallen from heaven into Lints's hands.[35] Thus somewhat covertly, the appeal to Scripture's interpreting Scripture turns out to be an appeal to "the divine and apostolic interpretation" (*FT* 279)—which, it seems, would be no interpretation at all. Indeed, what would be a "divine" interpretation? Does God need to interpret? Is God conditioned in such a way that interpretation is a necessity?

So the appeal to "the Scriptures themselves" is, as in Koivisto, an appeal to some kind of immediacy or clarity. This is a common evangelical construction, reiterated, for instance, in the "Chicago Statement on Biblical Hermeneutics" (1982), in which a collection of evangelical scholars made the following profession:

> *Article XIX.* We affirm that any preunderstandings which the interpreter brings to Scripture should be in harmony with scriptural

teaching and subject to correction by it. We deny that Scripture should be required to fit alien preunderstandings, inconsistent with itself, such as naturalism, evolutionism, scientism, secular humanism, and relativism.[36]

But first of all, is it not simply begging the question to assert that the criterion for interpreting the Bible is the Bible itself? How can we bring our preunderstandings under the judgment of "scriptural teaching" if we never have "scriptural teaching" apart from those preunderstandings? Is there not lodged in Lints's appeal to "the Scriptures themselves" an implicit notion of pure reading, of simply reading the Bible apart from interpretation? As soon as we appeal to *sola Scriptura* in this (second) sense, do we not only and always have interpretations and readings—what *my* Bible *clearly* says? The problem with this understanding of "Scripture interprets Scripture" is that the *interpreting* Scripture must be *interpreted;* there is no "pure" (i.e., noninterpreted) Scripture.

Further, to privilege the interpretive matrix of the Scriptures and apostles is simply to posit one interpretation over against another, one culture over another.[37] Lints's appeal to Scripture as the final interpretive lens fails to recognize this double effect of the ubiquity of interpretation: that we only "have" Scripture as interpreted and that, further, the Scriptures themselves are interpretations. Theology, then, is the translation of a translation—the Scriptures—which are themselves translations.

Des Tours de Babel: On Interpretation/Translation

The penchant for pure reading, *sans courrier* and without interpretation, is integrally connected to a belief in one true interpretation: an interpretation that is not an interpretation but a delivery of the truth from the hands of a veritable *facteur de la vérité* who in the end turns out to be God. This is rooted in what Mark C. Taylor describes as "monologic": an understanding of truth where "the true is never plural, multiple, and complex but always unified, single, and simple." This "monologism of truth is pre-scribed to ease the distress induced by the uncertainty that arises from the poly-morphous play of appearances."[38]

Against this horizon of immediacy and unity, plurality is a sin, yet another curse of the original sin in Eden; pluralism is some-thing endemic to a postlapsarian world. In contrast, the "perfect clarity" of Eden was accompanied by an unchallenged unity and uniformity. It is this underlying belief in and quest for unity that lies at the heart of Lints's critique of postmodern theology.[39] Theol-ogy, because of this plurality, is "intractably fragmented," owing to the fact that "we have gradually abandoned the goal of attempting to establish an 'objective' reading of the Bible and have as a result stranded theology in the quagmire of a thousand different frame-works" (*FT* 194).[40] Even though Lints calls for a "principled plural-ism," this plurality is linked to individual biases that must be overcome in order to appropriate the "unifying theology of the Scriptures. . . . We cannot find our way to truth unless we are will-ing to recognize our own biases" (*FT* 98).

If interpretation was the result of an Edenic trespass, this plu-rality is the heritage of the Babelian revolt and the attempt to ascend to God by human effort. According to traditional evangeli-cal thought, the multiplication of languages was a punishment that initiated the need for translation, which is closely linked to the need for interpretation.[41] Just as interpretation is linked to the Fall and an anormative state of affairs, the "origins" of plural-ity are cast against the horizon of a sinful rebellion; hence Lints's and the general evangelical disdain with regards to pluralist frameworks.

A second reading of the Babel story, however, will point to unity as the original sin and impetus for violence that Yahweh prevents pre-cisely by multiplication of languages, a *restoration* of plurality. It was a *lack* of difference that occasioned Yahweh's intervention in what was destined to be a violent story of oppression in the name of unity.[42] This is precisely the point emphasized in Derrida's illuminating essay on translation (which is, of course and necessarily, an essay on interpretation), signaling both the ubiquity of interpretation and the violence of unity.[43] For instance, with regard to *Babel* there is already confusion: Is this a proper name? Could this be translated *confusion?* Or does it rather mean the City of God, the City of the Father, as Voltaire suggested? Here, always and already, there is a confusion about confusion, a hermeneutical decision that must precede every translation (TB 245). Even further, when the people used brick *as* stone and tar *as* cement, there is already a traversing of a hermeneutical space, a field of construal. "That already resembles a translation," Derrida observes, "a translation of translation" (TB 247).

Derrida pushes this point by discussing Roman Jakobson's essay "On Linguistic Aspects of Translation,"[44] which, in a subtle way, offers a framework similar to Lints's. In the essay Jakobson distinguishes between three kinds of translation:

☐ intralingual translation, which interprets linguistic signs by means of other signs from the same language

☐ interlingual translation, which interprets by means of another language

☐ intersemiotic translation, which interprets linguistic signs by means of nonlinguistic signs

Jakobson goes on to translate the first and third kinds of translation: intralingual translation is described as "rewording," intersemiotic as "transmutation." But the second, interlingual translation, is not given such a "definitional interpretation"; it is, simply and clearly, "translation proper." As Derrida uncovers:

> in the case of translation "proper," translation in the ordinary sense, interlinguistic and post-Babelian, Jakobson does not translate; he repeats the same word: "interlingual translation or translation proper." He supposes that it is not necessary to translate; everyone understands what that means because everyone has experienced it, everyone is expected to know what a language is, the relation of one language to another and especially identity or difference in fact of language. If there is a transparency that Babel would not have impaired, this is surely it, the experience of multiplicity of tongues and the "proper" sense of the word *translation.* (TB 252)

Jakobson "presupposes that one can know in the final analysis how to determine rigorously the unity and identity of a language, the decidable form of its limits" (TB 252). But it is precisely this "determination," this interpretation of the boundaries of a language, that is made problematic by the Babel story. "Very quickly: at the very moment when pronouncing 'Babel' we sense the impossibility of deciding whether this name belongs, properly and simply, to *one* tongue" (TB 252-53). It is this undecidability, which precedes every decision and determination, that I am describing as the ubiquity of interpretation. Both Jakobson and Lints suppose there is a reading that escapes this, "a transparency that Babel would not have impaired" and that offers a pure reading *sans* (with-out, outside) interpretation. But as Derrida has pointed out, and as I have attempted to demonstrate in this chapter, such a vestige of immediacy is both impossible and dangerous.

It is this danger of immediacy and unity that occasions Yahweh's intervention on behalf of the others who do not speak the "one language" or the language of the One. In the name of unity, Derrida remarks, we are often faced with the most horrifying universals that are intent on excluding or executing those on the margins, the particulars that never quite fit into such grand schemes.

> In seeking to "make a name for themselves," to found at the same time a universal tongue and a unique genealogy, the Semites want to bring the world to reason, and this reason can signify simultaneously a colonial violence (since they would thus universalize their idiom) and a peaceful transparency of the human community. Inversely, when God imposes and opposes his name, he ruptures the rational transparency but interrupts also the colonial violence or the linguistic imperialism. (TB 253)

Yahweh, then, turns out to be a pluralist, one on the side of diversity and the multiplicity of others. And that is why creation is a pluralist idea and why a creational hermeneutic attempts to honor this diversity not as the original sin but rather as primordially good. Further, as a creational-*pneumatic* hermeneutic, my model relates the multiplicity of tongues not only to this Babelian trespass but also to the experience of Pentecost. For at Pentecost Yahweh's *pneuma* affirms the multiplicity of creation and the post-Babelian era, in direct contrast to the quest for unity that initiated the construction of the tower (Acts 2:1-12). It opens the door for an understanding of truth divorced from monologism, which in itself opens the door to those who have been shut out of the kingdom, so to speak—excluded because their interpretation was different. The truth, in creation, is plural.

In this chapter I have attempted to sketch the implicit relationship between hermeneutics and the Fall as construed in two representative evangelical interpretations of interpretation. Though there are differences in their theories, both Koivisto and Lints posit a model of immediacy, at least in certain aspects: for Koivisto, core orthodoxy stands outside interpretation; for Lints, the Scriptures themselves can be read apart from interpretation and thus can function as a standard for our interpretations. Further, the conditions of hermeneutics—tradition, culture, history—are construed as distortions, barriers and results of the Fall.

But if (as I will soon argue) being human means being necessarily located—situated in a tradition, as part of a culture and having a history—then these conditions are inescapable aspects of human existence. More specifically, hermeneutics will be seen as a constitutive element of human being-in-the-world as finite existence, in direct contrast to the evangelical dream of immediacy. But further, if traditionality is a fundamental and inescapable element of being human and if it is such as created by God, then to construe such conditions as barriers and distortions is to devalue a creational way of being that, if created by God, should be understood as primordially good.[45] Hermeneutics, then, is not a postlapsarian curse coming on the scene after Eden but is instead part of the original goodness of creation found in Eden as well.

Two

Through a
Mirror Darkly

O felix culpa, quae talem ac tantum meruit habere redemptorem!
[O blessed fault, which has brought about so great a redemption!]

EXSULTET
an ancient Latin liturgy

The quest for a primal immediacy that animates many evangelical hermeneutical theories has been exposed by others as a search
for a Holy Grail that cannot be found, that eludes its seekers and,
in the end, that turns into little more than an epistemological
wild-goose chase. But while claims to such pure, uninterpreted
readings are typical in evangelical contexts, the *hope* of immediacy
remains operative in a number of decidedly nonevangelical and
sophisticated engagements in philosophical hermeneutics. The
advent of historicism, particularly as it unfolded in Wilhelm
Dilthey and was transformed into "historicity" in Martin Heidegger,[1] has impacted all ensuing discussions in this century, by and
large excising any vestiges of realism, or at least pushing later
thinkers to focus much more attention on the influence history,
tradition and context have on knowing. The situationality and

locality of human existence as emphasized by Heidegger have also uncovered the perspectivalism of being-in-the-world. In short, it has emphasized that life is hermeneutical, that we survive by construal and interpretation and that these are inescapable aspects of being human.

Thus the figures addressed in this chapter—Wolfhart Pannenberg, Hans-Georg Gadamer and Jürgen Habermas—make no present claims to immediacy or pure reading as encountered in Rex Koivisto or Richard Lints (see chapter one). They all emphasize the provisionality and limits of human knowing based on the finitude of existence, the finitude of being human. However, as I will attempt to demonstrate, there remains in their thought a latent penchant for the unmediated, for a reading apart from interpretation. But because they recognize and honor the conditions of being-in-the-world, they project this immediacy into the future, into a future eschaton that will restore the hermeneutical paradise of Eden. That is, they find a way to both honor the conditionedness of human knowing *and at the same time* continue to posit a "knowledge" that overcomes this situationality.

This, of course, is a very Pauline idea, or at least it is an idea that the tradition has claimed as such: "For now we see through a glass darkly *[en ainigmati]*, but then face to face" (1 Cor 13:12 KJV). One day, they tell us, we will see face to face, without mediation, in a fusion of horizons, and we will no longer need to interpret: the curse (of hermeneutics) will be removed in this hermeneutical paradise from which interpretation is banished. They read Paul's "now" as defining the ontological status of finitude: now, to be a creature and to live in the world is to see darkly; but then, in the future, we will no longer see darkly, we will see face to face— which is understood as a kind of immediate understanding.[2]

Thus in the work of Pannenberg, Gadamer and Habermas, we will uncover what I have described as an *eschatological immediacy model*. John Caputo is pointing to the same framework when he (following Joseph Margolis) describes Gadamer's philosophical hermeneutics as a "closet essentialism": "'Closet'—because up front there is a lot of brave talk in Gadamer about history and change, time and becoming—but still 'essentialist'—because when the truth is told, that is all just a front for a theology of lasting essences."[3] *In the end,* in the eschaton and the consummation of history, this turns out to be a version of foundationalism and a veiled claim to immediacy,

> but of a more discrete, less obnoxious form, because it has done its best to accommodate the demands of history and finitude and to keep its distance from an outright transcendentalism. This is a theory of deep truth, which means that tradition—*the* tradition? a tradition? any tradition? what if there are many traditions, or many traditions within *the* tradition?—has the goods, both the *ousia* and the *agathon.*[4]

The difference between Koivisto and Pannenberg or between Lints and Gadamer is simply a disagreement as to *when* this mythical immediacy is restored and is not a fundamental difference in kind. Evangelicals adhere to something of a realized eschatology whereby we can presently step outside our human situation/ality and overcome the conditions of history and finitude. Pannenberg, Gadamer and Habermas offer a more nuanced reading, where the conditions of finitude are precisely the conditions for the possibility of overcoming finitude. The framework is always one of "both/and," where things are happening at the same time. While on the one hand that is an important concession, on the other it remains rather dangerous; further, it still results in a basic devaluing of being human and a construal of the finitude of human existence as something of a fall, a barrier that must be overcome.

The Fallenness of Creation: Pannenberg

That Wolfhart Pannenberg has become one of the theological giants of the late twentieth century is an inescapable fact. Nevertheless, I am concerned about Pannenberg's future, about his eschatological redemption, about his position in/on eternity. My concern is that this giant is destined to become too gigantic: im-mense, without measure, to the point of infinity. In Pannenberg's future, humanity is destined to become a race of Gigas larger than (human) life, no longer human, beyond finitude, perhaps even infinite, "in transcendence of their finitude" (*ST* 2:174). Of course, I have misread him. Pannenberg indefatigably insists that in the consummation of time, the participation of creatures in God is by no means a "violation of the distinction between God and creature" (*ST* 2:33). The "finitude of creatures, their distinction from God and one another, will continue in the eschatological consummation" (*ST* 2:95). But I will insist in this chapter that this, if indeed it is finitude, is a very strange finitude: a finitude that transcends finitude and escapes the temporal experience of time. It is an infinite finitude—the finitude of giants—and is destined to end in gigantomachy.

For Pannenberg, finitude itself is something of a fall, a fault, but it is a happy fault for it was the only means to redemption. This portrayal of human existence results in a devaluing of creation inasmuch as humanity is always already fallen, finite and in need of redemption; that is, creation is the first moment of redemption and the beginning of the process whereby humanity is destined for participation in the deity of God (*ST* 2:33, 176). Further, Pannenberg's portrayal makes evil a necessity for attaining the goal of creation, which is fellowship with God. "This goal is achieved only at the human stage, and even there not directly, but only as a result of a history in which human apostasy from God and all its consequences must be overcome" (*ST* 2:73). Because human finitude is conceived as a "lack," Pannenberg's discussion of the future of humanity in the eschatological consummation also devalues human life by positing that the goal of human existence is to overcome human existence, to transcend finitude and be "lifted above the natural world and even also above the social relations in which we exist" (*ST* 2:176). Since creation is itself in need of redemption—and thus humans simply as created stand in need of redemption—then redemption can be accomplished only by transcending the finitude of human existence. Redemption is not a restoration but a completion.

We must proceed carefully, however, in leveling these charges against Pannenberg; we shouldn't be too hasty in calling the police, for he inevitably has an alibi, an airtight system that makes him difficult to apprehend. James Olthuis and Brian Walsh have referred to this framework as Pannenberg's *contradictory monism*.[5] Contradictory monism is a *coincidentia oppositorum*, a unity of opposites, a system that devours difference in the name of difference. There are two simultaneous movements: one toward differentiation, the other toward unity. Thus "the finite and the infinite, the temporal and the eternal, existence and essence are simultaneously, mutually exclusive and mutually complementary. Simultaneously the direction of eternity and unity both validates and invalidates the opposing direction of temporality and differentiation."[6] Thus Pannenberg at once honors finitude and devalues finitude; finitude is a necessary evil—"necessary" because it is the only way to the true infinite, but "evil" because it must eventually be overcome. Throughout Pannenberg's corpus one encounters a both-and system that places his theory beyond critique.

However, *in the end* there seems to be a final resolution, a last reconciliation, a concluding *Aufhebung* that consummates the "end of history." I think it is very helpful to compare Olthuis and Walsh's "contradictory monism" with Caputo's "closet essentialism." Both, I would argue, are pointing to the same framework. In a manner very similar to Caputo's evaluation of Gadamer, Olthuis remarks that Pannenberg "seems to have a foundationalist concept of true universal reason that ignores, or at least does not take into account the current philosophical critiques of foundationalism. It is true that his is not a simple foundationalism. He insists not only that the question of truth remain open and our understanding of truth is always provisional *until the end,* but also that theology must begin and end with the majesty of God."[7] Up front there is a lot of

talk about provisionality, history and change, but *in the end* there is
a final determinative revelation of the essence of God.[8] "At the end
of history," Olthuis goes on to comment, "a hidden harmony will
be revealed in and through the contradictions."[9] In the end—when
time shall be no more—it is unity that overcomes the evil of diversity and multiplicity found in creation.

While this "end" is not straightforwardly historical or chronologi-
cal but rather *kairological,* his framework still posits a *moment* where
finitude is transcended, interpretation is overcome and the conditions of history are surmounted. Thus while I describe this model as
an eschatological immediacy model, it must be emphasized that the
eschaton is not simply chronologically future; in a sense the future
breaks into the present in the moment of *Aufhebung,* and it is in that
moment, which Pannenberg does describe as "future," that the conditions of hermeneutics are purportedly overcome.[10] While he may
not posit a "period of time" when this is the case, he nevertheless
assumes a (nontemporal) moment where this *Aufhebung* is effected.

In analyzing and engaging in criticism of Pannenberg, then, it is
necessary to proceed slowly. Some of my criticisms will appear to
be blatant misreadings and denials of explicit statements that he
makes. However, because of Pannenberg's contradictory monism,
or closet essentialism, it is imperative that we look to the future to
uncover his construals of interpretation. (One cannot call the
police until the end.) I will attempt to demonstrate these points by
first analyzing Pannenberg's understanding of creation and
humanity, which will lead to a discussion of evil in his system.
This will set the stage for showing the implications of these points
for his epistemology and hermeneutics. I will conclude with a critique and an alternate proposal.

Trouble in paradise. In Pannenberg, as we would expect, creation
itself points to the future, for finite beings exist in the nexus of
temporal sequence that "refers" to a future fulfillment, "a future
that transcends their finitude" (*ST* 2:7). "Creation and eschatology
belong together," he argues, "because it is only in the eschatological

consummation that the destiny of the creature, especially the human creature, will come to fulfillment" (*ST* 2:139). Creation's destiny—being in fellowship with God—was not possessed in Eden but rather remained a future fellowship to be established in the eschaton. Thus the second Adam does not *restore* a broken relationship; rather he *completes* a relationship that was deficient "in the beginning," so to speak (*ST* 2:138).[11] There is a contradiction between the state of creation (from the very *act* of creation) and the goal that the Creator has set for it, hence its groaning and pain until this contradiction is set aside in the eschaton (*ST* 2:137).

Creation, then, is lacking something that only the future can remedy. But this means creation *qua created* stands in need of redemption. There is a fallenness to creation that necessitates an addition or fulfillment. It is not surprising to find Pannenberg often approvingly citing Plotinus regarding the relationship between eternity and time,[12] and similar antecedents may be operative in Pannenberg's tradition, particularly in Luther.[13] But is it possible to speak of a "good" creation that is deficient? While Pannenberg would want to answer in the affirmative, the direction of his theology demonstrates that the two ideas cannot be maintained: either creation is complete (which does not mean "perfect") and therefore good or creation involves a lack that must be supplied, thereby impugning the original status of creation.

Pannenberg's system heads in the latter direction. This is seen, for instance, in his discussion of human finitude and time. Human beings, as created, are finite creatures; and as finite, they experience time as a sequence of events (*MIG* 87-88). But "with the completion of God's plan for history in his kingdom, time itself will end," and "God will overcome the separation of the past from the present and the future," which is a feature of cosmic time in distinction from eternity (*ST* 2:95). Juxtaposing these two ideas, Pannenberg is forced to ask, is time always related also to the finitude of creatures? That is to say, how will human beings—as finite creatures who are temporal beings that experience time as a sequence of past, present and future—exist in eternity, which is the end of time, and yet remain creatures and finite? "In the eschatological consummation," he answers:

> we do not expect a disappearance of the distinctions that occur in cosmic time, but the separation will cease when creation participates in the eternity of God. *Hence the distinction of life's moments in the sequence of time cannot be one of the conditions of finitude as such.* For the finitude of creatures, their distinction from God and one another, will continue in the eschatological consummation. Nevertheless, the distinction of life's moments in time has something to do with the finitude of creaturely existence, if only as a transitional feature on the way to consummation. (*ST* 2:95, emphasis added)

Pannenberg wants to keep his finite cake and infinitely eat it at the same time (in good Hegelian fashion).[14] Thus in the consummation humans remain finite (as Pannenberg insists),[15] yet they experience time as God experiences time, without distinction.[16] But we must consider the nature of finitude at this point. Finitude is both a temporal and a spatial limitation, or perhaps it is a temporal limitation rooted in spatial limitation. I experience time as a sequence because I am a situated person: I stand here, now. If, as Pannenberg contends, sequential experience of time ends with the eschatological consummation, is our spatiality also "overcome"? If not (and how could we remain creatures if it is?), how can spatially limited (i.e., finite) creatures experience time as anything other than succession, as a "separation of earlier and later by sequence of times, so that the present constantly sinks into the past (*ST* 2:95)"? Even if this is a kairological end, it still posits a moment when human beings transcend the human experience of time.

Allow me to present a little thought experiment, not on the "annihilation of the world"[17] but rather on the "consummation of the world," a picture of life in the new heaven and earth. On Pannenberg's accounting, humans remain finite beings in the eschaton, but they do not experience time as a succession of moments, distinguishing past, present and future. What then does their finitude consist of? If we continue with Pannenberg, "futural" finitude will consist in a distinction from the Creator and from one another (*ST* 2:95). We can at least say, then, that humans remain spatially limited beings in Pannenberg's new world; we do not, in the end, become omnipresent. But now, given that, can Pannenberg maintain the atemporality of redeemed humanity?

Let us consider Hendrikus, a human being occupying this new heaven and earth. As a redeemed creature (and as a Lutheran) he has attained the destiny that Pannenberg promised and has "transcended his finitude," but of course he is still not God. Hendrikus spoke with one of his redeemed sisters, Eta. But when did he speak with her? Yesterday? A moment ago? Do these questions not betray the reality that spatially limited beings must experience time as a succession of moments? Consider the conversation itself: Does the uttering of each word follow after one and precede another? Is that not constitutive of speaking? But again, do not the words *follow* and *precede* indicate an experience of time as successive, distinguishing the past, present and future? Indeed, is that not what Pannenberg describes as "our human experience of time" but an experience of time that he contends is *overcome* by eternity (*ST* 2:92)?[18] At this juncture we obtain a glimpse of the a-humanity, or supra-humanity, of Pannenberg's future. I agree with Pannenberg that humans do experience time as successive. But precisely for that reason it must be maintained that our future experience of time remains such; otherwise, we cease to be human and therefore cease to be God's privileged image bearers.

Pannenberg's theory regarding the *future* of humanity is the necessary correlate of his understanding of the *origin* of humanity. As a result of the creature's independence from the Creator in creation, there is a "tendency to disintegrate." Time, as the "condition of the attainment of independence by creatures" (*ST* 2:92), is at the same time that which dis-integrates the unity of life of the creature. Pannenberg's Plotinian borrowings are plainly evident here, as he confesses:

> According to Plotinus, even when the soul has lost the unity of its
> life and fallen victim to the succession of time, it is still related to
> eternity, and therefore to the totality of its life, but in the mode of
> endless striving after it, so that the lost totality can be regained only
> as a future totality (*Enn.* 3.7.11). Eternity as the complete totality of
> life is thus seen from the standpoint of time only in terms of a full-
> ness that is sought in the future. This was an important insight for
> Plotinus. (*ST* 1:408)

Pannenberg laments that Christian theology "let slip the chance"
to adopt Plotinus's analysis and goes on to mention that Heidegger
was the first to "recapture this insight," though he did so from an
anthropological rather than a theological standpoint.[19] Pannenberg's project is to retrieve this lost opportunity, hence his understanding of the creation of humanity as deficient and
disintegrating the unity of life. Humanity "falls victim" to temporality. Thus the "unity of life that we see only partially in the
sequence of moments in time, and that can find actualization as a
whole in eternal simultaneity, can be attained in the process of
time only from the future, which brings it to totality" (*ST* 2:102).
The emphasis on the future as completion and bringing about a
totality is the result of an emphasis on creation as something of a
fall, a lapse into temporality and finitude.

Creation as original sin. If the creature must attain independence
in time in order to attain future participation in God, and if that
independence can only be obtained in time, and if time is also the
condition of the dis-unity of life, then creation, in Pannenberg's
scheme, becomes a necessary evil for humanity's destiny. Though
"God did not will wickedness and evil," they are nevertheless
"accompanying phenomena" of creation and as such "are conditions of the realizing of his purpose for the creature" (*ST* 2:167).

The problem, as I see it, throughout Pannenberg's discussion of
creation is the fact that he fails to make a distinction between the
world *as it now is* and the world *as it was before the Fall*. For example, in an instance of questionable exegesis, he states that "accord-

ing to the Genesis record, the historical form and experience of humanity do not show unambiguously the goodness that the Creator ascribes to it. At the beginning of the flood story we read, 'And God saw the earth, and behold it was corrupt, for all flesh had corrupted their way upon the earth' (Gen. 6:12)" (*ST* 2:163). I am not an Old Testament scholar, but I do seem to recall that between the pronouncement of the goodness of creation (Gen 1:31) and the judgment of corruption in the flood narrative, a fairly momentous event occurred: the Fall of humanity (Gen 3).[20] But this corrupting of a good creation is pushed back, in Pannenberg, to a constitutive aspect of creation itself. Though he concedes that the biblical narrative points in the direction of an original perfect[21] creation, he feels that the eschatological motif of 1 Corinthinans 15:45-58, which points to a future completion of an incomplete humanity, is the ground for rejecting the notion of an original "perfect" state (*ST* 2:163).[22] Thus when God pronounced that his creation was "very good," it was really just "an anticipation of its eschatological consummation after it is reconciled and redeemed by the Son" (*ST* 2:168).

This "pushing back" of evil into creation itself comes to the fore when Pannenberg addresses the question, why did God permit wickedness and evil?

> To answer this question the theological tradition has pointed to the ontological constitution of created reality. In comparison with the Creator, the creature is mutable. Measured by God's eternal selfhood, the creature's mutability is an expression of its ontological weakness, of a lack of ontic power. (*ST* 2:169)

For Pannenberg, evil is rooted in the "ontological deficiency" of human beings (*ST* 2:169). "There is some truth," he continues, "in the tracing back of evil, including the moral evil of sin, to the conditions of existence bound up with creatureliness" (*ST* 2:170). But does this not mean that human beings as finite creatures, who are not gods, are at fault simply for being finite? Why must human fin-

itude be described as an original imperfection, unless, in fact, we
are expected to be gods? Pannenberg, relying heavily on Leibniz,
remarks that the creature is imperfect inasmuch as it "cannot
know all things, may be mistaken about many things, and can thus
be *guilty* of other failings" (*ST* 2:170, emphasis added). Guilty? Am I
guilty for not knowing everything and making mistakes? Am I
guilty for being a human being and for not being God?

Pannenberg does nuance this discussion, remarking that "the
limit of finitude is not yet itself evil." Yet he maintains a strong
relation between creaturehood and evil that in essence nullifies
this disclaimer; that is, the possibility of evil is still to be seen "in
the very nature of creaturehood." But rather than citing limitation
as the root, Pannenberg points rather to the "independence" of
creatures (*ST* 2:171).[23] But we must recall that earlier he insisted
that this independence is necessary for attaining the destiny of
humanity (*ST* 2:96). Evil remains, then, a structural element of
God's creation of human beings; or as Hegel said, Good Friday
must precede Easter Sunday. Olthuis has raised a number of serious questions at this point:

> Doesn't this make evil a necessary dimension of our nature as finite
> creatures? Is the "divided" self to be seen as a necessary, structural
> given of creation? Do not such views assume a fundamental "defi-
> ciency" in human nature from the beginning, that is, in principle,
> which makes it impossible for us to affirm wholeheartedly the good-
> ness of creaturely being? . . . If evil is as necessary to life as oxygen,
> does it ultimately make any sense to talk of human freedom and
> responsibility in respect to evil? If evil is a normal constituent of
> human existence, rather than a perverse condition, are we not legiti-
> mizing the very evils we are called to fight?[24]

It is against this background of creation's original deficiency that
we understand Pannenberg's insistence on creation as the first act
of redemption, only completed in the world's eschatological reconciliation (*ST* 2:173). Further, it is in connection with his discussion
of the fallenness of creation that we grasp another important fea-

ture of his theology: that "the incarnation is simply the theologically highest instance of creation." The sending of the Son[25] is the fulfillment of God's creative work (ST 2:144), a "fulfillment transcending our first weakness" (ST 2:211). Only in Christ do we see for the first time the completion of human nature, which seems to suggest that the completion of human nature is found in its divinization.

Thus creation, because it is deficient or lacking, is always already referred to in its future completion. This is seen, for instance, in Pannenberg's assertion regarding the "unfinished nature" of the image of God in humanity:

> In the story of the human race, then, the image of God was not achieved fully at the outset. It was still in process. This is true not only of the likeness but of the image itself. But since likeness is essential to an image, our creation in the image of God stands implicitly related to full similarity. This full actualization is our destiny, one that was historically achieved with Jesus Christ and in which others may participate by transformation into the image of Christ. (ST 2:217)

Humanity and creation, qua created, from the beginning required redemption, a completion not yet realized. As such we are driven by a "restless thrust toward overcoming the finite," recognizing that "the final horizon in which we see the true meaning of the data of life transcends the whole compass of the finite" (ST 2:228-29). A gigantic future awaits us in the eschaton.

Through a glass darkly, but . . . The same motif—the fallenness of creation—is uncovered in Pannenberg's epistemology and hermeneutics. Again, the understanding of finite human beings is (perhaps unwittingly) impugned, and we are constantly summoned to be gods and promised the hope of such in the consummation of history. In other words, Pannenberg is proffering an eschatological version of a "dim-mirror hermeneutic" (cf. 1 Cor 13:12), which posits an immediacy of understanding (without interpretation) in the future while at the same time affirming the present distortions and "brokenness" (*ST* 1:250) of human knowing. Thus Pannenberg will often speak of the "provisional" and "preliminary" nature of theological statements and interpretations "so long as time and history endure" (*ST* 1:16). They are provisional because of the limits placed upon them by the historicity of human experience, which, he continues, "forms the most important limit of our human knowledge of God."

Solely on account of its historicity, all human talk about God unavoidably falls short of full and final knowledge of the truth of God" (*ST* 1:55). Theological concepts and interpretations, then, must be understood as *anticipatory*: always referring to a future, definitive revelation. In his *Metaphysics and the Idea of God* this is tied more explicitly to the *finitude* of human existence (*MIG* 91-109), but in his *Systematic Theology* as well, he insists that the partiality of human knowing "is riveted as such to the conditions of finitude" (*ST* 1:54). Because we see through a mirror, enigmatically,

> the knowledge of Christian theology is always partial in comparison to the definitive revelation of God in the future of his kingdom (1 Cor. 13:12). Christians should not need to be taught this by modern reflection on the finitude of knowledge that goes with the historicity of experience. They can find instruction in the biblical account of our situation before God even as believers. Recognizing the finitude and inappropriateness of all human talk about God is an essential part of theological sobriety. (*ST* 1:55)

But . . . though our assertions and interpretations are provisional, preliminary and anticipatory, they nevertheless refer to a "future definitive revelation for which in the world faith is waiting" (*ST* 1:60). In the future the "definitive self-disclosure" of God will arrive, and it will overcome the conditions of provisionality and resolve all of the enigmas, "the final manifestation of what is yet hidden in God" that will constitute a "universal disclosure" (*ST* 1:207-8). In that day, we shall see "face to face." In that day, all of the essentialists will come out of the closet.

But . . . if the provisionality of human knowledge is riveted to the conditions of finitude and if—as Pannenberg insists—humanity remains finite in the consummation of history, then is it possible to ever overcome the provisional or "perspectival" nature of human knowledge? If the provisionality of knowing is overcome in the future, does this not require the overcoming of finitude? Does that not entail the overcoming of creaturehood? Is not even the face-to-face encounter mediated by a space of interpretation? That is, does not that face come to me through the space of vision? Do I not only see that which is other, that which is separated by a space, a space that requires interpretation? Do I not always already see the face "as" something, a seeing that is preceded by hermeneutics?

Coming to a juncture encountered earlier in the discussion of finitude and time,[26] Pannenberg is here forced to conclude that humans, despite their finitude, somehow overcome the perspectival and hermeneutical nature of knowing in the future, when time shall be no more. Again we must ask, how can spatially limited beings escape the situatedness of finitude? How can I avoid the fact that as a finite creature, I am standing here, now, and see things from this perspective? I think the dilemma is intensified for Pannenberg precisely because he grants that this is the case "in time and history" but not in the future; that is, he emphasizes finitude as the condition for its overcoming, but what does this kairological overcoming involve? Do we then cease to be human? Is not this future hermeneutical paradise (which is a paradise precisely because of the absence of interpretation) a land populated by giants who are larger than (human) life, beyond finitude and provisionality? And is that future not a rather in-human notion?

At a fundamental level, what is at issue is the relationship between creation and redemption. Within the context of such a question, it may be said that for Pannenberg, grace *completes* or *perfects* nature; redemption, then, consists in the completion of a deficient creation. This has been evident throughout the preceding

discussion, for instance, in Pannenberg's assertion regarding creation as the first act of redemption, the affirmation that the incarnation (the nexus of redemption) is the highest act of creation, the
notion of the "unfinished nature" of the *imago Dei* and the future
transcendence of finitude as the destiny of humanity. Redemption,
then, is not a remedial measure; rather it is necessitated by creation qua creation. The act of creation necessarily entails the crucifixion; the garden of Eden always already calls for the garden of
Gethsemane. The creation of "day" is intrinsically haunted by a
coming three hours of darkness, and seminally hewn from the tree
of life is a tree upon which the Son will hang, accursed.

But hasn't Pannenberg missed something here? Is redemption
necessitated by creation, or is it rather called for by a broken,
fallen creation, a creation corrupted and tarnished? Instead of
completing creation, does not grace *restore* a broken creation to its
original status?[27] Is it not a matter of *healing* rather than maturity?
The important effect of this emphasis on *restoration* rather than
completion is that it does justice to the original goodness of God's
creation and also emphasizes the ubiquity and radicality of evil
and suffering, in contrast to Pannenberg's system, which impugns
creation as already "fallen" and in need of redemption and which
also denies the horror of evil by integrating it into the necessity of
creation.

Finally, a theology of restoration, or a "creation theology,"
releases us from being guilty for being human beings. Because Pannenberg construes creation, and hence humanity, as deficient in
their created status, the impetus of his theology is driven towards a
suprahumanity and the "transcendence of finitude." On such
accounting, human life as finite is insufficient and must be overcome, and this also includes the situationality of human be-ing and
the accompanying ubiquity of hermeneutics. But is that not calling
us to be gods, or at least giants? And does that not entail a devaluing of human be-ing and a depreciation of the creational life that
has been granted to us by the Creator? Should we not rather be

content with our finitude, our humanity, as a gift from God? Should we not, with David (and against the giant), give thanks that we are so fearfully and wonderfully made (Ps 139:14)? Rather than construing creation and finitude as a fault *(culpa),* no matter how happy *(felix),* a creation theology challenges us to see in our finitude a gift that is not to be despised but rather enjoyed and even celebrated.

Ideal Fusion: Gadamer and Habermas

A brief consideration of Gadamer and Habermas (certainly unlikely bedfellows) will also mark their common affinity with an eschatological immediacy model such as Pannenberg's. While Habermas is a strident critic of philosophical hermeneutics and Gadamer stands as one of the fathers of the field, at root both seem to share a common interpretation of interpretation that *in the end* (whenever that may be) posits an overcoming of hermeneutics and the restoration or accomplishment of immediacy.

Painting such broad strokes, however, must be justified, particularly given Gadamer's impact on philosophical hermeneutics as perhaps the most influential post-Heideggerian philosopher with regards to questions of historicity and the conditionedness of knowing. Gadamer's project in *Truth and Method* was precisely to unveil the Enlightenment "prejudice against prejudice" *as* prejudice; Gadamer has demonstrated that the Enlightenment rejection of (religious) authority, while purporting to be a rejection of tradition in favor of reason, was really a rejection of one authority for another, of one tradition for a different tradition.

His own theory of hermeneutics, then, attempts a rehabilitation of tradition and an understanding of prejudice not as a barrier to knowledge but as its only avenue. Gadamer's two-sided project is illustrated well in the following:

> The overcoming of all prejudices, this global demand of the Enlightenment, will itself prove to be a prejudice, and removing it opens the way to an appropriate understanding of the finitude which dom-

inates not only our humanity but also our historical consciousness. Does being situated within traditions really mean being subject to prejudices and limited in one's freedom? Is not, rather, all human existence, even the freest, limited and qualified in various ways? If this is true, the idea of an absolute reason is not a possibility for historical humanity. (*TM* 276).

Gadamer stands very much on the side of finitude and situationality, laying out the conditions of hermeneutics as ubiquitous to human be-ing. This is especially seen in his discussions of tradition (*TM* 277-85) and the history of effect (*TM* 300-307) as the very conditions for the possibility of understanding. Unlike Lints, for instance, Gadamer does not think tradition is something that we could escape or overcome; rather, it is the very condition necessary for understanding. Far from being a "distortion" (Lints), tradition is that which enables us to understand.

Given this emphasis in Gadamer, many would find it an odd (or rather, erroneous) move to associate him with a model of hermeneutical immediacy, albeit an eschatological one. After all, is it not Gadamer that has pointed out to us the conditionedness and traditionedness of our understanding? Hasn't Gadamer, if anyone, sought to honor the reality of mediation? Is it not Gadamer who has opened our eyes to the fact that our understanding is always already an interpretation?

Yes and no. Gadamer certainly honors the historicity of knowing, and this book is indebted to him in many ways. However, by connecting Gadamer with a model of immediacy, I am emphasizing my hesitations regarding his understanding of plurality and difference; that is, I think behind Gadamer's hermeneutics—in the closet, if you will—there remains a deep monologism that ascribes unity to the Truth (and the Tradition). As such, there is a movement, in the process of conversation and interpretation, toward the *overcoming* of interpretation and finitude, but only, once again, via those conditions. Hermeneutics and interpretation are founded in difference and otherness; it is because I am unique, because I stand in another place and time, that interpretation is necessary.

But the task of Gadamer's hermeneutics, it seems to me, is to eliminate this otherness *in the end;* "understanding" for Gadamer seems to be constituted by the elimination of different identities.[28] This comes to the fore in his notion of the "fusion *[Verschmelzung]* of horizons," which arises in a section on temporal distance. Again, on the one hand I feel very near to Gadamer when he asserts that time "is no longer primarily a gulf to be bridged because it separates; it is actually the supportive ground of the course of events in which the present is rooted. Hence temporal distance is not something that must be overcome" (*TM* 297). Rather than being a yawning abyss, Gadamer adds, temporal distance is "filled with the continuity of custom and tradition."

It is his persistent (over-)emphasis on continuity that concerns me. As he goes on to develop, there is continuity because really, in the end, temporal distance is not composed of separate, closed horizons. *In the end* there is no difference: "Just as the individual is never simply an individual because he is always in understanding with others, so too the closed horizon that is supposed to enclose a culture is an abstraction" (*TM* 304). In the end we will see that what appear to be distinct horizons "together constitute the one great horizon that moves from within and that, beyond the frontiers of the present, embraces the historical depths of our self-consciousness" (*TM* 304). Thus for Gadamer, effecting understanding requires the transposing of ourselves—which involves "disregarding ourselves" and "rising to a higher universality that *overcomes* not only our own particularity but also that of the other" (*TM* 305, emphasis added). In fact, he argues, to acknowledge the otherness of the other is to suspend the other's claim to truth (*TM* 303-4). So *Verschmelzung* turns out to be a synonym of *Aufhebung,* another term bent on eliminating difference in the name of difference.

What ends up happening, it appears to me, is that identity is eliminated in the name of subjectivity and difference is obliterated in the name of commonality (*TM* 292). While Gadamer helpfully emphasizes the "miracle of understanding" (*TM* 292) in contrast to more radical deconstruction (pace Mark C. Taylor),[29] he does so at the expense of difference that grounds both hermeneutics and human existence. On the way to understanding and unity, interpretation is relegated to a transitional phase necessary for negotiating differences. I think Susan Shapiro is right when she observes that for Gadamer, "it is misunderstanding and misinterpretation that occasion the need for hermeneutics."[30] Gadamer himself seems to suggest the accidental status of hermeneutics when he alludes to the *solution* of the "hermeneutical problem" (*TM* 298). So as Caputo suggested, up front there is a lot of talk about change, difference and history, but in the end and in the closet, Gadamer's philosophical hermeneutics harbors a notion of deep monologic truth and a latent drive for immediacy which in fact seeks the overcoming of hermeneutics in a fusion of horizons. As Caputo remarks elsewhere:

> In the end, I think, Gadamer remains attached to the tradition as the bearer of eternal truths, which in a way does nothing more than modify Plato and Hegel from a Heideggerian standpoint. Gadamer's hermeneutics is traditionalism and the philosophy of eternal truth pushed to its historical limits. He offers us the most liberal form of traditionalism possible. He introduces as much change as possible into the philosophy of unchanging truth, as much movement as possible into immobile verity.[31]

There may be a case for the fact that Gadamer never believes hermeneutics will be overcome—that he is offering "not an *Aufhebung* which reaches or even aims at a final canonical state but an ongoing and continual *Aufhebung.*"[32] Nevertheless, his framework posits this as a hope and dream in the fusion of horizons and remains, as such, rooted in a deep monologism.

This attachment to the tradition is precisely the focus of Habermas's criticisms of Gadamer's philosophical hermeneutics.[33] He hears in Gadamer a dangerous submission to (the?) tradition that leaves one open to, and eventually ends in, violence. If, as Gadamer and hermeneutics suggest, we can never step outside our context—if we can only know based on context-dependent structures—then there is never possibility for critique, for one will never be in a position to challenge the tradition if one is enslaved to that tradition. If the tradition is distorted, hermeneutics will never permit one to recognize that distortion. This, Habermas contends, points out the limit of hermeneutics.

> The self-conception of hermeneutics can be shaken only if it becomes apparent that systematically distorted patterns of communication also occur in "normal"—that is to say, pathologically inconspicuous—speech. That, however, is true in the case of pseudo-communication, in which a disruption of communication is not recognized by the parties involved. *Only a newcomer to the conversation notices that they misunderstand each other.* (HCU 302)

It is this newcomer, this outsider or third party, who is able to point out the distortions; that is, these must be pointed out from outside the conversation—*outside the hermeneutical context.* If hermeneutical consciousness were truly universal, as it claims to be, then we would "have no universal criterion at our disposal which would tell us when we are caught up in the false consciousness of a pseudonormal understanding" (HCU 303). This is the limit experience of hermeneutics.

According to Habermas, Heidegger's and Gadamer's emphasis on our preconception formed by tradition as constitutive of knowing and impossible to escape—our "standing agreement" with our tradition—points to a consensus (which Habermas also wants) that is beyond critique (which Habermas is terribly frightened of).

> The inherently prejudiced nature of understanding renders it impossible—indeed, makes it seem pointless—to place in jeopardy the factually worked out consensus which underlies, as the case may be, our misconception or lack of comprehension. Hermeneutically, we are obliged to have reference to concrete preunderstandings which, ultimately, can be traced back to the process of socialization, to the mastery of and absorption into common contexts of tradition. . . . In

so doing, we resubmit ourselves to the hermeneutical obligation of accepting for the time being—as a standing agreement—whatever consensus the resumed conversation may lead to as its resolution. The attempt to cast doubt, abstractly, on this agreement—which is, of course, contingent—as a false consciousness is pointless, *since we cannot transcend the conversation which we are.* (HCU 313)

Habermas doesn't think (and I suspect he is right) that the tradition could ever be "wrong" or "deceptive" for Gadamer; that is, Gadamer fails to see that "the dogmatism of the traditional context is the vehicle not only for the objectivity of language in general, but for the repressiveness of a power relationship which deforms the intersubjectivity of understanding as such and systematically distorts colloquial communication" (HCU 314).

Habermas offers—in contrast to Gadamer's "ontologization of language"—a "critically self-aware hermeneutics . . . which differentiates between insight and delusion, assimilates the metahermeneutical knowledge concerning the conditions which make systematically distorted communication possible" (HCU 314). This critically self-aware hermeneutics finds consensus not in a standing agreement with what has been handed down but in the universal/shared principles of communication—"intersubjectively valid rules" (HCU 306)—which are the basis of all communication and which transcend every conversation. "Only this principle," he continues, "is able to ensure that the hermeneutical effort will not stop short before it has seen through deception (in the case of a forced consensus) and systematic displacement (in the case of apparently accidental misunderstanding)" (HCU 314-15). Because these shared principles transcend communication, they also stand independently of and outside our context and hence make critique possible. It is this "rationality" that provides the basis for critique of the tradition.

At this juncture we catch sight of Habermas's eschatology, his teleology of the ideal. This consensus, which is required for critique, "might be reached under the idealized conditions to be found in unrestrained and dominance-free communication, and which could, *in the course of time,* be affirmed to exist" (HCU 314, emphasis added). In the future lies "an ideal forum" where "communication can be carried through and made perfect" (HCU 315):

> An idea of the truth which measures itself against true consensus implies an idea of the true life. We can also say: it includes the idea of a coming of age. Only the formal anticipation of the idealized conversation as a future way of life guarantees the ultimate, contrafactual standing agreement which unites us provisionally, and on the basis of which any factual agreement, if it be a false one, can be criticized as a false consciousness. (HCU 315)

Language, then, is constituted by a systematic distortion; the negative effects of interpretation are *structural* elements of hermeneutics and are not accidental.[34] But the *overcoming* of such systematically distorted communication is envisioned in the future, in the realization of the ideal community in the kingdom of God, where a universal consensus is effected, eliminating the distortions inherent to interpretation. While Habermas is no evangelical—hoping to overcome mediation and "distortion" in the *present*—there remains nevertheless an eschatological bent that wakefully awaits the coming of the ideal speech community, which may even be experienced in the present (kairologically).

Ideally, I would disagree. However, Habermas's construal of the relationship between hermeneutics and distortion, against the horizon of consensus and universal reason, indicates that he too, though in a different way, offers an interpretation of interpretation not unlike Pannenberg's and Gadamer's. This eschatological immediacy model, in the name of historicity, delivers a deep monologic understanding of truth, a monologism that excludes all who are not the same *(monos).* In contrast, a creational-pneumatic hermeneutic offers space for different interpretations because it is rooted in a pluralist creation and a plural notion of truth. Thus a creational-pneumatic hermeneutic (developed more programmatically in part three) stands in direct contrast to the models in part one, models that link hermeneutics to fallenness and anormativity.

Part II

A Hermeneutics
of Fallenness

Three

Falling into
the Garden

P*art one of this book amounted to a hermeneutical hamartiology:*
an analysis of several interpretations of interpretation that linked
the meaning-ful negotiations of human communication to a story
of fallenness and, either presently or "in the end," promised
redemption from such structures. The state of affairs that necessitates interpretation (situationality, distantiality—in short, the finitude of human existence) is somehow overcome in order that
humanity might escape the plague of hermeneutics.

Our topic, while hermeneutical, is also anthropological: an
investigation into the nature of relations between persons (and
texts) in light of the "nature" of human be-ing.[1] As I have attempted
to demonstrate, both of the theories in part one, represented by
Rex Koivisto, Richard Lints, Wolfhart Pannenberg, Hans-Georg
Gadamer and Jürgen Habermas, result in a fundamental devaluing
of human be-ing by construing the conditions of such as something

to be overcome. Thus hermeneutics is anormative, accidental, fallen (hence the title of part one, "The Fallenness of Hermeneutics"). But if interpretation is a constitutive aspect of human experience and be-ing,[2] then it is impossible to overcome (without becoming gods); and further, the desire to escape the finitude of human existence itself marks the essence of the Fall, the quest to "be like God." The grasping of the forbidden fruit, rather than initiating the history of hermeneutics, was an attempt to overcome such mediation and to "know" as God does, *sans courrier.* A similar reversal in reading was offered with respect to the Babel narrative.

As we move into part two, however, we encounter several theoreticians who refuse to believe any such myth of immediacy or pure reading. It is precisely Martin Heidegger (and Jacques Derrida following him)[3] who has thematized the hermeneutical nature of human existence, as well as the inescapability of such. In short, Heidegger and Derrida are philosophers who accentuate what I have been describing as the "ubiquity of interpretation" with no dream of overcoming such a state of affairs. However, Heidegger and Derrida retain the category of fallenness to describe this state of affairs—not a fallenness in contrast to a primal paradise or heavenly city (as in part one) but rather an essential fallenness, a fall that is always already a fall *within* rather than a fall *from.* While the distantiality and situatedness of human be-ing are recognized as necessary and inescapable conditions of existence, they are nevertheless connected to a fallenness that issues in violence. Thus, instead of positing the "fallenness of hermeneutics," Heidegger and Derrida offer instead a "hermeneutics of fallenness."

But if hermeneutics and the space of interpretation are constitutive aspects of being human, why *must* this state of affairs be construed as violent? Further, if being human is to be a creature and if interpretation is an essential part of that creaturehood, then to construe such a state of affairs as essentially fallen is to ontologize the Fall and devalue the fundamental goodness of creation. While I agree with both Heidegger and Derrida that interpretation is part and parcel of being human, I disagree—precisely because of that view of interpretation—with their construal of this as necessarily or structurally fallen and violent. Further, I will argue that they understand it as such precisely because they continue to be haunted by a nostalgia for immediacy and the "ghost of full presence."[4]

In this chapter I will focus on Heidegger's early texts (1919-1927), attempting to outline both his positive contribution regarding the constitutive nature of hermeneutics as well as his construal of such as an aspect of the fallenness of human existence. This will require an extended consideration of Heidegger's anthropology and his analysis of intersubjectivity, followed by an attempt to mythologize otherwise than Heidegger. Crucial to this analysis will be a retrieval of the sources of Heidegger's thought in this regard, particularly the Christian antecedents in Martin Luther and Søren Kierkegaard. The chapter will close with a critique of these theological beginnings and a first attempt at reading the New Testament otherwise than Heidegger.

The Interpretedness of *Dasein*

The heart of Heidegger's early work, and that which has probably had the most impact on the subsequent history of philosophy in this century, is his disclosure of the interpretedness of human being-in-the-world; that is, the hermeneutical nature of human existence as conditioned by "being-there/here" *(Da-sein)*.[5] Though Heidegger's work is certainly indebted to previous research by Schleiermacher and Dilthey (and, to some extent, Nietzsche),[6] his project was a radicalization of their technical notions and an attempt "to locate interpretation originally in life itself."[7] While *Being and Time* (his most systematic presentation of these themes) fell as something of a bombshell on the philosophical community in 1927—seemingly without a genealogy—in recent years we have been made privy to the story of the genesis of this critical work, particularly with the publication of the young Heidegger's early

Freiburg lectures (1919-1923) in the still growing *Gesamtausgabe,* as well as the recovery of lost and unknown manuscripts.[8]

One of these early manuscripts is Heidegger's "Aristotle-Intro-duction" of 1922, which grants an early glimpse of his delineation of the "hermeneutical situation," or the conditions of interpreta-tion. Here he emphasizes that all interpretations "stand under determinate conditions of interpreting and understanding." Thus "every interpretation, each according to a particular field and knowledge-claim, has the following:"

> (1) a *visual stance* which is more or less expressly taken on and fixed;
>
> (2) a *visual direction* which is motivated by (1) and within which the "As-what" and the "That-with-respect-to-which" *[das "woraufhin"]* of the interpretation are determined. The object of the interpretation is grasped anticipatorily in the "As-what," and is interpreted according to the "That-with-respect-to-which";
>
> (3) a *visual breadth* which is limited with the visual stance and visual direction, and within which the interpretation's claim to objectivity moves." (PIRA 358)

Thus every interpretation is conditioned by these aspects of

1. traditionality, which hands down the possibilities for interpre-tation (the "forehavings" *[Vorhaben]* of *Being and Time*)

2. predelineation, whereby the interpreter understands some-one or something "as" something, which is conditioned by tradi-tionality (roughly the "foreconception" *[Vorbegriff]* of *Being and Time*)

3. the situationality or horizonality of human be-ing, which creates the horizons of the interpreter, beyond which he or she cannot see

Thus when I interpret something (a text, a sentence spoken to me by my wife), my interpretation is governed by several factors constitutive of finitude and being human. There are "limits" to interpretation that are both *handed down* by a tradition (such as the language I speak, the interpretations I have been taught at various levels of life, the sociocultural world in which I live, etc.) and *inhab-ited* as part of my finitude (the fact that I am here and not there). All of these aspects stand before every interpretation as "determinate conditions" that make interpretation possible, while at the same time governing the interpretive possibilities. There is no reading that is not at the same time a "reading-into" (PIRA 359).

Interpretation is always local, from a specific locale, a particular situation. In *Being and Time* Heidegger describes this as an "existential spatiality,"[9] which refers to what I have delineated as the situationality of human be-ing. This spatiality, or situationality, refers to a double-sided locatedness, a bivalent conditioning of human experience: (1) a *physico-spatial* limit inasmuch as I stand "here," "in this place," seeing things from this perspective; and (2) a *temporal* condition, inasmuch as I stand here "now," "at this time."[10] As he explains:

> The entity which is essentially constituted by Being-in-the-world *is* itself in every case its "there." According to the familiar signification of the word, the "there" points to a "here" and a "yonder." . . . Dasein's existential spatiality, which thus determines its "location," is itself grounded in Being-in-the-world. (*BT* 171)

Heidegger goes on to say that "by its very nature, Dasein brings its 'there' along with it."

Because human be-ing is characterized by this spatiality and situationality, the interpreter can never step outside of its locale, outside of its "there." I always see something "from here," from this perspective and this situation, the place where I stand: in relation to that which is interpreted, in relation to those to whom I am communicating and in relation to the traditions of which I am an heir. Inasmuch as this locale is not something I can choose (i.e., I cannot choose where and when I will be born, the culture into which I will emerge, the language I will be taught), Heidegger describes this being-in-the-world as *thrownness* (*BT* 174-83).

As humans existing in the world, the world is a constitutive aspect of our be-ing; the world is not something beside us or other than us, as the relation between subject and object or the distinction between the Cartesian *res cogitans* and the *res extensa*.[11] Thus we encounter "things" in the world not as things "in themselves" but as things that we use, as things *for* something. That is why the Greeks termed "things" as *pragmata*, things to be used in *praxis* (*BT* 96-97). Because we encounter entities in the world as things "for" something, we also encounter them always already *"as"* something.[12] Thus Heidegger refers (in his "Phenomenological Interpretations with Respect to Aristotle: Indication of the Hermeneutical Situation") to the "As-what," which in *Being and Time* becomes the "as-structure" whereby something "is understood in terms of a totality of involvements" (*BT* 189). It is this understanding of *something as something* that constitutes the fundamental interpretedness of existence, an interpreting that precedes every assertion.

> When we have to do with anything, the mere seeing of the things which are closest to us bears in itself the structure of interpretation, and in so primordial a manner that just to grasp something *free,* as it were, *of the "as,"* requires a certain readjustment. . . . In interpreting, we do not, so to speak, throw a "signification" over some naked thing which is present-at-hand, we do not stick a value on it; but when something within-the-world is encountered as such, the thing in question already has an involvement which is disclosed in our understanding of the world, and this involvement is one which gets laid out by interpretation. (*BT* 190-91)

At this point he returns to the three determinate conditions laid out in "Phenomenological Interpretations" as grounding this "everyday circumspective interpretation." In short, "whenever something is interpreted as something, the interpretation will be founded essentially upon fore-having, fore-sight, and fore-conception. An interpretation is never a presuppositionless apprehending of something presented to us" (*BT* 191-92). Every interpretation is a *decision* for a way of conceiving, a way of reading, "either with finality or with reservations" (*BT* 191).

This disclosure of the conditionedness of all interpretation and the role of presuppositions in hermeneutics are among the crucial contributions Heidegger has made to theory in the twentieth century. But the crux of his work lies not only in this discussion of the *nature* of interpretation but also in the *scope* of interpretation. Rather than confining hermeneutics to special disciplines such as law, aesthetics and theology, Heidegger's early corpus is devoted to signaling the primordial role of interpretation in all of human being-in-the-world. Hermeneutics is a negotiation not simply between a reader and a text but also between a carpenter and his hammer, or a wife and her husband. To be-in-the-world is to interpret. "Factical life," Heidegger states in 1922, "moves always within a determinate *interpretedness* which has been handed down, or revised, or re-worked anew. Circumspection gives to life its world as interpreted according to those respects in which the world is expected and encountered as the object of concern. . . . The interpretedness of the world is factically that interpretedness within which life itself stands" (PIRA 363).[13]

To be human is to interpret, to encounter the world and entities within the world "as" something—an encounter conditioned by the situationality of human finitude. In the language of phenomenology, interpretation is *pretheoretical* and thus precedes every thematization or theoretical articulation. The theoretical assertion, in fact, is a *derivative* mode of interpretation, made possible only by the primordial construal of existence. Heidegger's favorite example is a carpenter with his hammer:

> Prior to all analysis, logic has already understood "logically" what it takes as a theme under the heading of the "categorical statement"—for instance, "The hammer is heavy." The unexplained presupposition is that the "meaning" of this sentence is to be taken as: "This thing—a hammer—has the property of heaviness." In concernful circumspection there are no such assertions "at first." But such circumspection has of course its specific ways of interpreting, and these, as compared with the "theoretical judgment" just mentioned, may take

> some such form as "The hammer is too heavy," or rather just "Too heavy!" "Hand me the other hammer!" Interpretation is carried out primordially not in a theoretical statement but in an action of circumspective concern—laying aside the unsuitable tool, or exchanging it, "without wasting words." From the fact that words are absent, it may not be concluded that interpretation is absent. (*BT* 200)

Interpretation happens everyday, in the everyday, in every relationship. It often happens in the absence of words and largely in the absence of theoretical assertions. Life itself is a hermeneutical venture, and it is so because of the nature of human be-ing as finite, as located and situated. Heidegger represents something of a prophet of the ubiquity of interpretation, a prophetic tradition reaching back to Nietzsche. And as a prophet in this tradition he is, I would suggest, also recalling the tradition back to a more humane understanding of humanity, a more reasonable reason that honors the finitude (and createdness?) of human be-ing.

The Fallenness of the Everyday

However, having said that and despite all of the debts my creational hermeneutic owes to this prophet, a fundamental aspect of Heidegger's theory betrays that, in the end (although his philosophy is certainly a philosophy of finitude), his is a philosophy of the Fall. It is not a fallen philosophy[14] but a philosophy that sees the Fall as structural—an ontology or, if you will, an *ontologizing* of the Fall.

It is crucial that Heidegger's notion of fallenness (and earlier, "ruination")[15] be understood in connection with the hermeneutic structures outlined above. As noted there, Dasein encounters things "as" something "for" something because, as being-in-the-world, it is concerned and has a basic structure of care. But this "care for the world" has a built-in tendency to become absorbed in the world. Already in 1922 Heidegger proposes that

> there is alive in the movement of caring an *inclination* of caring towards the world as the *tendency* towards absorption in the world, a tendency towards letting-oneself-be-taken-along by the world. This

> tendency of concern is the expression of a basic factical tendency of
> life, a tendency towards the *falling away* from one's own self and
> thereby towards the *falling prey* to the world, and thus towards the
> *falling apart* of oneself. Let the basic character of the movement of
> caring be terminologically fixed as factical life's *inclination toward
> falling*. (PIRA 363)

This fallenness is not an "objective event" or something that
"happens"; instead it is "an intentional How" that is "constituent
of facticity" (PIRA 364; cf. *PIA* 133). Rather than living the factical
life of the *individual,* Dasein, as fallen, "moves instead within a
particular *averageness* of caring, of dealing, of circumspection,
and of grasping the world. This averageness is the averageness of
the *general public [Offentlichkeit]* at any given time, of the surrounding area, of the dominating trend, of the 'Just like the many
others, too.' It is 'they' *[das 'Man']* who factically live the individual life" (PIRA 365). A year later, in summer semester 1923, this
listening to the "they" (the "One," the "Anyone and Everyone") is
for the first time linked to the *everydayness [Alltaglichkeit]* of
Dasein (*OHF* 85).

It is this connection between fallenness, everydayness and the
"they"[16] that is explicated in *Being and Time.* It is important to recognize that this construal of fallenness is rooted in Heidegger's
anthropology and in his understanding of intersubjective relationships. "Being-with-one-another," he begins, "has the character of
distantiality" (*BT* 164). This is a necessary component of human
relationships inasmuch as human beings retain their identity in
relation—each is related but has its own space. However, Heidegger goes on to assert that this distantiality, which is constitutive of
Dasein, results in a fundamental violence.

> But this distantiality which belongs to Being-with, is such that
> Dasein, as everyday Being-with-one-another, stands in *subjection* to
> Others. It itself *is* not; its Being has been taken away by the Others.
> Dasein's everyday possibilities of Being are for the Others to dispose
> of as they please. These Others, moreover, are not *definite* Others.
> On the contrary, a n y Other can represent them. What is decisive is

just that inconspicuous domination by Others which has already
been taken over unawares from Dasein as Being-with. (*BT* 164)

Human relationships are constituted by a primordial violence
and domination. For Heidegger this happens whenever we read
the newspaper the others read or ride the subway on which others
ride. "This Being-with-one-another dissolves one's own Dasein
completely into the kind of Being of 'the Others,'" and it is because
of this subjection that Dasein falls prey to the "dictatorship of the
'they.'"[17] The "they" determines Dasein's possibilities; and as such
Dasein becomes bogged down in averageness, and its possibilities
are "levelled down" to what everyone else is doing. Dasein
becomes controlled by "the public" and the public's understanding
of the world. The "they," moreover, make things too easy; it "dis-
burdens" Dasein of the difficulty of life and Dasein becomes a
"nobody," "like everybody else." This surrender to the "they" is
directly related to Dasein's "absorption in the world" as an aspect of
fallenness and the tendency of care (*BT* 164-67).

Because Dasein's hermeneutical situation is determined precisely by what is handed down to it, Dasein is "proximally and for
the most part" mastered by the "they," takes the "they" at its word
and accepts its interpretation. But precisely at this point we see
that those determinate conditions constitutive of interpretation are
also, for Heidegger, instances of fallenness. That which is handed
down to Dasein as "traditioned" is now connected with the averageness of the public. For instance, language, rather than being understood as a necessary condition that makes interpretation possible
(while at the same time governing interpretive possibilities), is
construed as an "average intelligibility," an "interpretedness" to
which Dasein is "delivered over" (*BT* 212, 211). While a linguistic
tradition is a necessary aspect of human be-ing, it is at the same
time an instance of fallenness, another way that the "they" drags
the self into averageness and inauthenticity. Fallenness, in fact, is
"an essential tendency of Being—one which belongs to everyday-

ness" (*BT* 210). As such, "this everyday way in which things have been interpreted is one into which Dasein has grown in the first instance, with never a possibility of extrication. In it, out of it, *and against it,* all genuine understanding, interpreting, and communicating, all re-discovering and appropriating anew, are performed" (*BT* 213, emphasis added).

To be in-the-world, to be human, is to be fallen, for this is a "basic kind of Being which belongs to everydayness" (*BT* 219); in other words, "Being-in-the-world is always fallen" (*BT* 225). By becoming lost in the publicness of the "they," by listening to Others, Dasein has lapsed into *inauthenticity;* it has *"fallen into the world"* by becoming concernfully absorbed in the world (*BT* 220, emphasis added). Dasein does not fall *from* a "purer and higher 'primal status'" but rather is always already fallen: "Falling is a definite existential characteristic of Dasein itself. . . . Falling reveals an *essential* ontological structure of Dasein itself. Far from determining its nocturnal side, it constitutes all Dasein's days in their everydayness" (*BT* 220, 224). While Heidegger was one of the pioneers in underscoring the ubiquity of interpretation, we now see that his category of fallenness construes just those elements as inescapable moments of fallenness. Those elements of human be-ing that are the grounds for hermeneutics—the situationality, distantiality (and intersubjectivity) and traditionality of human existence—even though they are "constitutive" of human being, are at the same time depicted as those characteristics by which Dasein, as long as it *is,* "is sucked into the turbulence of the 'they's' inauthenticity" (*BT* 223).

Thus human relations (Being-with-one-another), which are part of Dasein's "constitution," are always already frameworks of domination whereby Dasein is mastered by the "they." *"The 'they,'"* he continues, *"is an existentiale; and as a primordial phenomenon, it belongs to Dasein's positive constitution. . . .* The Self of everyday Dasein is the *they-self,* which we distinguish from the *authentic Self*—that is, from the Self which has been taken hold of in its own way" (*BT* 167). But this makes things too easy, Heidegger laments; it takes the *Kampf* out of life—and Heidegger loves a good fight. When Dasein listens to the "they"—and it cannot help but do so—it becomes average, like everybody else. Heidegger, on the other hand, is calling us to be heroes, to stand up and fight, to be above average.

This same tension—the tension between the conditions of our existence and the fallenness of those conditions—can also be seen in the forestructures of interpretation. On the one hand Heidegger's work is devoted to demonstrating that every interpretation is governed by the determinate conditions of what is handed down to us (the visual stance), the way we learn to interpret (the visual direction) and the horizons these produce (the visual breadth). How we interpret depends on our locale and our tradition, our context.

However, when we are influenced by "the surrounding area" and "the dominating trend," we fall pray to the averageness of the public's interpretation (PIRA 365). "Thus Dasein's understanding in the 'they' is constantly *going wrong* in its projects," and it is this way of Being that dominates Being-with-one-another (*BT* 218-19). The traditionedness that is part and parcel of being human is the same characteristic preventing Dasein from being its own self, from being authentic. For this reason every "genuine" interpretation is a reading *against* (*BT* 213). Because of Dasein's essential tendency to fallen interpretation, from which it can never be extricated, genuine hermeneutics is "naturally" violent.

> The reason for this lies in care itself. Our Being alongside the things with which we concern ourselves most closely in the "world"—a Being which is falling—guides the everyday way in which Dasein is interpreted, and covers up ontically Dasein's authentic Being. . . . The laying bare of Dasein's primordial Being must rather be *wrested* from Dasein by following the *opposite course* from that taken by the falling ontico-ontological tendency of interpretation. (*BT* 359)

Because Dasein has fallen into the world, and this essentially so, "existential analysis . . . constantly has the character of *doing violence.*" This is not only true with regard to Heidegger's fundamental analysis of Dasein; "it belongs properly to any Interpretation" (*BT* 359) and is directed against the structures of everydayness that are an essential characteristic of human be-ing.

But if interpretation—and the determinate conditions of interpretation—are necessary and "essential" aspects of human existence, why must these be described as fallen and violent? How has Heidegger brought us to this point? When did these structures become moments of fallenness, and when did interpretation become violent? If we would trace our way back through this discourse, we will find that the fallenness of everydayness, and hence the violence of hermeneutics, is rooted in Heidegger's construal of intersubjective relationships as ipso facto frameworks of domination (*BT* 164-65). Because Being-with-one-another places Dasein in subjection, listening to the "they" becomes a lapse into inauthenticity. That is to say, behind Heidegger's interpretation of interpretation lies a rugged individualism, a militaristic self-affirmation that devalues intersubjectivity—a resolute individualism that took on a haunting, *Volklich* character in 1933.[18] I think Habermas is correct when he suggests that

> from the start he degrades the background structures of the lifeworld that reach beyond the isolated Dasein as structures of an average everyday existence, that is, of inauthentic Dasein. To be sure, the co-Dasein of others first appears to be a constitutive feature of being-in-the-world. But the priority of the lifeworld's intersubjectivity over the mineness of Dasein escapes any conceptual framework still tinged with the solipsism of Husserlian phenomenology.[19]

Robert Dostal has objected to reading Heidegger as a closet solipsist, arguing that "Being-with-others is basic to Heidegger's account of *Dasein*." In fact, he observes, "sociality or communality are constitutive of *Dasein* in the most fundamental way."[20] Indeed, Being-with-one-another is constitutive of Dasein, but it is at the same time *inauthentic* existence. As such, Habermas's analysis remains valid: to be authentically Dasein is to wrest yourself free from the influence of the "they," which requires that a person, in some sense, escape the domination of Being-with (though you never "can"). Because intersubjective relationships—which are part and parcel of being human—are construed as structures of violence and fallenness, Dasein is essentially fallen—always already fallen as a related, intersubjective Being-with.

But why must the "distance" between persons—the space of identity—be understood as "disturbing" (*BT* 164)? On what grounds is this violence of intersubjectivity smuggled in, or what lies behind its introduction? Have we indeed stumbled upon a vestige of the Cartesian subject, a "tinge of Husserlian solipsism"? Is *authentic* Dasein actually a closet *res cogitans?* Was Sartre perhaps a faithful reader of Heidegger after all?

I find little justification for this *interpretation* of intersubjectivity apart from those suggested above, namely, a lingering commitment to a detached, solipsistic self while at the same time recognizing the inescapable relatedness of human be-ing. But wouldn't Heidegger's own *Destruktion* of this ontology lead also to the deconstruction of such a construal of intersubjective relations? Only against the horizon of a latent individualism (*pace* Kierkegaard) are human relations understood as detrimental to the self, particularly when a person recognizes that he or she cannot escape these relations. With regard to the hermeneutical situation, it is this relatedness of human be-ing that lies behind the traditionedness of interpretation: I learn to interpret within a tradition of which I am a part and that is composed of the *community* of which I am a part. I interpret, by and large, the way "they" interpret. But why must this be portrayed as inauthentic if it is an inescapable aspect of being human? Is it not delineated as such only because Heidegger remains haunted by presence, albeit a presence that is never present, a *Geist* of full presence? That is to say, doesn't Heidegger's discourse—his interpretation of interpretation—allow itself to be governed by its ghost, though it has no dream of immediacy? Is it not the specter of presence setting the rules for the game? Doesn't Heidegger's critique of the modern subject remain confined within a modern paradigm?[21] Are we not permitted (called?) at this juncture to interpret otherwise than Heidegger,[22] to follow a different *Weg*?

What if being-in-relation were understood as a crucial aspect of being *authentically* human? It is this other reading of human intersubjectivity that lies at the heart of a creational-pneumatic hermeneutic, for if to be-in-relation is an aspect of being a creature, then it must be understood as a modality of creational goodness, of the goodness of creation. Rather than being always already dominated by the other, the Other and others are crucial to my be(com)ing human. It is precisely this other reading of "Being-with," a reading otherwise than Heidegger, that has been developed by James Olthuis in his construction of an anthropological model that honors the intersubjectivity inherent to being human and being a creature.[23]

> An individual person is always an "I" of the "We." Individuation—the Iself—and communality—the Weself—are not fundamentally opposed. They are the two sides, so to speak, of the differentiated unity of humanity. Doing injustice to either side distorts the other and destroys the whole. There is no lone self. Every self is a "connective self."[24]

Rather than being aspects of fallenness and inauthenticity, relationships with others are crucial for authentic existence, for being one's own self *(Eigentlichkeit)*. "Being human," Olthuis argues, in contrast to Heidegger, "is a thoroughly relational affair. And becoming a self is a process of interconnecting in a rich variety of ways and forms. A self is thus constitutionally a connective self in process, a fabric of many strands woven and being woven."[25]

Heidegger's construal of intersubjectivity remains confined within an ontology of power and domination, where "to be a self is to have enemies. Implicitly if not explicitly one is always at war."[26] But this of course is only one interpretation, conditioned by a certain ontological tradition, and it is one that is open to, even invites, question. If the world is creation—a good gift from the hand of God—and if being-with-others is a constitutive aspect of created goodness, then we may understand human relationships not necessarily as frameworks of domination (though there are certainly cases where they are) but rather as networks for connection that are as crucial to human life as the oxygen we breathe. Instead of being a violation of myself, being-with-others is to be human.

To be "by myself," to be "locked in myself, out of inner contact with others—loneliness—is against the human grain."[27] The "distance" and "distantiality" (*BT* 164) characteristic of Being-with-one-another are not "disturbing" gaps. Rather they are the "wild spaces of love," which is another way to read, another way to construe, the world, an alternative interpretation of interpretation (and intersubjectivity).

> Love as gift creates a space-which-is-meeting, inviting partnership and co-birthing, and fundamentally calling into question the deconstructive idea that structures are necessarily violent. It suggests a new thematization of meaning and truth as good connections, in contrast to both modernity's power, control and judgment, and postmodernism's disruption and dissemination of any claim of entitlement to meaning and truth. . . . We have an invitation to meet and sojourn together in the wild spaces of love as alternatives to both modernist distancing or domination, and postmodern fluidity and fusion.[28]

In this reading, the other is not necessarily a diminution of my being, or that by which I am dominated, but rather the other who enriches my being.

With regard to hermeneutics, then, we recover the traditionedness of human be-ing from the realm of "inauthentic everyday existence" to be honored as an important and enabling aspect of human intersubjectivity. The community of which I am a part is not the "they" who distort my interpretations but rather precisely the community that comprises the tradition(s) of which I am a part—the community that taught me to speak, read and write (my "linguistic tradition") and that thereby opens possibilities for interpretation. It is "they" who taught me to interpret, and without "them" I would be lost; in fact, I am never without "them." To listen to the "they" is simply to be human, though it will certainly be admitted that at times listening to the dominant interpretation is violent (as, for instance, in Germany in the 1930s). But it is not *necessarily* violent to read the newspaper or ride public transit as Heidegger contends (*BT* 164).

This other reading of intersubjectivity and the spatiality that necessitates hermeneutics is indeed an interpreting otherwise than Heidegger, but it is also a reading of Heidegger against Heidegger, a "demythologizing" of Heidegger that disrupts his construal of human relations with his understanding of the constitutive nature of hermeneutics for human be-ing.[29] The goal of this demythologizing is not the elimination of myth, as John Caputo emphasizes, but the production of another myth—a myth other than that of primordial violence. To interpret life as creation is just such a myth, a good story *(eu-angelion)*, a tale of healing. Creation is a liberating Hebrew narrative told from the margins—from exile[30]—and is precisely what Caputo (following Derrida) describes as a "jewgreek" myth of justice.[31]

Because it is a myth—an interpretation, a construal—some will be quick to dismiss creation. But it must be recognized that Heidegger's tale of fallenness and violence is also a myth, a hermeneutical decision haunted by undecidability. We must choose between myths and interpretations, for

> it is not a question of getting beyond myth or of laying aside mythologizing altogether, which is no more possible than getting beyond or laying aside metaphysics, but rather of inventing new and more salutary myths, or of recovering other and older myths, myths to counter the destructive myths of violence, domination, patriarchy, and hierarchy.[32]

As John Milbank has argued, Heidegger and Derrida's "differen-

tial ontology is but one more *mythos*" to which we offer a counter-
myth, "an 'ontology of peace,' which conceives differences as
analogically related, rather than equivocally at variance."[33] Milbank
asks precisely the question that I have put to Heidegger's construal
of intersubjectivity:

> Does one need to interpret every disturbance, every event, as an
> event of war? Only, I would argue, if one has transcendentally
> understood all differences as negatively related. . . . If one makes no
> such presupposition, then it would be possible to understand the act
> of affirmative difference, in its passing over to the other, as an invita-
> tion to the other to embrace this difference because of its objective
> desirability.[34]

If we begin with a different decision, with a decision to interpret
and believe differently, then the relationships between entities,
which are the condition for hermeneutics, may be understood as
primordially and fundamentally "good" or "peaceful" (Milbank) yet
nevertheless open to the possibility of violence. But violence, in
contrast to Heidegger, would not be a constitutive aspect of such
relations; its intrusion, in war, is read "as an absolute intrusion, an
ontological anomaly" that has no "place" in creation.[35]

Heidegger's Disclaimers

Thus far I have suggested another reading of intersubjectivity in an
attempt to read otherwise than Heidegger's myth of intersubjective
violence and latent individualism, which undergirds his construal
of the fallenness of Dasein. But there would seem to be yet another
myth at work behind his discourse on fallenness: namely, a certain
reading of the traditional Christian doctrine of the Fall and original
sin. Of course, I have misread him, for Heidegger's early corpus is
filled with disclaimers that preclude just such a suggestion. The
interpretation of fallenness offered in *Being and Time* is "purely
ontological in its aims, and is far removed from any moralizing critique of everyday Dasein" (*BT* 211). Further, the category of fallenness and its manifestation in idle talk, curiosity and ambiguity is

not meant to "express any negative evaluation" (*BT* 220, 265); it is simply part of Dasein's essential ontological structure (*BT* 224). "So neither," he continues, "must we take the fallenness of Dasein as a 'fall' from a purer and higher 'primal status.' Not only do we lack any experience of this ontically, but ontologically we lack any possibilities or clues for Interpreting it" (*BT* 220). Dasein has not fallen *from* something or somewhere but is rather always already fallen— essentially and existentially—"into the world."

Above all, the ontological analysis of the fundamental structures of Dasein must not be confused with an ontical/theological discourse on the fall of humanity.

> It follows that our existential-ontological Interpretation makes no ontical assertion about the "corruption of human Nature," not because the necessary evidence is lacking, but because the problematic of this Interpretation is *prior* to any assertion about corruption or incorruption. Falling is conceived ontologically as a kind of motion. Ontically, we have not decided whether man is "drunk with sin" and in the *status corruptionis,* whether he walks in the *status integritatis,* or whether he finds himself in an intermediate stage, the *status gratiae.* But in so far as any faith or "world view" makes any such assertions, and if it asserts anything about Dasein as Being-in-the-world, it must come back to the existential structures which we have set forth. (*BT* 224)

The characteristics Heidegger describes as fallen are essential to Dasein, and therefore they precede any theological commentary on sin; the interpretation of fallenness in *Being and Time* is fundamentally neutral, before any faith commitment and hence untainted by it. He was most emphatic about this point in the lecture course of summer semester 1925, where he adamantly asserts that

> what is involved here is a pure consideration of structures, which *precedes* all such considerations. Our consideration must be differentiated quite sharply from any theological consideration. It is possible, perhaps necessary, that all of these structures will recur in a theological anthropology. I am in no position to judge how, since I

understand nothing of such things. I am of course familiar with theology, but it is still quite a way from that to an understanding. Since this analysis time and again incurs this misunderstanding, let me emphasize that it proposes no covert theology and in principle has nothing to do with theology.[36]

Across the campus at Marburg, Rudolf Bultmann was buying the story—the tale that lies behind his own myth of demythologizing, the goal of which was to sort through the layers of myth in the New Testament to unveil the essential structures of the gospel to express to the modern world. Because for Bultmann it is patently obvious that it is "impossible to use electric light and the wireless and to avail ourselves of modern medical and surgical discoveries, and at the same time to believe in the New Testament world of spirits and miracles,"[37] it is necessary to strip the kerygma of its mythical framework to arrive at a nonmythical expression of the gospel. The three-layered cosmos, the notion that death is the punishment of sin, the doctrine of the atonement and the resurrection of Jesus are all problematic aspects of the New Testament that are unacceptable to "modern man." Bultmann's project was to disclose the New Testament interpretation of human *existence* and to then determine whether that understanding is true. The faith that claims this understanding is true "ought not to be tied down to the imagery of New Testament mythology."[38]

Bultmann's project was at root apologetical. In essence it would appear that he was working with a revised natural theology, a kind of Protestant fundamental theology whereby he wanted to strip the New Testament of myth and arrive at its interpretation of existence in order that it might be "acceptable even to the non-mythological mind of to-day."[39] To then demonstrate that this interpretation of existence was true, which is the "real question,"[40] Bultmann turns to the "pure" discipline of philosophy to act as arbiter. This is not entirely unlike the traditional Thomist project of turning to philosophy—that is, natural reason—to confirm the preambles of faith. Thus one may read Bultmann's "New Testament and Mythology" as something of a twentieth-century *Summa Contra Gentiles,* a project erected with the hopes of beckoning a generation to faith by establishing a point of contact in reason (i.e., philosophy).[41] Just one refers to "the Philosopher," the other refers to the testimony of "the philosophers" for support.

What happens in the process of this demythologization is a remarkable tale: surprisingly enough, when all the demythologizing is said and done, Bultmann is startled by the fact that the New Testament, in mythical language, is saying precisely what Heidegger was saying in the earlier twentieth century in the neutral language of philosophy. "Above all," he remarked, "Heidegger's existentialist analysis of the ontological structure of being would seem to be no more than a secularized, philosophical version of the New Testament view of human life."[42] But because Bultmann was buying Heidegger's story about the neutrality and a-theological nature of his philosophy, Bultmann knew that it *wasn't* a secularization of the New Testament. It was, on Heidegger's accounting, a strictly neutral, even atheistic, analysis of ontological structures. Bultmann goes on to say:

> Some critics have objected that I am borrowing Heidegger's categories and forcing them upon the New Testament. I am afraid this only shows that they are blinding their eyes to the real problem. I mean, one should rather be startled that philosophy is saying the same thing as the New Testament *and saying it quite independently.*[43]

Thus when Bultmann finally arrived at the fundamental structures of the New Testament kerygma as encapsulated in anxiety and authenticity, he was assured that this was not simply mythology but instead part of the very structures of human existence since Heidegger was saying the same thing and saying it "quite independently."

But Bultmann's demythologizing worked only because he believed Heidegger's myth of religious neutrality in philosophy, which is rooted in his earlier methodological work where he developed the notion of "methodological atheism." This is not a simple atheism but perhaps even a Christian atheism, the atheism of one who has a knack for being both a philosopher and a Christian, which means being both an atheist and yet religious. What is at stake is the relationship between faith and philosophy, and it is here that Heidegger preaches atheism. For instance, in winter semester 1921-1922 Heidegger insisted that

> questioningness *[Fraglichkeit]* is not religious, but it may nevertheless lead me to a position where I must make a religious decision. I do not behave religiously in philosophizing, even if I as a philosopher can be a religious man. "But here is the art": to philosophize and thereby to be genuinely religious, i.e., to take up factically its worldly, historical task in philosophizing, in action and a world of action, not in religious ideology and fantasy. Philosophy, in its radical self-positing questioningness, must be in principle *a-theistic.* (*PIA* 197)

Philosophy is radical questioning, but to really question—to push one's questioning to the brink of the abyss—one must be an atheist, for faith gives answers too soon. Even into the next decade, in 1935, Heidegger maintained this principle of methodological atheism, arguing that

> anyone for whom the Bible is divine revelation and truth has the answer to the question, "Why are there essents rather than nothing?" even before it is asked: everything that is, except God himself, has been created by him. . . . One who holds to such a faith can in a way participate in the asking of our question, but he cannot really question without ceasing to be a believer and taking all of the consequences of such a step. He will only be able to act "as if." [44]

Faith and philosophy are mortal enemies; in fact, "faith is so absolutely the mortal enemy that philosophy does not even begin to want in any way to do battle with it." [45] "The philosopher does not believe" [46]—she or he cannot believe, because faith is in radical opposition to the very nature of philosophy as questioning. If phi-

losophy is going to "make factical life speak for itself," it must be
fundamentally atheistic' (PIRA 367). That is why the idea of a
"Christian philosophy" is a "square circle" and a "round square."[47]
Further, and most important for the present consideration, this is
why the ontological analyses of fallenness, care and conscience
must not be confused with theological accounts. Heidegger's discourse is a "pure" one, untainted or decontaminated of any vestige
of faith and religion.

Heidegger's Faith

I, for one, am not buying the story. As the research of Theodore
Kisiel, John van Buren and Caputo has demonstrated, Heidegger
did not come upon these structures quite as independently as Bultmann had assumed. From 1917 on, Heidegger turned to reading
Protestant theology and became particularly enamored with the
work of Luther.[48] His "Aristotle-Introduction" took its task of "phenomenological destruction" from "Luther's early theological
period"; indeed, the entire analysis was rooted in the implications
of "Reformation theology" (PIRA 372-73). Further, it is in Luther's
Lectures on Romans, Heidelberg Disputation and *Commentary on Genesis* that we find many of the terms used in Heidegger's description
of fallenness including *fall, care, anxiety, flight* and *conscience.*[49] And
most recently we see the genesis of Heidegger's "ontological" analyses in his work with Augustine's *Confessions.*[50]

It is not necessary in the present context to recite the mass of
data pulled together by Kisiel and van Buren. It is now beyond
question in Heidegger studies that his theological reading in Paul,
Augustine, Luther and Kierkegaard had a decisive influence on
Heidegger's early thought, a point that he himself maintained in
1959 when he remarked that without his theological background,
he would never have come upon the topic of hermeneutics.[51] However, Heidegger insisted that his philosophical conclusions were
reached "quite independently" of theological or religious influences. After all, this is philosophy, and philosophy has nothing to

do with faith. It seems, perhaps, that Heidegger most adamantly denies that which lies at the very heart of his project.[52]

But once again I am not buying the story, precisely because I do not buy the story of methodological atheism. *Being and Time* amounts to precisely what some had suggested but what Bultmann rejected: namely, a secularization (Heidegger would say a "formalization") of the New Testament. As Caputo well summarizes:

> When Christian theologians looked into the pages of *Being and Time* they found themselves staring at their own image—formalized, ontologized, or, what amounts to the same thing, "demythologized."
> . . . When Bultmann "applied" *Being and Time* to Christian theology he was "de-formalizing" the existential analytic and articulating it in terms of a historically specific, existentiell ideal, viz., historical Christianity. The reason this deformalization worked so well was that the existential analytic was in the first place and in no small part itself the issue of a formalization of Christian factical life. Bultmann was largely reversing the process that had brought *Being and Time* about in the first place.[53]

Once this is appreciated, it turns out that Heidegger's interpretation of fallenness—his interpretation of interpretation and his construal of intersubjectivity—is not so "neutral" or "pure" after all. Rather it is a myth that invites de- and remythologization.

At this juncture we may set about a second demythologization of Heidegger, reading Heidegger against Heidegger, dispelling the myth of religious neutrality. For is philosophy so pure? Is not the notion of an autonomous philosophy precisely the demon that Heidegger's own work was engaged in battling? Was it not Heidegger who insisted on the role of presuppositions and preunderstanding in philosophy? Is not this excising of faith from Dasein akin to the reduction to a transcendental-logical ego—the animal that Heidegger declared to be mythical? Can I stop believing when I philosophize? Do I?

Here I would propose that Heidegger, when discussing faith and philosophy, draws back from where the trajectory of his own thought would lead. The whole of Heidegger's early work is bent on demonstrating that we are not disembodied egos but rather human be-ings who are in the world and who cannot extrapolate ourselves outside of that environment. Philosophy, then, is not a pure, unalloyed, transcendental science, though it is a theoretical discipline *(Wissenschaft)*. As his own work has demonstrated, theory is not free from prejudice, from "extra-philosophical" commitments, and yet it is precisely this young Heidegger who insists on excluding the influence of faith from philosophy. But do we not find at this juncture yet another vestige of Enlightenment rationalism in the work of this one who played such a pivotal role in its dismantlement? Would not a more insistent hermeneutic phenomenology honor the role played by faith in philosophizing?[54]

Reading the New Testament Otherwise Than Heidegger

My goal in the preceding section was to unveil the myth—the religious commitment—at work behind Heidegger's purportedly neutral reading of intersubjectivity and hermeneutics. I did this in order to open space for a different myth, an other story of intersubjectivity. But secondly, having appreciated that Heidegger's interpretation of interpretation owes its impetus to the Christian tradition, one must emphasize that this influence comes from a particular *side* of the Christian tradition, a tradition within the tradition, albeit one of the most influential traditions. The genealogy of this tradition stems back to Paul, as interpreted by Augustine, Luther and Kierkegaard—a lineage traced in *Being and Time:* "Augustine . . . Luther . . . Kierkegaard . . ." (*BT* 492 n. iv)—echoing Luther's genealogy in the opening of the *Heidelberg Disputation,* where he appeals to "St. Paul, the especially chosen vessel and instrument of Christ, and also from St. Augustine, his most trustworthy interpreter."[55] Thus Heidegger's reading of historical Christianity and the New Testament was through the lens of a particular interpretive tradition, a tradition that excludes other tellings of the story. While Kisiel and van Buren claim that Heidegger was recovering "primal Christianity," I would ask, *whose* primal Christianity?

In the chapters that follow, I will suggest that Heidegger's dependence on this particular interpretive tradition leads to his devaluing of human be-ing by absolutizing and ontologizing the Fall and its effect on interpretation. However, it is important to remark that such an interpretive tradition, claiming to be in the lineage of Paul, seems to represent a selective reading of the Pauline corpus. And more importantly for my project, the claims to an "Augustinian" heritage constitute distortions of Augustine that fail to see the way in which the biblical impetus of his thought undermines the Neo-Platonic categories he employed. In chapter five, I will suggest that this mis-reading of Augustine can be traced to the Port Royal tradition of Blaise Pascal and Antoin Arnauld, disciples of Jansenius's *Augustinus*—which in the name of Augustine presents us with a very un-Augustinian "system." The result is what we might describe as a "naturalizing" or "ontologizing" of the Fall.

My goal will be to read the New Testament otherwise than Heidegger, through the lens of a different—and therefore suppressed and marginalized—interpretive tradition other than this privileged line. This different interpretive tradition, with a genealogy that includes the names of Jacobus Arminius and John Wesley, is uncovered through an archaeology of subjugated knowledges (voices from the margin), particularly the Pentecostal and Holiness traditions.[56] This alternative or counter-history itself offers another reading of Paul, questioning the Lutheran interpretive lineage marked above: that is, Heidegger's retrieval is not a simple retrieval of "primal Christianity"; it is not even a simple appropriation of the Pauline tradition, for Paul and the Pauline tradition itself constitute a pluriform corpus.

While Heidegger followed Luther in his *Destruktion* of Aristotelian Christianity, he left its Platonism untouched. Hence to be in the world is to be fallen, to be absorbed in the world. The Fall is a rather Plotinian fall into the Garden itself, inasmuch as the world/creation is essentially and structurally fallen, and hence the state of affairs that necessitates hermeneutics is fallen and violent.[57] Following Luther, in summer semester 1923 Heidegger emphasized that the Fall is "as such *constitutive!*" (*OHF* 27), and in his notes to the course he describes the Fall as "absolute" and refers "above all" to Paul (*OHF* 111). Being-in-the-world, for both Luther and Heidegger, is characterized by an essential fallenness, a notion that both attribute to Paul.

The attribution of such ideas to Paul is not entirely without warrant. As Jürgen Becker has observed, in Paul, as in Heidegger, there is no consideration of a world before a Fall; Paul's Adam is already a representative of a fallen humanity.[58] And while this would represent only a "side" of Paul, it is a side of the tradition that persists in Luther and Heidegger, to the extent that Milbank hears in Heidegger echoes of Valentinus:

> In trying to discuss the ontological difference in non-metaphysical, and non-ontological terms, Heidegger seems only to have succeeded in inventing his own religion. Indeed, in the notion of an ontological rather than a historical fall, there are many echoes of Valentinian gnosis, with its idea of primal disaster within the divine *pleroma,* or of Jacob Boehme, with his ideas of evil as arising within the workings of desire in the Trinity itself.[59]

Hermeneutics, then, is an inescapable aspect of human be-ing, but for Heidegger the Fall is also a constitutive or structural moment of the world. While this reading draws on a side of Paul or the Pauline tradition, my creational-pneumatic hermeneutic attempts a retrieval of an alternative, non-Platonic interpretive tradition also stemming from Paul and *another* Augustine but then tracing its genealogy down a more marginal path. In this tradition (which will be discussed more fully in chapter five) the Fall is not a structural or ontological aspect of the world but rather a historical and accidental brokenness that befalls a good creation. As such, hermeneutics is not construed as necessarily violent but rather as the space that opens the possibility for connection. Interpretation is not a sign of falling into the Garden; rather it is an invitation to commune with the other.

Four

Edenic Violence

$\mathbf{M}$*artin Heidegger's interpretation of interpretation represents the* seed for what I earlier described as a violent mediation model of hermeneutics, which affirms the ubiquity of interpretation as an inescapable aspect of being human but at the same time construes such conditions as the source of inevitable violence. "In the beginning is hermeneutics," Jacques Derrida writes.[1] That is, in Eden, in creation, there is interpretation, the negotiation of human be-ing, Adam interpreting (and misinterpreting) Eve (and God).

However, Derrida's interpretation of interpretation is not yet my creational-pneumatic model, for, as this chapter will attempt to demonstrate, when he asserts that "in the beginning there is hermeneutics," he is simultaneously declaring that "in the beginning there is violence." While interpretation is *in Eden*—unlike in the models in part one, which relegated hermeneutics to an accidental postlapsarian history—Eden itself is always already contaminated by the Fall, albeit a fall *within* and not a fall *from*. The garden is always already plagued by violence, and human intersubjective relations are "essentially" and necessarily a violation of the other. To be human is to be a savage hermeneut, always already and inescapably culpable for reading and thereby doing violence.

In this chapter I want to explore Derrida's interpretation of hermeneutics, focusing especially on the early *Of Grammatology* but also making reference to other essays. The first part of the chapter will be largely an exposition of the link between writing, violence and intersubjectivity in Derrida (and secondarily, Emmanuel Levinas), followed by a critique of Derrida's infinitist metaphysics of the supplement, attempting to catch sight of a spirit/ghost that continues to haunt his proposal.

Derrida's Reading of Writing

It must be emphasized that when we turn to Derrida's construal of writing and interpretation, his discourse is a sustained reading of a particular philosophical and theological tradition that then shapes his own "constructive" proposals. Thus his thoughts on writing are expressed against the horizon of what he describes as the "logocentric" tradition of Western metaphysics. It is a painstaking task to sort out the voices in this deconstructive mode of criticism, but such labor is necessary in order to avoid attributing to Derrida precisely what he is dismantling.

From Plato's *Phaedrus* to Hegel's *Encyclopaedia* to Saussure's *Course in General Linguistics,* Derrida sees the Western philosophical or onto-theo-logical tradition privileging *voice* over *writing,* sanctioning voice as the site of immediate access to "full presence," where presence is linked to comprehension and the denial of mystery. Western explorations into the relationship between thought, speech and writing would seem to be a series of footnotes to Aristotle's dictum:

> Spoken words are the symbols of mental experience and written words are the symbols of spoken words. Just as all men have not the same writing, so all men have not the same speech sounds, but the mental experiences, which these directly symbolize, are the same

for all, as also are those things of which our experiences are the images.[2]

Speech "directly symbolizes" thought, whereas written words are symbols of symbols, twice removed from reality, site of a degenerative secondarity. In the framework of Saussurean linguistics, speech is the signifier of a signified, whereas writing is signifier of a signifier.[3] Voice *(phone)* is thought to be a mirror of reality, delivering the world as it "really" is. In this history of logo/phonocentrism, writing is confined to a secondary and instrumental position:

> translator of a full speech that was fully *present* (present to itself, to its signified, to the other, the very condition of the theme of presence in general), technics in the service of language, *spokesman,* interpreter of an originary speech itself shielded from interpretation. *(OG* 8)

In the tradition, then, writing is linked to interpretation and mediation, whereas speech is thought to have unmediated access to "things" apart from interpretation. "The epoch of the logos," he continues, "thus debases writing considered as the mediation of mediation and as a fall into the exteriority of meaning" *(OG* 12-13). "Thus, within this epoch, reading and writing, the production or interpretation of signs, the text in general as fabric of signs, allow themselves to be confined within secondariness" *(OG* 14). Writing, and so interpretation, is relegated to a fallen secondarity and derivative status, merely "a sign signifying a signifier itself signifying an eternal verity, eternally thought and spoken in the proximity of a present logos" *(OG* 15). Inasmuch as speech is thought to be free of interpretation, human intersubjective relations are also thought to be free of interpretive superstructures and the mediacy of hermeneutics, a plague brought on by writing. It is this "contamination by writing" that is denounced by the preacher from Geneva (Saussure) as a violent heresy, "an archetypal violence: eruption of the *outside* within the *inside,*" a violence brought about by the body's usurping of the soul (*OG* 34-35).

Writing, in the tradition, comes upon language as a violence, though perhaps, as Jean-Jacques Rousseau intimates, a necessary violence, a supplement to speech that ends up replacing speech (*OG* 144-52). Writing, while an inevitable development, marks the corruption of the purity of speech; it is *exterior* to language, accidental, on the outside making its way in. "Rousseau," Derrida remarks, "considers writing as a dangerous means, a menacing aid, the critical response to a situation of distress. When Nature, as self-proximity, comes to be forbidden or interrupted, when speech fails to protect presence, writing becomes necessary. It must *be added* to the word urgently." Writing is "not natural. It diverts the immediate presence of thought to speech into representation" (*OG* 144). Writing is derivative because re-presentative.

This logocentrism of the Occident is the horizon against which Derrida takes up his project. His deconstruction sets out to disturb this myth of a pure voice—a speech uninhibited by interpretation and mediation—by unveiling the interpretedness of all human discourse; that is, "the secondarity that it seemed possible to ascribe to writing alone affects all signifieds in general, affects them always already" (*OG* 7). The *signified* is always already a *signifier,* so "signifier of the signifier"—the traditional definition of writing—"no longer defines accidental doubling and fallen secondarity"; on the contrary, it is the very origin of language and thus also characterizes speech (*OG* 7). Derrida does not question the traditional definition of writing and its link to violence; what he is challenging is the ascription of this only to writing "in the ordinary sense."

> Deconstructing this tradition will therefore not consist of reversing it, of making writing innocent. Rather of showing why the violence of writing does not *befall* an innocent language. There is an originary violence of writing because language is first, in a sense I shall gradually reveal, writing. "Usurpation" has always already begun. (*OG* 37)

His "revelation" to us is that there is a writing—and hence a necessity for interpretation—that *precedes* speech, which he describes as "arche-writing" (*OG* 56), a writing of which all language is composed. Writing, rather than being exterior to a pure speech, is always already interior to language, essentially rather than accidentally, as its very possibility (*OG* 52).

While the logocentric tradition debases writing as "accidental" and a "fall" inasmuch as it is mediated and re-presentative, Derrida pushes this back to language itself. While Rousseau understood the supplement of writing as exterior, Derrida's analysis attempts to reveal that supplementarity is inherent to language, that there is always already mediation, that "in the beginning there is hermeneutics." *"There is,"* he insists, in italics, *"nothing outside of the text,"* no referent at which language "stops" (*OG* 158). There has never been anything but writing; "there have never been anything but supplements, substitutive significations which could only come forth in a chain of differential references, the 'real' supervening, and being added only while taking on meaning from a trace and from an invocation of the supplement, etc." (*OG* 159). Rather than marking an accidental moment, supplementarity is a *structural* matter (*OG* 219): "Originary differance is supplementarity as *structure*" (*OG* 167).

The "Fall"[4] then, for Derrida, is structural—a theme that recurs elsewhere. In the collection of "Envois" in *The Post Card*, for instance, he emphasizes that "as soon as there is, there is differance . . . and there is postal maneuvering, relays, delay, anticipation, destination, telecommunicating network, the possibility, *and therefore the fatal necessity* of going astray, etc." (*PC* 66, emphasis added).[5] But when did a possibility become a "fatal necessity"? Why, because it is possible that a letter will not arrive, is it necessary that it not arrive?

Derrida admits he cannot demonstrate that something never arrives at its destination; rather, he will always say, "a letter *can* always *not* arrive at its destination." That is certainly a weaker reading, but in the end he doesn't really mean it. He betrays such in a postscript (to a postscript), noting that "in order *to be able* not

to arrive, it must bear within itself a force and a structure, a stray-
ing of the destination, such that it *must* also not arrive in any way"
(*PC* 123). The problem, for Derrida, is built into the very *structure*
of the postal system, which is also to say that it is an inherent element of the structure of the sign and the system of signifiers. The
"possibility" of going astray is a structural matter, which means that
it must (necessarily) be the case.

The mediation of hermeneutics, which the tradition relegated
only to writing "in the ordinary sense," is pushed back to the very
"origin" of language. But for Derrida this means that the origin is
fractured from the beginning.[6]

> If we consider the difference which fractured the origin, it must be
> said that this history, which is decadence and degeneracy through
> and through, had no prehistory. Degeneration as separation, sever-
> ing of voice and song, has always already begun. We shall see that
> Rousseau's entire text *describes* origin as the beginning of the end, as
> the inaugural decadence. Yet, in spite of that description, the text
> twists about in a sort of oblique effort to act *as if* degeneration were
> not prescribed in the genesis and as if evil *supervened upon* a good
> origin. (*OG* 199)

Derrida's project is to give up acting "as if" and to face the reality
of originary decadence. Thus *Of Grammatology,* he suggests, might
be read as a "theory of the structural necessity of the abyss" (*OG*
163). Arche-writing constitutes the fissure and rupture at the origin
of language, the "harsh law of spacing" that is "an originary acces-
sory and an essential accident" (*OG* 200).

Throughout this deconstruction, then, Derrida continues to
accept the traditional analysis of writing as representative, mediated and therefore calling for interpretation; his "twist" (*tours,*
"trick, turn, trope") is to emphasize that these elements are constitutive of language itself, and therefore he posits an arche- or pre-
originary writing. A second aspect of the tradition that he
appropriates is the link between writing and violence. While Rousseau and Claude Lévi-Strauss understand writing as a violation of

fully present speech, Derrida contends that arche-writing, before speech, retains this violent character. "Not for a moment" challenging Rousseau or Lévi-Strauss, he emphasizes that violence

> *does not supervene* from without upon an innocent language in order to surprise it, a language that suffers the aggression of writing as the accident of its disease, its defeat and its fall; but is the originary violence of a language which is always already a writing. Rousseau and Lévi-Strauss are not for a moment to be challenged when they relate the power of writing to the exercise of violence. But radicalizing this theme, no longer considering this violence as *derivative* with respect to naturally innocent speech, one reverses the entire sense of a proposition—the unity of violence and writing. (*OG* 106)

Rather than being accidental, violence is originary; thus we may "write" *writing/violence*—"violence is writing, . . . a fatal accident which is nothing but history itself" (*OG* 135). In a necessarily related manner, to read and interpret is also to do violence.

Intersubjective Violence
The violence of writing/interpretation, or writing/interpretation as violence, is rooted in the primordial war, "the essential confrontation that opens communication between peoples and cultures" (*OG* 107). This consideration arises in the midst of an extended dialogue with Lévi-Strauss on the impossibility of the proper name. The springboard for the discussion is a page from Lévi-Strauss's notebooks, compiled during his stay with the Nambikwara on an anthropological study—which was complicated by the fact that the Nambikwara are not allowed to use proper names. European visitors, then, impose nicknames upon them for sake of convenience. But as he recounts:

> One day, when I was playing with a group of children, a little girl was struck by one of her comrades. She ran to me for protection and began to whisper something, a "great secret," in my ear. As I did not understand I had to ask her to repeat it over and over again. Eventually, her adversary found out what was going on, came up to me in a

rage, and tried in her turn to tell me what seemed to be another secret. After a little while I was able to get to the bottom of the incident. The first little girl was trying to tell me her enemy's name, and when the enemy found out what was going on she decided to tell me the other girl's name, by way of reprisal. (cited in *OG* 111)

As Lévi-Strauss interprets the scene, this violent naming is occasioned by a foreigner, a spectator from the West. It is a violence induced when natural goodness is interrupted by something or someone from *outside*. The purity of the tribe is contaminated by the presence of an outsider. From this Lévi-Strauss draws a "writing lesson": the violence of naming, occasioned by the foreigner, is akin to the violence of writing, itself foreign to language, representing its exteriority, its "outside." But as such, the violence of writing is *accidental*.

Just as Derrida challenges the construal of writing as "outside" language, so analogously he deconstructs the notion of violence as accident befalling a fundamental goodness. Rather, the proper name represents the first violence. *Before* "empirical" violence there is the violence of arche-writing, which stands as its possibility. The impossibility of the absolutely proper name—and hence every naming is a violation of uniqueness—is inscribed in the very structure of language.

> The death of absolutely proper naming, recognizing in a language the other as pure other, invoking it as what it is, is the death of the pure idiom reserved for the unique. Anterior to the possibility of violence in the current and derivative sense, the sense used in "A Writing Lesson," there is, as the space of its possibility, the violence of arche-writing, the violence of difference, of classification, and of the system of appellations. (*OG* 110)

Inasmuch as writing/language does not allow the other to stand as "pure" other (*OG* 110-11), its naming is a violation of the other, a violence done to the other. Further, this is an inescapable violence, one essential to being human, for we cannot step outside of language, nor can we refrain from naming.[7]

> There was in fact a first violence to be named. To name, to give
> names that it will on occasion be forbidden to pronounce, such is the
> originary violence of language which consists in inscribing within a
> difference, in classifying, in suspending the vocative absolute. To
> think the unique *within* the system, to inscribe it there, such is the
> gesture of the arche-writing: arche-violence, loss of the proper, of
> absolute proximity, of self-presence, in truth the loss of what has
> never taken place, of a self-presence which has never been given but
> only dreamed of and always already split, repeated, incapable of
> appearing to itself except in its own disappearance. (*OG* 112)

"A first violence to be named"; a first violence: to be named—a violence beginning at birth, a violation of the parents against their
children that plagues them throughout their existence, one
re-enacted each day.

It is, in the end (or rather from the beginning), a violence inherent to intersubjective relations, a violence of being-with-others, an
almost familial violence. Writing—that is, arche-writing—is "the
exploitation of man by man" (*OG* 119). This is followed by a confession: "If it is true, as I in fact believe, that writing cannot be
thought outside of the horizon of intersubjective violence, is there
anything, even science, that radically escapes it?" (*OG* 127). Here
we have Derrida's "Confessions," following in the tradition of Rousseau (and Augustine),[8] his profession of faith, what he "in fact"
believes: "writing cannot be thought outside of the horizon of intersubjective violence."

Intersubjectivity marks the very origin of the self, but it is an
origin that is at once an originary corruption: "Affecting oneself by
another presence, one *corrupts* oneself (makes oneself other) by
oneself" (*OG* 153). Once again Derrida makes a confession: "I do
not *profess* that writing may not and does not *in fact* play this role
[of violence], but from that to attribute to writing [in the ordinary
sense] the specificity of this role and to conclude that speech is
exempt from it, is an abyss that one must not leap over so lightly"
(*OG* 133, emphasis added).

In his construal of intersubjectivity we get a glimpse of how Levinasian Derrida's thought has been throughout its course since 1967, rather than "shifting" to such in the later work.[9] With Derrida (and before Derrida), Levinas shares a philosophical commitment to the primordiality of war, and thus the relationship with the Other is one of violence (as in Heidegger). That war is the result of a totality, of the Other's being crammed into a system against her will, made to "fit." Thus when Derrida remarks that language prevents the Other from being recognized as pure Other, he echoes Levinas's opening to *Totality and Infinity,* where he writes, "War does not manifest exteriority and the other as other; it destroys the identity of the same. The visage of being that shows itself in war is fixed in the concept of totality, which dominates Western philosophy" (*TI* 21). Levinas's project is to show that this totality is interrupted by infinity; the interiority of the egoist self is disturbed by the exteriority of the Other, the transcendent face of the Other that comes from "on high."

For Levinas this relationship with the Other is "primordial," which we may roughly translate (in accord with previous terminology used in this book) "constitutive of human being." Infinity is "as primordial as totality" (*TI* 23). This means then that totality is primordial, and inasmuch as totality represents violence, we come upon an "essential violence" (*TI* 27). While for Levinas I am always already called to responsibility for the Other, which means that intersubjectivity is "essential" to human be-ing, this call is one that always comes violently upon me, disturbing my egoistic "enjoyment." The analysis of intersubjective relations begins with the purported necessary egoism of the self, of the "I."

> In enjoyment I am absolutely for myself. Egoist without reference to the Other, I am alone without solitude, innocently egoist and alone. Not against the Others, not "as for me . . ."—but entirely deaf to the Other, outside of all communication and all refusal to communicate—without ears, like a hungry stomach. (*TI* 134)

It is because I am egoist in my enjoyment, Levinas argues, that the face of the Other comes upon me violently, taking me hostage,

disturbing my "being at home with oneself" (*TI* 39). "To be I, atheist, at home with oneself, separated, happy, created—these are
synonyms" (*TI* 148). However, it is precisely the interiority of
enjoyment that is the condition for the possibility of the Other's
coming upon me: "Interiority must be at the same time closed and
open" (*TI* 149).

Levinas contends that because of the enjoyment/egoism of the
"I," the face of the Other comes as a violation. But in *Otherwise than
Being or Beyond Essence* the order of necessity seems to be
reversed: I must be egoist because the Other comes as a violation.
Of course, I know I have things backwards; I know that the Other
comes violently upon me *precisely because* I am joyously egoist.
That is, Levinas insists upon the violence of the Other's coming
upon me *given that* I am egoistic. His descriptive analysis has disclosed that I am complacent in my interiority and enjoyment, and
therefore the Other comes as a burglar, as a thief in the night. But it
would seem that Levinas sometimes flips the order. Note his comment that

> [signification] is the passivity of being-for-another, which is possible
> only in the form of giving the very bread I eat. But for this one has to
> ["must"] first enjoy one's bread, not in order to have the merit of giv-
> ing it, but in order to give it with one's heart, to give oneself in giving
> it. Enjoyment is an eluctable moment of sensibility. (*OBBE* 72)

Here the necessity of egoism's preceding the passivity of signification is posited in order to make sense of Levinas's thesis. It is
necessary for his thesis, but of course it is also a given, or given. We
are egoist, he describes (and never prescribes). But is this the case?
What I am attempting to point out is that Levinas's entire thesis
regarding the violent or asymmetrical relationship with the Other
assumes his discussion of enjoyment and the egoism of "me." But
could my living be described as otherwise than egoistic enjoyment,
as beyond interiority? Must we assume his description is correct?
Is it necessary?

This same construal of intersubjectivity lies at the heart of Levinas's critique of hermeneutics (as does Derrida's). When the face of the Other is taken "as a theme for interpretation," it is violated and placed in a totality of involvements rather than announcing itself *kath-auto* (*TI* 65).[10] Every thematization or conceptualization is necessarily an act of violence that reduces the other to the same. "Thematization and conceptualization," he continues, "which moreover are inseparable, are not peace with the other but suppression or possession of the other" (*TI* 46). At the same time this thematization is "inevitable" (*OBBE* 151). (At this juncture we also hear Derrida's discussion of the inescapable violence of the proper name.)

But is my relationship with the Other necessarily one of violence? Is it not construed as such only against the horizon of Levinas's interpretation of the self as primordially egoistic? At the level of "intersubjective violence," have we not arrived at Derrida's supporting myth, his *belief* "in fact"? Are we not free to interpret otherwise, to believe otherwise?

> One could make him say quite a different thing. And [Derrida's] text must constantly be considered as a complex and many-leveled structure; in it, certain propositions may be read as interpretations of other propositions that we are, up to a certain point and with certain precautions, free to read otherwise. [Derrida] says A, then for reasons that we must determine, he interprets A into B. A, which was already an interpretation, is reinterpreted into B. After taking cognizance of it, we may, without leaving [Derrida's] text, isolate A from its interpretation into B, and discover possibilities and resources there that indeed belong to [Derrida's] text, but were not produced or exploited by him, which, for equally legible motives, he *preferred to cut short* by a gesture neither witting or unwitting. (*OG* 307)[11]

I have attempted to isolate A from B, to demonstrate that there is a first interpretation regarding the violence of intersubjectivity that is then read into B, the violence of interpretation. But at the level of this first interpretation we are "free to read otherwise," able to offer an alternative myth of intersubjectivity, much as was offered above with regards to Heidegger. Indeed, do we not uncover here, as with Heidegger, a peculiar vestige of the tradition that he is attempting to deconstruct, a "falling back" (*OG* 14, 21) into the tradition?

What Derrida and Levinas have inherited from modernity is precisely what needs to be challenged.[12] Derrida is honest about not challenging for a moment Rousseau's and Lévi-Strauss's reading of violence; his own analysis is only a "radicalization" of their thesis (*OG* 106). And it would seem that Levinas's framework is also a wholesale adoption of a modern ontology (as found, for instance, in Thomas Hobbes), if only to invert it. But as I have attempted to argue above, intersubjectivity is violent only if one maintains something of a latent Cartesian solipsism or egoism. But if, in contrast, we understand human be-ing as essentially inter-relational, then that may be understood as "good," as an instance of a good creation and not fundamentally violent. Admittedly, that is a "belief," but so too, we have discovered, is Derrida's interpretation.

The Infinite and the Ghost of Metaphysics Past

Naming, reading, interpreting, speaking, writing—all of these are violence, Derrida argues. But on what grounds is naming a child violence? Or why must interpretation be violent? Further, if this is an inescapable aspect of being human—as Derrida believes—then why must this be construed as necessarily a violation? I would suggest that his interpretation of interpretation as violent betrays another vestige of the modern tradition of immediacy, for it is only if one is looking for immediacy and full presence that the finitude of interpreting "as" something is considered a lack, a fall, an impurity. The logic of supplementarity, despite all of Derrida's intentions, remains a kind of metaphysics of infinity. This is not to say that Derrida is looking for full presence or that he has any dream of immediacy, of escaping the interpolation of the postal system or of stepping outside of the space of interpretation. He has given up any "dream of a full and immediate presence closing history, the

transparence and indivision of a parousia, the suppression of contradiction and difference" (*OG* 115). The dream has died.

However, its ghost continues to haunt his work. Of course, "a
ghost does not exist" (*OS* 62); presence *is* not, is *not*, never was. But
its ghost remains, a specter lurking behind his discourse, unwittingly shaping the plot of the story. A dream that has become a
ghoulish *[Geistlich]* nightmare, a recurring haunting of a nostalgic
longing. It is a ghost he has caught sight of in the discourse of others: "Metaphysics always returns, I mean in the sense of a *revenant*
[ghost], and *Geist* is the most fatal figure of this *revenance* [return-
ing, haunting]" (*OS* 40). It is the *Geist* that Heidegger was unable to
avoid. But Derrida fails to see this phantom lurking in his own
work, "the phantom of subjectity" (*OS* 41).[13]

For instance, writing was traditionally construed as fallen and
violent because it sacrificed full presence. Derrida's radicalization
of this is to push it back to the origin of language, to the very structures of language. But is that not to maintain full presence as a
horizon? Elsewhere, he connects the violence of language to the
fact that it prevents the recognition of the other as *pure* other,
because purity is impossible (*OG* 110). Or as Levinas would say,
interpretation fails to do justice to the infinite and in fact violates
the alterity of the other.[14] Violence marks the very origin of language because it initiates the "loss of the proper" (*OG* 112).

But what if we were to give up an expectation of purity? What if
we refused to be haunted by this ghost of full presence and gave up
any pretensions to purity? Why must this be counted loss? Is not
interpreting it as such to harbor a notion of finitude as limitation
against the infinite? Is it not in fact Derrida who follows up his discourse with "the most traditional metaphysics of infinity" and "a philosophy of the unlimited"?[15] This seems to become clear in his
"Force of Law," where the ethical decision is an interpretive violence
because it is a decision that is "structurally finite" and can never
meet the demands of an "infinite 'idea of justice'"—"by nature"
unjust.[16] The decision is violent because it is finite; every decision

is an incision only because it cannot measure up to infinity, "cannot furnish itself with infinite information and the unlimited knowledge of conditions."[17]

But is that not to make finitude a violence, and is this not violence only if we are expected to be gods, even if it is impossible—only a dead dream? What if, instead of construing interpretive decisions as finite *incisions*, the hermeneutical moment was understood as "all we have," an inescapable aspect of being of which nothing more is expected? I am not suggesting that we "give up the infinite" or our attempts to do justice to the alterity of the other. It is not a matter of "giving up the infinite" but rather of giving up the assumption that the only way to "do justice" to the infinite is to speak of it in its infinity—which, of course, is impossible.[18]

What I am suggesting is that we give up a certain criterion for interpretation: namely that inasmuch as it is finite, it is a violation. Instead, and following Derrida, we might understand the "as-structure" of interpretation as a structure of *respect*, as a way of doing justice to the other by recognizing that it exceeds our finite comprehension.[19] Would not such a finitude be something like differance without being haunted by the ghost of full presence or the infinite ghost of metaphysics past? Following from such a construal, interpretation is not a violation of purity but rather a way of connection, a way of being-with that is essential to be(com)ing human. Rather than being the first violence, to be named is to be loved, is to be part of a community.[20] Once the myth of essential intersubjective violence is relinquished—that is, once we mythologize differently—then the ground for the violence of hermeneutics is transformed into the possibility of connection and the wild space of love—the field of creation and the ground of a creational hermeneutic.

Part III

Toward a Creational Hermeneutic

Five

Interpreting
the Fall

*The system which generally goes by the name
of Augustinianism is in great part a cruel travesty
of Augustine's deepest and most vital thought.*

JOHN BURNABY
*Amor Dei: A Study of the Religion
of Saint Augustine*

At this juncture I am obligated to fulfill a number of promises, to validate a number of promissory notes scattered throughout earlier chapters regarding my own proposal, which was repeatedly postponed to the fifth chapter. It is my hope that the shape of my own proposal has been sufficiently sketched or intimated in the first two parts of this book in order to provide grounds for my critiques. The task of parts one and two (chapters one to four) was to expound two basic interpretations of interpretation: a model of immediacy or presence (part one) and a violent mediation model (part two). Within these basic models, two variations were considered, such as the evangelical model of present immediacy and Wolfhart Pannenberg's eschatological immediacy model.

Those interpretations of interpretation, once expounded, were subjected to critique against the horizon of my own constructive proposal, which here, in chapter five, will be more programmatically developed. My own proposal—a creational hermeneutic—does not stand in dialectical relationship to the models in parts one and two; that is, it must not be understood as a new synthesis constituted by the sublimation *(Aufhebung)* of an evangelical thesis and a deconstructive antithesis. As I hope will become clear, my proposal stands in contrast to both and yet indebted to both; it is both very near to and yet very far from Richard Lints *and* Jacques Derrida. Thus the close reader will refrain from dismissing my creational-pneumatic model as either *simply* evangelical *or* deconstructive.

Toward an Augustinian Hermeneutic

My creational model is neither *simply* evangelical *nor* deconstructive precisely because it attempts to step "outside" (inasmuch as that is possible) the paradigm that I believe nourishes or grounds both of those models. I would argue that all of the earlier interpretations of interpretation considered in this book, from Rex Koivisto to Derrida, stand within a very distinct and formidable interpretive tradition whose genealogy stems from the beginnings of Western philosophy, to the beginnings of Christianity, to the beginnings of the medieval church, to the beginnings of the Reformation, to the beginnings of the modern era.

At root (and roots, of course, are usually buried, unseen and hidden) the linking of interpretation to fallenness may be understood as the product of a dominant Western interpretive tradition, a broadly Neo-Platonic understanding of creation and Fall, an understanding that is itself *an interpretation.* I believe that this tradition, which has significantly influenced aspects of the Christian tradition, remains plagued by an incipient Neo-Platonism (or gnosticism) which continues to construe creational finitude and human be-ing as "essentially" fallen and therefore ties hermeneutics to such a corrupted condition.

The immediacy model of evangelicals, Pannenberg and modern

philosophy rests on a dream of full presence,[1] of ascending to the Absolute Infinite Unconditioned, the *Eidos* or its Christianization as the "God of metaphysics."[2] Thus John Milbank writes (approvingly, I should add) of "Platonism/Christianity" and of the "neo-Platonic/Christian infinitization of the absolute" that characterizes the dominant Christian tradition.[3] With regard to the violent mediation model of Martin Heidegger, it became evident that his thought owed a number of unpaid debts to Martin Luther and Luther's tradition, namely, a *certain* "Paul" as mediated by a *certain* "Augustine." Even if Heidegger was enacting a recovery of "primal Christianity," as Theodore Kioiol and John van Buren suggest, it must be noted that it was a recovery of only a certain side of a pluriform Pauline Christianity that bore the marks of a Neo-Platonic devaluing of creation and provided the seeds for gnosticism, which Marcion exclusively adopted.[4]

This is then reflected in an influential understanding of original sin (deemed to be "Augustinian") that understands sin as original, constitutive, absolute—an essential aspect of being human.[5] This tradition then culminates in Heidegger, for whom fallenness is constitutive of finitude (*OHF* 27, 111)—what I have described above as an "ontologizing" of the Fall, whereby the Fall becomes "natural." While I do not have the space here to trace the genealogy of this tradition, I would suggest that the impetus for this understanding, beyond Luther, is found in the Port Royal tradition of Blaise Pascal and its patriarch, Jansenius. Jansenius's *Augustinus* is a paradigmatic example of John Burnaby's remark that "the system which generally goes by the name of Augustinianism is in great part a cruel travesty of Augustine's deepest and most vital thought."[6]

But as Paul Ricoeur suggests, there is a sense in which we must deconstruct Augustine in the name of Augustine; we must read the Augustinian affirmation of the goodness of creation *against* the received understanding of Augustine's notion of "original sin."[7] This is necessary because the development of a creational hermeneutic receives its impetus from a fundamentally Augustinian theme: the goodness of creation. Thus my project in this chapter is to effect a "deconstruction" of this Augustinian heritage in order to show that there is another side to the story—even "another Augustine." By a "deconstruction of Augustine" I do not mean a *destruction,* or leveling, but *another* reading of Augustine, a reading of Augustine against himself; more specifically, it is a deconstruction of Augustine's *Neo-Platonism* in the name of Augustine's *Christianity.*

As is always the case, a deconstructive reading is ultimately a productive reading that here seeks to produce an integrally Christian (and Augustinian) account of human finitude and hermeneutics. What will be at stake is precisely an interpretation of the Fall; drawing on Augustine's understanding of the goodness of creation, it will be a matter of *neither* identifying finitude with fallenness (as in Neo-Platonism and the models in part one) *nor* identifying finitude with violence (contra Heidegger and Derrida).

In addition to using this other (biblical and Christian) side of Augustine, my proposal attempts to draw on an alternate history— another story relegated to the margins, a collection of subjugated voices long identified not only with the margins but with the "outside" of the Christian tradition, at times with the heretical fringe. First, my creational model stands in contrast to those of the previous chapters precisely because it is rooted in a different paradigm. That is, mine is a more Arminian (but not precisely Arminian) understanding of the Fall and its implications for philosophical hermeneutics; it draws not on the received and dominant tradition but rather on the interpretive tradition traced in the likes of Grotius, Erasmus, Jacobus Arminius, Wesley and Miley[8] as mediated in its reinterpretation in early Pentecostal experience and later Pentecostal theology (inasmuch as it attempts to retrieve its Wesleyan-Holiness roots rather than a more Reformed-Baptistic framework).[9]

This tradition attempts to honor the goodness of creation *in the midst of* and *in spite of* the Fall; in contrast to Luther and Heidegger, this tradition holds that the Fall is not absolute nor constitutive (contra *OHF* 27, 111), though it is pervasive and ubiquitous. However, creation is not destroyed but rather marred, broken, diseased. As Augustine himself emphasizes, "We must remember that the image of God in the human soul has not been so completely obliterated by the stain of earthly affections, that no faint outlines of the original remain therein."[10] The Fall, then, is *not* "natural" (i.e., constitutive of creaturehood); rather, "the fault in man is contrary to his nature, and is just that which grace heals. . . . Grace is the mending of nature."[11] Redemption, then, is neither the completion of a deficient creation (Pannenberg) nor the recreation of an absolutely corrupted "nature" (Luther), but rather the *restoration* or healing[12] of a broken creation

The Fall, therefore, is

☐ historical rather than ontological
☐ accidental rather than essential or constitutive
☐ ubiquitous rather than absolute or total

The world is not the result of a primal disaster nor the site of unmitigated evil; the world, in short, is not "by nature" evil and fallen, given over to "the evil one." The world, though broken, yet remains creation. Interpreting the Fall is crucial for a creational hermeneutic because our understanding of the Fall indicates something of our understanding of *creation.* By emphasizing, with Augustine (and Arminius and Wesley) that the Fall does not completely change nature, we affirm that the goodness of creation persists in the midst of and in spite of fallenness.

Second, my model departs from the dominant tradition insofar as it does not identify finitude or hermeneutics with fallenness. While I disagree with the dominant tradition's understanding of the Fall, I am also disagreeing with what is connected with the Fall or seen as its result. Here we are concerned with a rejection of the Neo-Platonic elements of the tradition, seeking to mark a radical distinction between creaturehood and fallenness. There are strong currents within the Christian tradition—even within Augustine, as we will see—that identify the two, that see finite, physical, temporal existence as a penalty for sin. By affirming the goodness of creation (following Augustine) I am seeking to affirm the goodness of physical, temporal, bodily existence—that which makes language and interpretation both possible and necessary.

In the development of this framework, the shorthand of which may be simply described as "the goodness of creation," I am drawing on several (related) traditions. The first and most fundamental is the side of Augustine I have discussed above. The second is the neo-Calvinian tradition as it follows Abraham Kuyper in his reinterpretation of John Calvin: a reinterpretation, I would offer, that is actually a demythologizing, a reading of Calvin against Calvin as a mode of deconstructing Calvin*ism*. Kuyper's retrieval of the goodness of creation and of the world *as* creation stands in contrast to the dominant dualism of Christian thought.[13] The doctrine of total depravity, Kuyper remarked, remains disturbed by the experience of goodness; this is a result of what Kuyper describes as "common grace."[14] At this point the Kuyperian heritage intersects with a second source of my proposal, the Wesleyan-Arminian-Pentecostal tradition and the notion of prevenient grace. I would suggest that in Wesley's prevenient grace, we hear an analog of Kuyper's common grace and also that underlying both is a belief in the goodness of creation not as a pristine Edenic original but as a persisting present creation in the midst of the fallenness we experience. In the theology of my son's children's praise tapes, "God don't make no junk," and if God made this world, "it ain't junk."

The task of the remaining sections of this chapter is to unpack an Augustinian creational hermeneutic by means of a deconstructive reading of Augustine on language and interpretation, seeking to delineate the trajectory of his most biblical and Christian insights for a contemporary philosophical hermeneutic.

The Time of Language: The Fall to Interpretation in Early Augustine

The time of the Fall. In the early[15] Augustine we find a narrative similar to those sketched in part one above: the necessity of interpretation is occasioned by *language* (both oral[16] and written) and the order of signification; further, language itself functions only within the "medium" or "horizon" of *time*, or more specifically, temporal succession. Thus, interpretation is a task for temporal, finite creatures who must communicate by means of signs.[17] As language is the condition for interpretation and as time is the condition for language, so, it will become evident, the Fall is the condition for temporality. That is, the "distention" of the soul that constitutes the temporal condition of human beings, Ronald Teske observes, "is not merely the being of creatures; it is also our condition of having been separated or having fallen away from the One. Our being in time, it seems, is a penalty for sin."[18] And insofar as this "fall into time" is the condition for language, which necessitates interpretation, hermeneutics itself is only a postlapsarian task that befalls humanity as a consequence of sin.

Despite this link between time, language and the Fall (to be demonstrated below), there is another "side" to Augustine that would affirm the goodness of creation and thus ought to affirm the goodness of temporal, finite existence. And if finitude (i.e., being located in space and conditioned by time) is constitutive of creaturehood or creaturely existence, and if such finitude demands an "experience" of time as temporal succession, then would not time and language both be a creational good rather than something befalling humanity? And would this not indicate that interpretation is part of pre-Fall creaturely life and not a "punishment" to be overcome?

The fall to language: interiority and signification. Language, which for Augustine constitutes the condition for the necessity of interpretation, finds its origin in a "space" construed as a rift, an abyss between interiorities.[19] Signs are required in order to express the

soul's desires and intentions, since others "have no means of entering into my soul" (*CSA* 1.6.8), which is radically interior and thus
inaccessible. The infant, for example, "manifests" her wishes and
desires by uttering sounds that function as *external* signs of *interior*
desires. Thus it is by means of signs more generally, and language
in particular, that the soul's interiority is expressed: "Even at that
time I had existence and life, and already at the last stage of my
infant speechlessness I was searching out signs by which I made
my thoughts known to others" (*CSA* 1.6.10). The movement from
infancy to childhood is a shift from the use of nonverbal signs to
verbal signs, namely, words.[20] This permitted Augustine to better
"express the intentions of my heart" and so "communicate the
signs of my wishes to those around me" (*CSA* 1.8.13).

   In this opening narrative of the *Confessions,* Augustine reiterates a
fundamental aspect of signs as developed in *De magistro,* namely,
the mediating function of signs (and language) as that which
expresses an interiority to another who is exterior. Words (as signs)
are *external* manifestations of *internal* thoughts or desires. In *De magistro* this arises in a consideration of prayer: if, as Augustine suggests,
the purpose of all speaking is to either teach or remind, then what is
it that we teach God when we pray? As Adeodatus concludes, "We
certainly speak while we're praying, and yet it isn't right to believe
that we teach God or remind him of anything."[21] But we are commanded to pray, Augustine replies, "in closed chambers" (Mt 6:6),

> a phrase that signifies the inner recesses of the mind—precisely
> because God does not seek to be taught or reminded by our speaking
> in order to provide us what we want. Anyone who speaks gives an
> external sign of his will by means of an articulated sound. . . . There
> is accordingly no need for speaking when we pray. That is, there is
> no need for spoken words—except perhaps to speak as priests do, for
> the sake of signifying what is in their minds: not that God might
> hear, but that men might do so and by remembering might, with one
> accord, be raised to God.[22]

Speaking, and language in general, is an *external* sign of an *inte-*

rior desire or intention to those who are *exterior* to the soul, to other persons. In the case of God, however, who is able to know our innermost thoughts, language and speech are unnecessary.[23] Thus language is necessitated by the inaccessibility of the self's interiority and must function as a mediator between persons— between "interiorities":[24] "So as I make my confession, they wish to hear about my inner self, where they cannot penetrate with eye or ear or mind" (*CSA* 10.3.4). Words indicate, but do not "present," an a-lingual interiority that cannot be fully disclosed in speech but that nevertheless can be "expressed" or "manifested." The secret life of the soul can never be fully present in language.

Thus in *De doctrina christiana* Augustine asserts that spoken words *(verbum)* are the most characteristic form of "conventional" (as opposed to "natural") signs,

> which living creatures give one another in order to show, *as far as they can,* their moods and feelings, or to indicate whatever it may be they have sensed or understood. Nor have we any purpose in signifying, that is in giving a sign, other than to bring out and transfer to someone else's mind what we, the givers of the sign, have in mind ourselves.[25]

Language is required in order to express that which is interior to the soul by means of something external *(verbum)*; thus language "makes public" the "private" intentions and desires of the self; words are therefore "common property," belonging to a community.[26] Language must span a gulf between interiorities, precisely because the other has "no means of entering into my soul." The "space" between souls requires the mediation of signs, which in turn require interpretation.

But for Augustine this very state of affairs—the order of external signification and mediation—already signals a fall or distortion of a previously enjoyed *im*-mediacy, both between humanity and God and between human beings.[27] Signs and language are indications of a ruptured immediacy previously enjoyed, and they signal a rift opened between *signa* and *res.* In commenting on Genesis 2:4-5, for instance, Augustine interprets the rain that falls upon the earth as "words which sound and pass away after they strike the air."[28] However, the "field" requires nourishment by rain only *after* the fall of the soul:

> It was not already this way before the soul sinned, that is, before the green of the field was upon the earth. "For God had not yet made it rain upon the earth, and there was no man to work on it." For the rain from the clouds, which we have already mentioned, is necessary for man who is laboring on the earth. After sin man began to labor on the earth and to have need of those clouds. But before sin God made the green of the field and food, and we said that this expression signified the invisible creature. God watered it by an interior spring, speaking to its intellect, so that it did not receive words from the outside, as rain from the aforementioned clouds. Rather it was satisfied from its own spring, that is, by the truth flowing from its interior.[29]

Words, as *external* signs, are required only after the interruption of an interior dialogue with God wherein the soul communicated with God by means of an immediate intuition "flowing from its interior." Thus language already represents a rupture, a disruption of immediacy and an interruption of a private interiority.[30] The very order of external signification is a result of the Fall and will be overcome by redemption: "Man as he labors on the earth, that is, as he has become dried up by his sins, has need of divine teaching from human words, like rain from the clouds. However, such knowledge will be destroyed. For while seeking our food, we see now in an enigma, as in a cloud, but then we will see face to face, when the whole face of our earth will be watered by the interior spring of water springing up."[31] What is restored, then, is a prelapsarian immediacy where language, and hence interpretation, is absent; hermeneutics, as the interpretation of signs, is construed as a task of fallen humanity who "labors on the earth," a task from which we await redemption.

The fall into time: language and temporal succession. While language necessitates interpretation, we have seen that for Augustine it is mediation of subjective interiority that calls for language. We must further note at this point that the need for mediation is linked to the temporal existence of humanity as its condition; in other words, language functions only within the medium or horizon of *time.*[32] Temporality is constitutive of creaturehood,[33] and thus language is required as a mediator for those subjectivities located, or rather *limited,* in space and time; in short, language is constitutive of *finitude.* Beings within the finite, temporal order of creation are subject to change and impermanence: "When things rise and emerge into existence, the faster they grow to be, the quicker they rush towards non-being. That is the law limiting their being" (*CSA* 4.10.15). As limited by this law of finitude they "do not all have their being at the same moment"; that is, they are characterized by "passing away and by successiveness."

Augustine continues, "that is the way our speech is constructed by sounds which are significant. What we say would not be complete if one word did not cease to exist when it has sounded its constituent parts, so that it can be succeeded by another." Temporal succession is, for Augustine, a necessary aspect of language that is itself operative only for finite beings; and it is this temporal succession that signals the difference between external human words and that interior Word spoken in simultaneity. Thus later he again emphasizes that this temporality indicates the deficiency of creation as that which "suffers change and variation" in contrast to God's unchanging Being. So also human speech, in which syllables sound and pass away in "temporal succession," stands in contrast to the Word of God spoken in "the simultaneity of eternity" (*CSA* 11.4.6-11.7.9).

Just as Augustine posits the soul's redemption from the necessity of external signs, so he also asserts that the soul is promised release from its temporal conditions and, hence, a liberation from human language, which is constituted by temporal succession. The soul's ascent in its return to God climbs out of the temporal order and rises to the eternal, "where there is no past and future, but only being, since it is eternal" (*CSA* 9.10.24). This redemption is "tasted" in the ecstatic experience at Ostia, where the souls of Augustine and Monica "were lifted up by an ardent affection towards eternal being itself. . . . We touched it in some small degree [only to then return] to the noise of our human speech *where a sentence has both a beginning and an ending*" (*CSA* 9.10.24). Thus it is not only the mediating function of language that is overcome but also the very *temporality* of language. This can only be possible insofar as the soul transcends time itself, which requires the transcendence of finitude.[34] Finitude—location in space and time—is precisely that from which the soul seeks redemption.

But if time is created along with the rest of creation, why would the creature seek to overcome its temporality—that is, its location and delimitation in time? Would this not be a desire to overcome creaturehood, and is this not the essence of sinful pride?[35] Or is this longing for redemption from time an indication that time itself is fallen, that the soul falls *into* time?

The fallenness of temporality unfolds in books 11 and 12 of the *Confessions*; it becomes clear that Augustine posits a prior state of the created soul "before sin" in which the soul is not subject to temporal conditioning and hence is not subject to the temporal succession of language. Thus the desire for *redemption* from time is simply the *restoration* of a previously enjoyed state of the soul in the "heaven of heaven,"[36] wherein the intellect "participates in [God's] eternity" and thus "escapes all the revolving vicissitudes of the temporal process."[37] While not coeternal with God, the intellect nevertheless "suffers no variation and experiences no distending in the successiveness of time" precisely because it "lies outside time" (*CSA* 12.11.12; 12.12.15). As a result, the soul in the "heaven of heaven" is not plagued by the necessity of interpretation or the mediation of signs; rather, "the intelligence's knowing is a matter of simultaneity—not in part, not in an enigma, not through a mirror, but complete, in total openness, 'face to face.' This knowing is not of one thing at one moment and of another thing at another moment, but is concurrent *without any temporal successiveness.*"[38]

It is through the soul's "wandering" and "detachment" that it "slips away into the changes and successiveness of time"—a movement that is "a fault and a sin" (*CSA* 12.11.12; 12.15.19; 12.11.12). In other words, finitude itself marks a fall insofar as the soul has been "justly restrained to a *part* of the universe" as a "punishment."[39] It is because of this delimiting or confinement in time and space that we know by means of "physical perception," and the "words we speak [the soul] hears by the same physical perception." In other words, the embodiment of the self in space and time, the subsequent experience of time as successive and the employment of language conditioned by time are all attributed to a fall from an originary simultaneity and immediacy "before the soul sinned."

Thus we understand the "treatise" on time in book 11, in which time is finally "defined" as "simply a distention . . . of the mind itself" in which "I am scattered" (*CSA* 11.26.33; 11.29.39). *Distentio* ("distention"), Teske notes, carries a decidedly negative connotation, "indicating a spasm or distortion, similar to the description of the soul's 'swelling' *(tumor)* into a body."[40] "Stretched" by a multiplicity of distractions, the soul is scattered and dissolved in time, which also threatens to devour the self (*CSA* 11.29.39; 8.10.24; 9.4.10). The soul, then, falls *into* time as a fall *away* from eternity and immediacy.[41] Thus as suggested above, "since our presence in time is the penalty of our fall, Augustine sees the purpose of Christ's coming as to set us free from time. . . . Hence, the distention that is time is not merely the being of creatures; it is for us at least the penalty of sin from which Christ must set us free."[42] Temporality is not constitutive of creaturehood per se but is rather characteristic of *fallen* creation.

The fall to interpretation: summary. We are now in a position to sketch Augustine's understanding of hermeneutics as only a postlapsarian task. First, interpretation, we will recall, is demanded precisely by the mediation of language. Before the employment of external signs, interpretation was not needed; the soul was taught by direct intuition. Second, language is occasioned by two related states of affairs: (1) the incommensurability between subjective interiorities requiring external signs and (2) the temporal horizon of physical perception. Both of these states of affairs, we have discovered, are linked to the fall of the soul into time: the finite creature—located in space and time[43]—is limited in its being as a punishment for sin. As a result, hermeneutics and the necessity of interpretation are aspects of only a fallen creation, a disrupted immediacy, from which we look for redemption in a paradise where interpretation is absent and immediacy is restored.

Deconstructing Augustine: Toward a Creational Hermeneutic
Time, space and the goodness of creation. Having arrived at an account of Augustine's philosophical hermeneutics, we are left with questions that need to be asked of Augustine. First, if the soul "is distended in the creation of the world, is not the soul's fall into time the same as the creation of the world? Or in Christian terms, do not creation and original sin coincide?"[44] Second, would this not make finitude itself fallen? And would this not jeopardize the central distinction between Creator and creature—for how can we be other than finite and yet not pretend to divinity? Does not the portrayal of finitude and temporality as fallen erase any distinction between "creaturehood" and sin? Does this not push evil back to creation itself? Are we guilty for being human *(homo)?* And finally, do we not locate here a tension with a fundamentally Augustinian affirmation of the goodness of creation?

What is most lacking in Augustine's account of time and language is an affirmation of the primordial goodness of *embodied* human existence. And yet it is precisely this embodied, finite, temporal existence that Augustine ought—on his own terms—affirm as basically good. As Etienne Gilson comments, a medieval Christian philosophy grounded in an understanding of *creation* must grapple with the fact that the "very limitations and mutabilities for which nature is arraigned [in a Platonic tradition], are metaphysically *inherent in the very status of a created thing as such. . . .* If therefore we insist on calling evil the ineluctable law of change in nature, we must recognize that the possibility of change is a necessity from which God Himself could not absolve His creation."[45]

But insofar as it is not only the spiritual creation but the physical, bodily creation that is pronounced to be "very good" (Gen 1:31), a Christian philosophy must withdraw such an evaluation of finitude and temporality. "From you," Augustine notes, "the One, the supreme Good, they have being and are all 'very good'" (*CSA* 13.2.2). In a fundamental divergence from the Platonic schema, Augustine's Christian commitments lead him to affirm the general goodness of existence and thus the goodness of creation. The affirmation that "existence is good because it is thy work"[46] is located in Augustine's earliest works. With regards to the physical creation, Augustine attests that

> a corporeal object has some concord between its parts, otherwise it could not exist at all. Therefore, it was made by him who is the head of all concord. A corporeal object enjoys a certain degree of peace, due to its having form. Without that it would be nothing. Therefore he is the *creator of matter*, from whom all peace comes, and who is the uncreated and most perfect form. Matter participates in something belonging to the ideal world, otherwise it would not be matter. . . . For all existence as such is good.[47]

As such, fallenness is not to be attributed to matter *qua* matter nor to the embodied human person *qua* embodied or finite. Rather than such a "substantial" understanding of sin and evil, Augustine unceasingly emphasizes an "intentional" understanding of sin; that is, bodies are not sinful *qua* their ontological status as corporeal matter but insofar as they are "enjoyed" rather than "used." Augustine never offers us an *ontology* of sin but rather a *phenomenology* of sin.[48]

This "tension"—even "contradiction"—in Augustine's thought does not call for a solution or leveling; it is not a matter of harmonization. Rather, it invites us to take up Augustine's thought in a productive reading that reads Augustine on his own terms: a demythologizing or deconstructing of Augustine, which ought never to be understood as a *de*-struction, but much rather as a *pro*-duction that grants us another Augustine.[49] With regard to Augustine's hermeneutics, we would seek to critically read his devaluing of temporality, finitude and language against the horizon of his fundamental affirmation of the goodness of creation, producing an Augustinian hermeneutics that affirms embodiment and understands interpretation as a "creational" task.[50] In the final section that follows I will briefly sketch such an Augustinian hermeneutic that might be described as a "creational" hermeneutic.

An Augustinian philosophical hermeneutic. The import of the affirmation of finitude for hermeneutics is this: If hermeneutics is a constitutive aspect of human be-ing as creational, then

☐ It is not accidental but an inescapable aspect of human existence.

☐ It is a state of affairs that is *affected by* the Fall but not completely corrupted by fallenness nor the product of the Fall.

☐ It is an aspect of human be-ing that is primordially good and remains such in a postlapsarian world, and therefore it is not to be construed as necessarily violent nor understood as a state of affairs to be "overcome."

Creation, in this model, should not be identified with either a pristine "perfection" (or immediacy) or with a primal disaster or violence.

A demythologized Augustinian hermeneutic would link his insights on the temporality of human be-ing and language with his affirmation of the fundamental goodness of creation; the result is an understanding of the *status* of interpretation as a "creational" task—a task constitutive of finitude and thus not a "labor" to be escaped or overcome. Such an "interpretation of interpretation" *revalues* embodiment and ultimately ends in an ethical respect for difference as the gift of a creating God who loves difference and who loves differently. The heart of a "creational" hermeneutic is also rather "Pentecostal," creating a space where there is room for a plurality of God's creatures to speak, sing and dance in a multivalent chorus of tongues. It is to an explication of the hermeneutical structure of creation that I now turn.

Six

Interpretation
in Eden

In the beginning is hermeneutics.

JACQUES DERRIDA
"Edmond Jabès and the Question of the Book"

Having located the impetus for a creational hermeneutic in the trajectory of Augustine's thought, my task in this final chapter is a systematic analysis of the conditions of hermeneutics as constitutive of creaturehood (see "Human Be-ing and the Conditions of Hermeneutics"), understanding such structures as fundamentally good and not necessarily violent (see "The Goodness of Creation"). Finally, I will consider the question of plurality of interpretation within this framework (see "Before Interpretation" and "The Ethics of Interpretation"), sketching a correlative hermeneutics of trust grounded in the guidance of the Spirit (see "Of Spirit: 'Yes' and Amen").

Human Be-ing and the Conditions of Hermeneutics
Situationality and intersubjectivity. To be human is to interpret—to

negotiate understanding between two or more finite entities. Interpretation, then, is called for by a "state of affairs" in which we find *finite*[1] or situated beings *in relation*. These two elements—finitude and intersubjectivity—are the conditions for hermeneutics; but as will be noted, they are at the same time conditions that are part and parcel of being human and living in the world. Hermeneutics—the need for negotiation of understanding between finite entities—is therefore an inescapable aspect of being human and not an accidental or fallen way of being.

As finite human beings we never have (nor ever will have) access to the thoughts of another as immediately present, as Dante's Adam proclaimed. Instead, I always hear another or read a text from "where I am," translating the other's discourse into one that I can understand. Every act of reading or listening is an act of translation: a negotiation between two (or more) universes of discourse, two (or more) traditionalities, two (or more) ways of understanding the world. To use a more popular metaphor, I always read a text or see the world through the lens of an interpretive tradition from which I cannot extricate myself for it is part of what it means to be human.[2]

The ubiquity of hermeneutics, then, rests first of all on the *intersubjectivity* of human existence. We live with others—spouses, children, colleagues—and communication is necessary not only for survival, but also for our enrichment and growth as human beings. If there were no communication between entities,[3] there would be no need for interpretation. But intersubjectivity *alone* would not necessarily require interpretation of communication if both (or all) of the communicants shared the exact same language, identical vocabularies, the same thought processes and immediate access to another's thought (which would be identical to one's own). If this were the case, however, one would wonder if even something like communication would be necessary, let alone possible.

But precisely because human beings do not share the same language, possess identical vocabularies or have the same thoughts, interpretation is inescapable. This *difference*, which necessitates interpretation, is rooted in the *finitude* of human be-ing, the second condition of hermeneutics. Finitude, or what I have earlier described as *situationality*, signals the locality of being human, the fact that I hear or read from a specific locale, a certain situation—what Martin Heidegger described as the "hermeneutical situation."[4] This understanding of finitude should not be understood as a kind of negative limitation; rather it should be understood in a more Aristotelian sense of being located, bounded, with boundaries *(peras)*.[5] This locality or spatiality is both temporal and physicospatial and determines the possibilities of how one reads or hears.[6] It may also be described as the historicity of human be-ing, in the sense that I do not share *my* history and that this personal history shapes my language, my vocabulary, my "way of reading" and so on.

While the "ubiquity of interpretation" refers to the conditions of interpretation as a constitutive aspect of being human, it also refers to the *scope* of interpretation. Interpretation is not something that happens only when one reads a text; instead, interpretation occurs at every level of communication and is not limited to the textual or even the verbal (for even "body language" requires interpretation).[7] Interpretation "happens"—*es gibt* interpretation—at every level of relationship between situated beings. Every reading of the newspaper, every conversation at the dinner table, every rude gesture on the highway must be interpreted before it is understood. Every communication is filtered through a series of questionings, largely implicit, asked with the goal of understanding.

But the questions asked are determined by the situation and traditionality of the interpreter. Interpretation is not relegated or confined to writing (a notion that Derrida described as *logocentrism*) but rather stands at the origin of language and thus inhabits speech and gesture as well. For instance, if three hunters are walking to the blind in the middle of the marsh and one of the hunters shouts "Duck!" one hunter may raise his gun searching for the incoming fowl, while the other may dive to the ground in a desperate attempt to avoid an approaching projectile. The exclamation was "heard" differently, interpreted differently. This "universalizing" of hermeneutics beyond textual reading has been one of the crucial insights of Heidegger and Gadamer, moving hermeneutical discussions from specialized fields such as law, theology and aesthetics to the question of general hermeneutics (the project of Gadamer's magnum opus, *Truth and Method*).

Traditionality and intersubjectivity. Inasmuch as intersubjectivity and situationality are necessary elements of human be-ing that necessitate interpretation, the possibilities for interpretation are conditioned by the *traditionality*[8] that results from both intersubjective relations and the finitude of existence. As a finite creature I am part of a community, the inheritor of a way or ways of "seeing" the world, part of an interpretive tradition. We are always traditioned. We are always part of a tradition and always see through a tradition—that is, we are human.

In fact, we are the inheritors of a plurality of traditions: a linguistic tradition, a sociocultural tradition, a geographic tradition, a religious tradition and so on. For instance, I was taught to speak English (and in a certain sense, being born in rural Ontario, Canada—which I did not choose—I had no choice in the matter), which creates the possibility for both communicating and interpreting yet at the same time conditions the possibilities inasmuch as I can only say so much. My language is a finite collection, and my vocabulary uses only a small fraction of the possibilities within that language, which then limits my possibilities both for understanding and for communicating. However, even the notion of "limiting" betrays a nostalgia for infinity, thus I prefer the word *conditions.*[9] My linguistic tradition determines how I will interpret and determines "beforehand" the questions I will ask in the negotiation of idioms that constitutes hermeneutics. My sociocultural tradition (as a middle-class rural male), my geographic tradition (as a Canadian Westerner), my religious tradition (as a Christian) all condition how I will read a text, how I will hear a statement, how I will understand a communication.

While more Nietzschean deconstructionists such as Mark C. Taylor seem to suggest that there is no limit to the ways in which the world can be interpreted,[10] these conditions of traditionality do prescribe possibilities: a plurality of possibilities to be sure, but a plurality does not an infinity make. A similar suggestion may be found in an early critic of metaphysics, David Hume:

> Nothing, at first view, seems more unbounded than the thought of man, which not only escapes all human power and authority, but is not even restrained within the limits of nature and reality. . . . But though our thought seems to possess this unbounded liberty, we shall find, upon a nearer examination, that it is really confined within very narrow limits, and that all this creative power of the mind amounts to no more than the faculty of compounding, transposing, augmenting, or diminishing the materials afforded us by the senses and experience.[11]

The possibilities for construal are conditioned by what has been handed down as possibilities: that is, a person's tradition (*paradosis*). This is not to be confused with a mere repetition, for there are certainly possibilities for new interpretations; but there are only so many possibilities, a limited number of options with respect to the possibilities handed down. In Paul Ricoeur's language, only those "innovations" handed down by one's tradition are possible.[12] Traditionality is a *heritage* that one both receives and shapes. As Claude Geffre suggests, it is this idea of heritage that both "culture" and "religion" have in common: "Belonging to a culture is being rooted in particular tradition. It is being invited to live in the world in a certain language."[13]

A bibliography, for instance, is an indicator of such traditionality: the list of texts discloses one's tradition or one's exposure to a host of different traditions. However, though a bibliography may represent a diversity of reading areas, it nevertheless remains a finite collection that marks the constellation of one's thought.

Other books that lie outside of the bibliography may raise questions and interpretive possibilities I have not envisioned, and thus my reading remains conditioned by my situation. Further, the very location of texts happens within determinate limits: the books I will possibly read are limited to the languages that I have learned; I will have often read books upon suggestion of others—my teachers, for instance; or at the very least I will have read only those books that I have had *time* to read, which marks another condition. Traditionality, then, is marked by physico-spatial and temporal conditioning (as with situationality), but it is also made up of an inheritance from others (which is grounded in intersubjectivity).

Every interpretation, then, happens within an interpretive tradition, and within that interpretive tradition there is an accepted hermeneutic functioning as the normative or traditional hermeneutic, the standard of hermeneutic orthodoxy. We may see a similar state of affairs described in Thomas Kuhn's groundbreaking work *The Structure of Scientific Revolutions*. There he argues that scientific research into the structure of the world functions within a paradigm: a constellation of "commitments that govern normal science."[14] Purportedly objective scientific research proceeds "on the assumption that the scientific community knows what the world is like"; thus science works on a notion of precedent, and a paradigm functions very much like an "accepted judicial decision."[15] "Normal science" is that accepted standard within a paradigm which is taken as normative for guiding research; it is "research firmly based upon one or more past scientific achievements that some particular scientific community acknowledges for a time as supplying the foundation for its further practice."[16]

Classic examples would be the geocentric or Ptolemaic understanding of the universe, an interpretation of the world that was accepted as a paradigm for further research until its crisis in the Middle Ages.[17] Normal science is the research orthodoxy within a given paradigm. But the paradigm itself, Kuhn argues, is an interpretation, and as such normal science is a series of interpretations resting on a paradigmatic "reading" of the world. In the same way, every interpretation happens within an interpretive tradition—a paradigm, if you will—and the interpretive tradition shapes how interpretation happens. But as with the paradigms of scientific research, interpretive traditions, while necessary and inescapable, are nevertheless themselves construals of the world that are open to revision, conversion and rejection.

It is this traditionedness that is denied in immediacy models, particularly in evangelical theology, which proposes to read Scripture apart from the "distortion" of presuppositions or biases and which claims that "Scripture itself" can stand over and correct our presuppositions. But "empirically" (as in a Foucauldian genealogical analysis) it will be seen that purportedly objective readings function with an accepted interpretive tradition and that "everything but the most esoteric detail of the result is known in advance, and the typical latitude of expectation is only somewhat wider."[18] This was seen above whenever Rex Koivisto and Richard Lints proposed to deliver the "crisp unadorned voice of God" and their definitions of the gospel. I am not, it should be remarked, faulting evangelical theology for operating within an interpretive tradition, for it is impossible to stand outside of such—it is a constitutive aspect of human be-ing. The problem with much of evangelical theology is that it does not perceive itself as being governed by such an interpretive tradition, much as scientific research claims to deliver the world as it "really" is (scientists themselves have not been fond of Kuhn's conclusions). The myth of a pure, objective reading prevents evangelicals from appreciating the impact of their tradition on their reading, particularly with regards to the Bible.

A case in point would be recent evangelical engagements with Catholic thought, precipitated by the document "Evangelicals and Catholics Together: The Christian Mission in the Third Millennium" (1994, drafted by Richard John Neuhaus and Charles Colson), to which conservative evangelical responses came hard and

fast.[19] All of the evangelical responses are grounded in the Reformational commitment to "justification by faith alone" as disclosing
the *essence* of the gospel. What they fail to recognize in their
hermeneutical essentialism is that justification constitutes only
one interpretation of the gospel and that their own development is
mediated by Martin Luther's interpretation of Paul.

While they claim to deliver the essence of the gospel, *sans courrier,* what we receive is actually an interpretation of an interpretation, a reading shaped by a certain tradition and committed to a
certain mono-logic. When Luther defines the gospel as justification
by faith, he seems to have forgotten that the apostle John also
wrote about the gospel without ever mentioning such a forensic
notion. This distillation of the essence turns out to be the privileging of a certain tradition (the Pauline) to the exclusion of or at least
ignorance of the Johannine and Petrine traditions, and notori-
ously, the witness of James. The mono-logic of purported objectivity results in a leveling of the plurality of traditions within the New
Testament itself.[20]

Traditionality, or traditionedness, is simply an aspect of being
human, of living in the world as a finite being in relation with others. Rather than being a distortion or barrier to understanding, it is
our heritage, which opens up the very possibility of interpretation
while at the same time standing as the determinate condition of
interpretation.[21] Thus Heidegger remarked that every reading is, in
a sense, a "reading-into" (PIRA 359)—a reading shaped by one's situation, one's personal history and heritage, one's language and
one's faith. There is always already interpretation in every relationship, which means that there is also room for *plurality,* or
rather, plurality is the necessary result of irreducible difference.
We abandon, in addition to the myth of "objectivity,"[22] the
mono-logic of a hermeneutics of immediacy that claims to deliver
the one, true interpretation. But if interpretation is part of being
human, then its analogue is a creational diversity: a multitude of
ways to "read" the world. This is not to give up the notion of truth,

but it does abandon a certain understanding of truth; further, to say that everything is a matter of interpretation is not to abandon *criteria,* but it does require a reconsideration and reformulation of what those criteria will be (see "Before Interpretation" and "The Ethics of Interpretation," below).

Undecidability. A final structural moment of the hermeneutical nature of human be-ing that I want to briefly consider relates to the plurality and revisability of interpretation just mentioned. Every interpretation "takes a read," as it were, and thus involves a certain "commitment" to an understanding based on conditioned knowledge—in short, the judgment of a finite creature. One of the correlates of the situationality of interpretation and human life is an *undecidability* with regards to interpretation. This is because the space of interpretation, which opens up the possibility of understanding, is also the space that opens the possibility for *mis*-understanding, which is a necessary aspect of being finite, of being human, of being a creature. There is, if you will, a possibility for misunderstanding built into the very fabric of human life; there is the possibility of misunderstanding *in Eden.* This is neither sin nor evil, though after the Fall it becomes the space that evil and violence inhabit; that is, it was not a sin for Adam to misunderstand Eve, to think she said "three" when she said "tree." He simply misheard her, misunderstood, misinterpreted. As part of the structure of creation and the finitude of creaturehood, this should not be understood as sin; the goodness of creation is not perfection.

Therefore, the space of interpretation that is opened up in the very be-ing of being human is the space of a hermeneutic judgment made by a finite creature, and as such, it may be "wrong." In fact, in the end I would argue that every hermeneutic judgment is a kind of leap of faith, a certain trust or commitment, a belief that gropes beyond mere presence. Every interpretive judgment, then, should be accompanied by a corresponding hermeneutic humility or uncertainty.[23] Here again we turn to Augustine who, in finding a plurality of truths within the Scriptures, admonished humility on the part of interpreters: "Among many truths which are met by inquiring minds in those words which are variously interpreted, which of us can discover your will with such assurance that he can confidently say, 'This is what Moses meant'?" (*CSA* 12.24.33).[24] Thus our claims ought not be those of the "proud" (*CSA* 12.25.34), who claim to have the one, true, objective interpretation; rather, we ought to "equally respect another true interpretation as valid."

This tentativeness of the hermeneutical decision is captured in Derrida's notion of undecidability.[25] The hermeneutic decision—which is at root a commitment of faith—is a belief, not a metaphysical certainty of presence. As Søren Kierkegaard, in the persona of Johannes Climacus, remarks, "Faith is always in conflict, but as long as there is conflict, there is the possibility of defeat. Therefore, with regard to faith, one never celebrates triumphantly ahead of time, that is, never in time, for when is there the time to compose songs of victory or the opportune occasion to sing them!"[26] The hermeneutic decision remains haunted by uncertainty, for undecidability (not indecision) is the ground of the decision, just as doubt is the necessary correlate of faith. As Kierkegaard jots in his journal, "It is really Christianity that has brought this doubt into the world, for in Christianity this self received its meaning.—Doubt is conquered not by the system but by faith, just as it is faith that has brought doubt into the world."[27]

Faith and hermeneutics are inherent to creation, aspects of human life in its goodness; but inasmuch as hermeneutics indicates the necessity of interpretation—mediation—it also includes the possibility of misinterpretation. Also, faith implies its correlate, doubt. Interpretation and the hermeneutic project introduce a mediation that necessitates faith, that does not erase uncertainty but makes a decision "in spite of."[28] As such, there is built into the hermeneutical structure of creation an uncertainty, an undecidability with regards to hermeneutical judgments (i.e., interpretations), which ought to result in a more tentative offering of interpretations rather than a triumphant proclamation of having arrived at or having received from God the one, true, definitive reading.[29]

The Goodness of Creation

The goal of the preceding section was to disclose the *structures* of human life that (1) constitute the state of affairs (intersubjectivity, situationality, traditionality) grounding hermeneutics and the call for interpretation and (2) are constitutive aspects of human be-ing. The project was one of describing the nature and scope of hermeneutics and its inescapability in contrast to models of immediacy, which understand hermeneutics as accidental and fallen. So far the discussion has differed little from and relied heavily on the development of hermeneutics in Heidegger and its radicalization in Derrida.

However, as I remarked at the outset of this chapter, my model is not a simple reiteration of hermeneutic phenomenology or deconstruction, even though, as has been seen, it lies close to both. The point at which my model diverges from Heidegger and Derrida is in the construal of these structures: while we are agreed that these are "essential" to human be-ing and, as a result, so is hermeneutics, we are disagreed inasmuch as Heidegger and Derrida describe these structures as inherently violent. On the other hand, because I affirm the goodness of creation, I understand these structures as good and not inherently violent, though they may and do become such in a fallen and broken world. But I do not think they are "necessarily" so precisely because I believe the Fall to be a historical, accidental moment rather than an ontological, essential origin of human existence. In other words, I am proposing a fundamentally non-Plotinian account of physical, temporal, bodily existence that does not see temporal embodiment as an originary evil; rather, evil is parasitic, a corruption of "nature," and therefore fundamentally *un*-natural. Finitude is not evil and therefore is not essentially violent.[30] As a result the hermeneutical *structures* grounded in creational finitude are also fundamentally good.[31]

That is what I "in fact" *believe* (cp. *OG* 127), and it is perhaps destined to be rejected by some as a lapse into "theology," and a rather
naive theology at that. However, as we discovered as we looked at
Heidegger and Derrida (chapters three and four), their assertions
regarding the necessary violence of human existence and interpretation were grounded in "myth," in a fundamental commitment or
faith, a primordial way of reading the world. At this juncture we
have arrived at the level of fundamental construals, a very religious realm (though it is denied to be such by both Heidegger and
Derrida) of incommensurability. A similar juncture is seen in John
Caputo's *Radical Hermeneutics*, where he considers two primary
responses to our experience of suffering: the Nietzschean "tragic"
response and the Kierkegaardian "religious" response.[32] Undecidability, he remarks, prevents the privileging of either. But it seems
that, ironically, Caputo privileges the Nietzschean by describing
the religious response as a "construal," a *hermeneusis* that "has
looked down the dark well of suffering and found there a loving
power which takes the side of suffering."[33] More recently he says:

> Faith is a matter of a radical hermeneutic, an art of construing shad-
> ows, in the midst of what is happening. Faith is neither magic nor an
> infused knowledge that lifts one above the flux or above the limits of
> mortality. Faith, on my view, is above all the *hermeneia* that Some-
> one looks back at us from the abyss, that the spell of anonymity is
> broken by a Someone who stands with those who suffer, which is
> why the Exodus and the Crucifixion are central religious symbols.
> Faith, does not, however, extinguish the abyss but constitutes a cer-
> tain reading of the abyss, a hermeneutics of the abyss.[34]

Faith is only a construal which is enveloped and haunted by
undecidability; Abraham is haunted by Zarathustra's laughter. The
construal of the religious response is simply a way to cope with the
cold reality of the flux by construing it as something warm.

But doesn't this characterization already deny undecidability?
Isn't his characterization of the flux as "cold" already a privileging
of Nietzsche? Isn't the tragic also a construal, a *hermeneusis* that is

also exposed to undecidability? As suggested earlier, though Abraham certainly hears the echo of Zarathustra's laughter, I wonder whether Zarathustra ever lies awake at night wondering if Abraham is right. Is that not a more insistent understanding of undecidability? Caputo puts the burden of proof upon the religious response, which must answer to Nietzsche. But doesn't Nietzsche also have some explaining to do? Both the religious and the tragic responses are construals: interpretations of factical life.

Caputo continually insists on the frigidity of the world while seeing the necessity of a religious response; but this privileging of the tragic interpretation seems to convey that Nietzsche knows what the world is *really* like (which is a very realist notion). Only a hermeneutic that recognizes the creational nature of faith can truly recognize the all-the-way-downness of undecidability. Thus instead of undecidability's making it impossible to choose between the two, it is precisely undecidability that requires that we choose, in spite of the fact that our decision of faith is haunted by undecidability. Undecidability does not mean indecision; rather it is the condition for the possibility of decision, that which beckons for a decision. Undecidability means we can't put all of the data and options into a computer and let it generate a decision; we do not have time to wait for the machine to tabulate all the data, nor could the machine ever be supplied with "all" the data. But we must decide.

My construal of the world as creation is just such a construal: an interpretive decision in spite of a number of experiences that would seem to point otherwise, to the inevitable or essential violence of human life. But I would offer, the construal of the world as structurally violent is also a decision fraught with undecidability, confronted by experiences that would point otherwise. While for every interpretation of the world as creation "there is an Auschwitz or a Hiroshima, a killing field somewhere, in South Africa or South America, which silences God's voice,"[35] for every construal of the world as structurally violent there is the smile of a child, a birth, love. In fact, I would suggest that it is only a construal of the world as creation that can do justice to evil *as evil,* as that which should not be, as a horrendous and horrifying violence that should be opposed and from which we are promised redemption. If violence is understood as "natural"—an originary Hericlitean *polemos*—then on what ground could it be opposed? If human be-ing is essentially violent, what criteria could be offered to renounce violence? By affirming the goodness of creation we can also account for our opposition to violence and oppression as a state of affairs that "ought" not be, that demands of us not a "greater good defense" but protest and lament.[36]

Certainly creation is a different story than the one Heidegger and Derrida are telling, but it is only a different myth, a mythologizing differently. With regards to hermeneutics, this belief in the fundamental and persistent goodness of creation means that one is not doing violence to interpret, to construe something as something. However, a creational hermeneutic also recognizes that hermeneutics *can* become violent in a fallen world and that some readings have been responsible for the most horrific violence.[37] But again, it rejects that this is "necessarily the case," that this is a structural matter (contra *PC* 29). While Derrida offers a "structural theory of the abyss," my creational hermeneutic contends that the abyss is not structural but directional, a historical but not an essential reality of the world. A creational-pneumatic hermeneutic is something of a structural theory of the goodness of creation.

Before Interpretation
The postmodern condition. Given the structures of human be-ing and hermeneutics explored above—situationality, traditionality, undecidability—one may be left with the nagging sense that all is lost, that a creational hermeneutic is something of a religious cloak for a rampant relativism. If, as has been argued above, "interpretation is the only game in town"[38] and all of human life is at root hermeneutical, then it would appear that human be-ing is doomed

to arbitrariness and that the universality of hermeneutics signals the demise of any notion of normativity. If all norms, canons and standards are only construals and only operate within an interpretive tradition from which we cannot extricate ourselves, then any hope of adjudicating between different interpretations is lost. The very notions of a "good" interpretation and a "wrong" interpretation are themselves interpretations: construals made from a particular locale and from within a situated tradition. Furthermore, at root and beneath the surface, every interpretation or truth claim will be understood as the imposition of one interpretive tradition over another, and hence every assertion must be heard suspiciously, heard in such a way as to unveil the power structures at work in its production. If we take the ubiquity of interpretation seriously, we must be honest with ourselves and confess that, if the truth be told, there is no truth.[39]

That *may* be the case, but it is by no means necessarily so. The burden of this section is to challenge just such a construal of the implications of hermeneutics. While the ubiquity of interpretation does require a rethinking of truth, it by no means signals the abandonment of truth; that is, to say that everything is interpretation is not to say that all is *arbitrary*. Or in other words, to emphasize that understanding is relative to one's situationality is not to espouse a *relativism* (which is largely understood as arbitrariness). Further, the situatedness or perspectivalism of human be-ing need not issue in a fundamental hermeneutics of suspicion. In this and the following sections, I will counter these two basic proposals by (1) exploring the criteria of interpretation (as phenomenological and ethical) and (2) arguing for a primordial hermeneutics of trust as an inescapable element of human discourse—though this primordial trust, which makes suspicion both possible and necessary in a broken world, is nevertheless derivative.

The bulk of this book (particularly part three) has been devoted to demonstrating that interpretation is a constitutive aspect of human be-ing and that human life is inescapably one of construal.

We inevitably "see" the world through the lens of an interpretive tradition that delivers it "as" something; our reading of texts and our hearing of others are conditioned by our situationality (our topographic and temporal locale) and traditionality (those possibilities and ways of reading handed down to us). No discourse or interpretation is able to "overcome" these conditions so as to be able to deliver the world as it "really" is, to provide a normative interpretation that is "purified" from such conditions. To privilege one reading as normative (*the* one correct interpretation) would be to privilege one contingent situationality or tradition over another—a move that would be impossible to justify precisely because of the locatedness of any such justification. There is not *a* reading that is *the* reading of the world or a text.

But are we not then left with a state of affairs that precludes the exclusion of any interpretation and prescribes all interpretations be given equal status? Are we not then given over to a carnivalesque or Dionysiac celebration of diversity, where the construals of Isaiah and Hitler are just that: only interpretations and therefore construals from within a tradition that cannot be adjudicated?[40] It is at this juncture, in the realm of ethics, that the ubiquity of hermeneutics raises an acute problem: if every "reading" or claim is an interpretation, then is every interpretation legitimate? Can any interpretation be excluded as "false"? And if so, on what grounds, since every framework of justification rests on a contingent interpretive tradition? Here we have arrived at the dilemma of a pluralist society: (a) given that within a society there are competing truth claims, (b) recognizing that those claims are rooted in different interpretive traditions or worldviews that *found* those claims, and (c) understanding that criteria for evaluation always and only function *within* such a paradigm, how are competing claims arbitrated?

This dilemma is what Jean-François Lyotard means to describe by the notion of the "postmodern condition." While the term *postmodern* has of late been justly questioned and even discarded as overused and abused, it nevertheless remains helpful as a heuristic term for describing important shifts in Western culture and society.

As I will employ the term (following Lyotard), *postmodern* indicates the irreducibility and incommensurability of worldviews, "paradigms" (Kuhn) or "language games"[41] (Wittgenstein) that shape both knowledge and moral claims.[42] Rather than indicating a historical epoch, "postmodern" refers to a gestalt:[43] grounded in a recognition of the historical and contextual determination of thought, postmodernity signals the collapse of any myth of either Reason or Religion as a universal guarantor of Truth. That is, in postmodern society and culture we are confronted by a plurality of competing visions of the world without appeal to either an Enlightenment rationality or a religious revelation to settle the score. Being without recourse to either a premodern homogeneity of a *Volk*, which accepts the story without requesting legitimation (*PMC* 18-23), or a modern "metanarrative," which claims to provide universal legitimation through consensus (*PMC* 23-27), postmodernity experiences a "delegitimation" (*PMC* 37-41).

What is most characteristic and most challenging about postmodernity, then, is what we may describe (following both Lyotard and Habermas) as a "legitimation crisis" or "problem of legitimation" (*PMC* 8). Confining ourselves, for the present purpose, to the reality of deep *moral* diversity and competing visions of the Good, postmodern society is at a loss to adjudicate the competing claims. There can be no appeal to a higher court that would transcend a historical context or language game; there is no neutral observer or a "God's-eye view" that can *legitimate* or *justify* one paradigm or moral language game above another. If all moral claims are conditioned by paradigms of historical commitment, then they cannot transcend those conditions; thus every moral claim operates within a "logic" conditioned by the paradigm. Or in other words, every language game has its own set of rules. As a result, *criteria* that determine what constitutes "evidence" or "proof" must be *game relative:* they will function as "rules" only for those who share the same paradigm or participate in the same language game (see figure 2).

Language Game A
Logic A
Criteria
-
-
-
Arguments

Language Game B
Logic B
Criteria
-
-
-
Arguments

Figure 2. Language games

Arguments or defenses of moral claims operate on the basis of *intra*-paradigm or *intra*-game criteria; as such, the arguments carry force only insofar as the "addressee" shares the same paradigm; in this case there would be a "consensus between the sender and addressee of a statement" (*PMC* xxiii). If, however, the "sender" of the argument and the "addressee" live in different language games, then the argument is bound to be lost in the mail (cf. *PC*). The incommensurability of language games means that there is a plurality of logics that precludes any demonstrative appeal to a "common reason." Or again, in the model of language games the rules for distinct games are not proportional (*JG* 22). The pragmatics of justification, which requires a reversibility (i.e., consensus) between the sender and addressees (*JG* 23), is precisely that which is denied between language games.

"The problem," Lyotard notes, "is indeed one of translation and translatability. It so happens that languages are translatable, otherwise they are not languages; but language games are not translatable, because if they were, they would not be language games" (*JG* 53).[44] Recognizing the incommensurability of language games means that there is no consensus, no *sensus communis* (*JG* 14).

This postmodern condition, then, is felt most acutely in the confrontation and clash of worldviews, paradigms or traditions. Insofar as the paradigms remain isolated, the challenge of pluralism is absent: communities and traditions simply carry on with the logic granted by the paradigm. In what Lyotard describes as "narrative cultures," narratives enjoy an "immediate legitimation" and thus carry an inherent authority within the "people," *Volk* or tribe. It is important to note that it is precisely the homogeneity of "the people" which is the condition for the auto-legitimation of narratives: "Narratives, as we have seen, determine criteria of competence and/or illustrate how they are to be applied. They thus define what has the right to be said and done in the culture in question, and since they are themselves a part of that culture, they are legitimated by the simple fact that they do what they do" (*PMC* 23).

As Lyotard later suggests, this represents a certain "tribalism": the language game, or "genre," is a comfortable, "homey," very *Heimlich* space where narrative grants a homogenous identity and affords peace: "The *Volk* shuts itself up in the *Heim*."[45] However, this " 'internal' peace is bought at the price of perpetual differends on the outskirts." (The differend is always that which lives in the *pagus*—the border zone between genres or games—and thus never "at home" in a game. The differend is precisely the "victim" who suffers a "wrong," for which she has no appeal to rules precisely because she is denied space in the *Heim*.)[46]

But these communities can operate in isolation only as long as there is no attempt to form a common government. Thus Lyotard points to the formation of civil law or public policy as one of the sites in which we see this crisis of legitimation: "Take any civil law as an example: it states that a given category of citizens must perform a specific kind of action. Legitimation is the process by which a legislator is authorized to promulgate such a law or norm" (*JG* 8). The formation of a society or, more particularly, a state—which is responsible for the establishment and enforcement of laws—necessitates a confrontation of these plural logics *within* one body politic. "Contact between two communities," Lyotard suggests, "is immediately a conflict, since the names and narratives of one community are exclusive of the names and narratives of the other."[47]

Between the genres "there is an abyss" that marks the condition of pluralism. Pluralism, we might say, is the globe brought home; with recent mobilization and trends in migration (all aided by the development of technology), challenges once posed only by cross-cultural and international relations are now intranational dilemmas. In fact, this reproduction of the globe within the typical nation-state produces an even more critical dilemma insofar as the state is responsible for establishing laws or standards within its domain—laws to which a plurality of paradigms or cultures will be subject. This "abyss" between games or genres is the site of public policy and civil law, and it is an abyss precisely because there is no "metalanguage"—"and by metalanguage, I mean the famous theoretical discourse that is supposed to ground political and ethical decisions that will be taken as the basis of its statements" (*JG* 28).

The unique challenge posed by this situation is that law must be backed up by *force:* law is imposed upon a society by the state and is enforced in the case of transgression (wherever there is a policy, there is a police/force). In democratic societies, law or policy backed up by force must be *justified* or *legitimated;*[48] in short, the state must be able to provide some kind of argument that defends the legitimacy of the law. But as I have suggested, legitimation can happen only *within* a paradigm or language game; arguments will necessarily appeal to *a* logic from a plurality of logics. Law, however, demands a kind of justification that functions *across* paradigms and thus functions for all. But where would we locate such "transparadigm" or "crossparadigm" criteria? Can we ever have criteria that are not linked to a particular, contextual, historical logic functioning within one language game? And if not, then how can law or policy ever be legitimated in the pluralist state? Could there ever be a policy without differends? How can we adjudicate between competing and conflicting interpretations of justice? At stake here is just the question we have raised: does a creational hermeneutic, which recognizes the hermeneutical structure of human existence, result in a loss of criteria? Does a creational hermeneutic preclude judgment?

The world as limit: A phenomenological criterion. At this point I would like to introduce an important distinction: to deny that there are *normative interpretations* is not to deny that there are *interpretive norms.* Every assertion or articulation of truth functions within very specific conditions of human finitude; that is, every truth claim is an interpretation, and it is conditioned by the situationality and traditionality of the interpreter, meaning that the interpreter cannot transcend space and time. Therefore, interpretations cannot be normative if by "normative" we mean universal or all-encompassing—*the* one, true interpretation. However, *what is interpreted* remains a norm for every interpretation; there is something or someone who stands *before* all of our interpretations and is binding upon every construal. This interpretive norm, which stands before (or even "outside of") interpretation, constitutes the *phenomenological criterion* of every construal; there *are* universals that are binding upon interpretation. But these universals are better understood as *empirical transcendentals* than a priori transcendent criteria.[49]

By "empirical transcendentals" I simply mean worldly states of affairs—the world as given and experienced. The tree outside my window is, from a phenomenological perspective, transcendent to consciousness and imposes itself upon me. As "outside" of me, or transcendent, the tree is not "mine" to be manipulated. As such it imposes upon me limits for its interpretations; bad interpretations will be precisely those construals that transgress those limits. For instance, if I interpret the tree as a chimera and attempt to run through its trunk, my interpretation will quickly prove itself wrong. With respect to texts, the text itself is present to me and is "transcendent" in this sense, as is what the text is speaking about (its topic).[50] As such both the text and the topic to which it refers constitute a transcendence that imposes itself upon my experience and thus represents a limit to its interpretation. But the limits placed upon interpretation do not prescribe a *single* "correct" interpretation but only preclude an infinite number of interpretations.

Empirical transcendentals have the status of what Edward Farley describes as *existential* or *determinate universality*, meaning "simply what is universally present, even if it is not present as an a priori or generic term, or is not grasped through a universally accessible instrument of cognition."[51] There is a given/gift—creation—that every interpreter encounters. In the phenomenology of Edmund Husserl and Heidegger, it is "the things themselves" *(die Sachen selbst)* that stand before every construal and function as that which limits interpretation and prevents arbitrariness.[52] Truth, then, is not something uncovered; it is instead the process of *uncovering.* Truth *happens;* it is itself the uncovering that discloses something to us, something of a world that is given *(BT* 262-63). But it must also be recognized that it is the interpreter (Dasein) that does the uncovering; thus, in a radical sense, truth is "subjective." That is, it is *dependent* on the uncovering role of Dasein *(BT* 270).

But does not this conception of truth once again deliver us into the hands of arbitrariness? It is precisely this question to which Heidegger turns:

> *Because the kind of Being that is essential to truth* [i.e., uncovering] *is of the character of Dasein, all truth is relative to Dasein's Being.* Does this relativity signify that all truth is "subjective"? If one interprets "subjective" as "left to the subject's discretion," then it certainly does not. For uncovering, in the sense which is most its own, takes asserting out of the province of "subjective" discretion, and brings the uncovering Dasein face to face with the entities themselves. And only *because* "truth," as uncovering, *is a kind of Being which belongs to Dasein,* can it be taken out of the province of *Dasein's* discretion. Even the "universal validity" of truth is rooted in the fact that Dasein can uncover entities in themselves and free them. Only so can these entities in themselves be binding for every possible assertion—that is, for every way of pointing them out. *(BT* 270)

Thus on the one hand truth is re-lative to human be-ing, to the role of the interpreter as the being that uncovers the things themselves. So "what is primarily 'true'—that is, uncovering—is Dasein" (*BT* 263). Dasein is the being that uncovers, and because truth (and this must be heard as a verb rather than as a noun) is relative to Dasein's being, "*'There is' truth only in so far as Dasein i s and so long as Dasein i s*. . . . Before there was any Dasein, there was no truth; nor will there be any after Dasein is no more" (*BT* 269).

But on the other hand, to emphasize that truth is relative to Dasein is not to say that truth is "subjective," left to the interpreter's private discretion. Instead, that which is interpreted—the things themselves—stands before every construal as "binding for every possible assertion." Thus the interpretedness of human be-ing ought not be understood as founding a system of arbitrariness but rather as emphasizing that while every interpretation of the world is just that, an *interpretation* of the world, it is also simultaneously an interpretation *of the world*.

In this phenomenological framework there is a renewed appreciation for the givenness of the world. For instance, in an unpublished manuscript entitled "Contra Heidegger," Husserl emphasizes that

> theoretical interest is concerned with what is; and that, everywhere, is what is identical through variation of subjects and their practical interests, i.e., the same things, the same relations, the same changes, etc., which are there in themselves, i.e., there for "everybody." . . . Whatever is cognized, it is a being that is cognized; and a being is something identical, something identifiable again and again, and ultimately, something identifiable for everybody.[53]

The world is a fundamentally given, objective world that is shared by all, though it will be construed differently by those who share it as a lifeworld. This is worked out most explicitly in Husserl's "principle of all principles": the doctrine of *intuition*.[54] Intuition gives the phenomenon, and the phenomenon gives itself through intuition. It is on this basis that Husserl urges a return to the things themselves, because "to judge rationally or scientifically about things signifies to conform *to the things themselves* or to go from words and opinions back to the things themselves, to consult them in their self-givenness and to set aside all prejudices alien to them."[55] The heart of the principle of all principles is that *everything originarily . . . offered to us in 'intuition' is to be accepted simply as what it is presented as being.*[56]

While Husserl's doctrine of intuition seems to carry on the modern project of immediacy by granting the world as it "really" is, that is not the case. Rather, as this passage emphasizes, the world, which is given, is always given *as* something.[57] The given is constituted and presented against a horizon or as-structure. As Caputo remarks:

> We are not arguing that there is no given in Husserl or that he has no theory of intuition, but only that these notions are not naively formulated by him, that he has a critical sense of the limits of intuitionism. For him, to intuit the given means to know how to construe what presents itself, failing which there is only the flux. The injunction to remain with the given includes the reminder that the given is given only *as* something.[58]

Thus in Husserl's development of intuition we may find the seed of an *inter-mediacy*, which emphasizes at once the "objectivity" of that which is being interpreted (the interpretive norm) and also the "subjectivity" of the interpreter as the being that construes the given "as" something, a construal conditioned by situationality and traditionality.

Herman Dooyeweerd, a contemporary of Heidegger and fellow phenomenologist, offers a similar framework and perhaps goes even further in working through its details, though in a slightly different language. The distinction I have made between *interpretations* and *interpretive norms* is analogous to what Dooyeweerd distinguishes as the *subjective* a priori and the *structural* a priori. Thus there is both a "law" and "subject" side to the world as interpreted, and the "law" (that which is interpreted) is binding upon its "subject" (the interpreter).

There is an *a priori* complex in the *cosmological* sense of the *structural horizon of human experience*. This *a priori* as such has the character of a *law*. And there is also a *merely subjective a priori complex* in the *epistemological sense of the subjective a priori insight into that horizon*. We can distinguish the two complexes simply as the *structural* and the *subjective a priori*. Only the subjective a priori can be true or false in an epistemological sense. As it is *subjective insight* expressing itself in judgments, it necessarily remains enclosed within the cosmological a priori horizon of human experience. In other words, the subjective a priori always remains determined and delimitated by the a priori *structure* of all human experience.[59]

The structural horizon—that which is interpreted—is binding upon every subjective insight into and assertion about that structure, inasmuch as "all human experience is bound to some horizon which makes this experience possible."[60] The "state of affairs" considered in theory functions as an a priori in theoretical abstraction, but precisely because of this the state of affairs "can never be *actual* in its theoretical abstraction."[61] Translated into the language used above, while every interpretation stands in determinate relation to that which is interpreted—a "state of affairs"—the interpretation is not itself the state of affairs; it does not deliver the world as it "really" is but is rather a subjective insight into that structure. Nevertheless, it is only in interpretation that we gain access to that which is interpreted: "We only gain *access to* [this structural horizon] in a subjective-theoretical way" and the *"insight* into this horizon is the *subjective-fallible a priori* of all epistemology."[62]

The bindingness or "law" character of the structural horizon prevents arbitrariness, even though "truth" is, as in Heidegger, only possible from the "perspective" of the self.[63] Thus Dooyeweerd must address the same question addressed by Heidegger above, namely, the issue of arbitrariness given the subjectivity of truth. "My answer," Dooyeweerd retorts, "is that [truth] is not *dependent* on this insight in the sense of being *determined* by it or *subjected* to it. But without my subjective insight into theoretical truth, its structure will remain hidden from my cognitive selfhood."[64]

Truth is dependent on the self for uncovering the structural horizon of human experience, and within this horizon "the structural states of affairs founded in this order urge themselves upon everyone who is seriously confronted with them." Just as assertions, for Heidegger, must uncover the things themselves, so for Dooyeweerd interpretations "must also vindicate their claim to relative truth, viz. in a process of *transcendental experience* in the forum of the Divine world-order. For in the latter are founded the structural states of affairs which are undeniable when they have been laid bare to theoretical insight."[65]

I draw on these phenomenological discussions as that which undergirds my distinction between interpretations (assertions, insights) and interpretive norms ("the things themselves," the structural horizon). We only have access to the world or a text through the lens of interpretation, which is conditioned and "fallible"; yet this does not end in a ubiquitous arbitrariness because of the binding character of that which is interpreted—that which stands "before" or even "outside of" interpretation (though our access to it is only through the mediation of an interpretation). These empirical transcendentals urge themselves upon a plurality of interpreters and resist capricious construal,[66] allowing for a plurality, but *not* an infinite number, of interpretive possibilities. Thus the binding character of the things themselves does not mean that one correct interpretation is prescribed by the world or a text; it means only that interpretation is not merely a subjective appropriation: it is a subjective construal of an objective reality.[67]

Dooyeweerd perhaps best emphasizes the *pragmatic* character of good interpretation: it has to work. Insights and construals of the world must vindicate themselves *in the world,* "in the forum of the Divine world-order."[68] Again, while this does not guarantee the elimination of misinterpretation, it does mark the distinction between the ubiquity of hermeneutics and a perceived arbitrariness. Interpretation is indeed the only game in town, but there are rules to the game—not rules concocted by a council and printed in a rule book but a rule as simple as this: you have to play on the field, staying within the boundaries. And it is the same field for all of us.

The Ethics of Interpretation

In the previous section I have attempted to point to the world (the structural *a priori*) as a phenomenological criterion that "limits" interpretation. To turn to this limit "before interpretation" is to attempt to locate a limit "outside" the hermeneutical circle, as it were. As discussed above, we can locate what might be described as "empirical transcendentals" (Dooyeweerd's structural a priori), which are *before* interpretation and *resist* misinterpretation. Here I would turn to the work of Emmanuel Levinas and his suggestion that this transcendence—the empirical transcendental—that confronts and disrupts every horizon is precisely the face of the Other, the face that makes me ethically responsible and demands justice.[69] As such, the Other is precisely the transcendence that places *limits* on interpretation; now the question of interpretation is also a question of justice (cf. chapter four, "The Infinite and the Ghost of Metaphysics Past"), and the question of limits on interpretation is an ethical rather than simply an epistemological matter. Interpretation becomes not so much a matter of "correctness" as *responsibility;* the interpreter has an obligation to "do justice" to the transcendence of that which is interpreted.

The force of Levinas's corpus is that ethics is not about abstract norms or theory but rather about faces and withered hands (Mt 12:9-14). Ethics is not found in divine-command theory; it is found in the face that commands me, calls me, makes me responsible, before any ethical theory or law, and comes from *je ne sais d'ou.* "The face," Levinas remarks, "is present in its refusal to be contained. In this sense it cannot be comprehended, that is, encompassed" (*TI* 194). In other words, the face cannot be contained in theory, cannot be thematized in an interpretation or reduced to a concept (*OBBE* 101). The call of the face and my responsibility to the face (and her body) is an-archic, before any *arche,* by which I am commanded to obey before hearing the order—like creation *ex nihilo* (*OBBE* 101, 113). Rather than assigning value, I am under an assignation and obligation to which I did not give consent.

The Other—the face that confronts me and demands justice—is not theoretical; it is located before theory, in pretheoretical experience, or what the young Heidegger described as "facticity." Thus for Levinas the Other commands absolutely and universally, and yet it is, in a sense, empirical. Thus we might suggest, not without warrant, that the Other is a kind of "empirical transcendental,"[70] a site functioning as a transcendent criterion because it exceeds the horizons of the interpreter and is *binding* upon every construal or interpretation. This of course is a rather odd transcendence, but it is a rigorously phenomenological transcendence. As an empirical or pretheoretical transcendence it is fundamentally distinct from theoretical criteria. To speak of this in Husserlian terms, theoretical criteria are *Irreal* or *ideal,* which means that they function only within consciousness and therefore offer no resistance to the intentionality or horizons of the interpreter.[71]

Levinas's Other, however, is a *real* phenomenon (transcendent, not transcenden*tal*) and thus by definition cannot be encompassed or contained by consciousness or intentionality. As such, the Other resists manipulation or distortion, prohibits violent "interpretations" and thus functions as a limiting criterion for interpretation.[72] Heidegger suggested the same when he emphasized that "the things themselves" are "binding" upon every possible interpretation, thereby *limiting* the possibilities (*BT* 270). In Levinas, however, this takes on an ethical imperative: the interpreter must do justice to the other that resists manipulation.[73]

The notion of an ethical limit on interpretation is also a rather Augustinian idea. In Augustine's manual on biblical interpretation, *De doctrina christiana,*[74] interpretation is to be grounded in the "right order of love." Distinguishing between things to be "used" (*uti*) and things to be "enjoyed" (*frui*), Augustine establishes an order of love in which the world is to be used in order to love that alone which is to be enjoyed, namely, God.[75] Things then are to be used; God is to be enjoyed. But what of our neighbor?[76] Is the Other a thing to be used? While there are difficulties at this juncture,[77] Augustine answers that we love God *in* the neighbor.[78] Thus we have an account of the dual commandment to love God and love our neighbor as ourselves; and that, Augustine notes, is the sum of what the Scripture teaches.[79] "So," he concludes, "if it seems to you that you have understood the divine scriptures, or any part of them, in such a way that by this understanding you do not build up this twin love of God and neighbor, then you have not yet understood them."[80] In fact, he continues by saying that so long as our interpretations build up this love of God and neighbor, the question of authorial intent is secondary.[81]

The criterion for interpretation, Augustine suggests, is a practical or ethical one: whether our interpretations "build up" love of God and neighbor. It is this ethical criterion that is to guide the interpreter when one encounters ambiguities: "So this rule will be observed in dealing with figurative expressions, that you should take pains to turn over and over in your mind what you read, until your interpretation of it is led right through to the kingdom of charity. But if this is already happening with the literal meaning, do not suppose the expression is in any way a figurative one."[82] Indeed, a plurality of interpretations is permitted, so long as this ethical criterion of love is maintained. This point arises in Augustine's reading of Genesis in book 12 of the *Confessions,* where he is confronted by "many truths" within the text.

> "Let us love the Lord our God with all our heart, with all our soul, with all our mind, and our neighbor as ourselves." On the basis of these two commandments of love, Moses meant whatever he meant in those books. . . . See how stupid it is, among so large a mass of entirely correct interpretations which can be elicited from those words, rashly to assert that a particular one has the best claim to be Moses' view, and by destructive disputes to offend against charity

itself, which is the principle of everything he said in the texts we are attempting to expound. (*CSA* 12.25.35)

Within the limits of charity, there is room for plurality, which, Augustine admonishes, ought to issue in a hermeneutical humility that makes room for difference but that does not eliminate criteria (*CSA* 12.24.33).[83] The ethics of interpretation, for Augustine, is a hermeneutics of love.

Of Spirit: "Yes" and Amen

I have emphasized "the things themselves" (empirical transcendentals) as binding for interpretation in an attempt to counter the charge of arbitrariness that is leveled against a creational hermeneutic emphasizing the ubiquity of interpretation. But this discussion also deprivileges a "hermeneutics of suspicion" inasmuch as it argues that interpretation is not left to the caprice of the interpreter[84] because it is confronted by a structural or "objective" reality—a world outside of or before interpretation. While interpretation is rooted in the situationality and traditionality of the interpreter, it is not produced only by those conditions; interpretation is not simply the effect of the will to power. In this section I will argue that a second criterion, or "check," on interpretation is rooted in a fundamental hermeneutics of trust as the correlate of a belief in the goodness of creation. At this juncture we will finally explore the pneumatic pole of my creational-pneumatic hermeneutical model inasmuch as this hermeneutic trust is linked to the guidance of the Spirit.[85]

The site of this pneumatic discourse may be located in a little treatise on spirits: *ruah, pneuma, esprit* and, especially, *Geist*. Derrida's *Of Spirit* is a discourse on both trust and suspicion, "spirit" and "avoiding" or, more specifically, *Geist und vermeiden* and how Heidegger (unsuccessfully) attempted to avoid this spirit in his work and life. A life and work haunted by ghosts—is this Heidegger or Derrida? Of course within Heidegger's *Gesamtausgabe* there lurk a number of disturbing specters: spirits that both disturb this corpus and arise from this corpus to disturb us. Derrida's goal in his little spirit-filled treatise is to reveal that, despite all of his protests and attempts, Heidegger failed to avoid this tormenting *Geist*:

> *Geist* is always haunted by its *Geist:* a spirit, or in other words, in French [and English] as in German, a phantom, always surprises by returning to be the other's ventriloquist. Metaphysics always returns, I mean in the sense of a *revenant* [ghost], and *Geist* is the most fatal figure of this *revenance* [returning, haunting]. . . . Is this not what Heidegger will never finally be able to avoid *(vermeiden)*, the unavoidable itself—spirit's double, *Geist* as the *Geist* of *Geist*, spirit as the spirit of the spirit which always comes with its double? (*OS* 40-41)

But again we may ask: Is there not also a spirit, let us say *l'esprit*, that Derrida cannot avoid, which is the unavoidable? Is there not a specter lurking behind and underneath Derrida's corpus, his body (of writings), his writing body?

We need not consult the witch of Endor to conjure up this spirit, for it is sighted in a startling way later in the text, when Derrida considers the origins of language as promise, a passage hovering between commentary and autobiography.[86]

> It remains to find out whether this *Versprechen* is not the promise which, opening every speaking, makes possible the very question and therefore precedes it without belonging to it: the dissymmetry of an affirmation, of a *yes* before all opposition of *yes* and *no*. . . . Language always, *before any question,* and in the very question, comes down to the promise. This would also be a promise *of spirit.* (*OS* 94)

Following on the heels of this passage is an extended note (which, not without significance, he offers as a pledge), an attempt to understand this uninvited visitation of (the) spirit. Here the spirit of promise—of the "pledge"—returns as that which must precede any question. Thus before any hermeneutics of suspicion (which is at heart a hermeneutics of radical questioning), one must place one's trust in the promises of language.

> Language is *already* there, in advance at the moment at which any
> question can arise about it. In this it exceeds the question. This
> advance is, before any contract, a sort of promise of originary alle-
> giance to which we must have in some sense already acquiesced,
> already said *yes,* given a pledge, whatever may be the negativity or
> problematicity of the discourse which may follow. (*OS* 129)

This pledge, he goes on to say, is a "commitment" to what is
given in the promise itself. Questioning—the heart and sole of suspicion—does not have the last word, precisely because it does not
have the first word, because it is itself grounded in *trusting* a promise (*OS* 130). This pledge happens "before" the question, even
before language, in time immemorial: "before the word, there is
this sometimes wordless word which we name the 'yes.' A sort of
pre-originary pledge which precedes any other engagement in language or action" (*OS* 130).

As Derrida notes, then, there is a trust that is more primordial
than suspicion precisely because, I have been attempting to argue,
goodness is more primordial than evil. Going beyond (or at least
otherwise than) Derrida, I would argue that the state of affairs
composed of deception and false consciousness is an accidental
way of being, not an essential one. The *pharmakon* (poison/cure) is
not original nor constitutive, but rather it is a contingency result-
ing from the brokenness of a fallen world.

But before this Fall, and now in spite of this Fall, there is a primordial "yes": a "wordless word," a living *logos* who was "in the
beginning," who tabernacles with us in flesh and whose spirit
resides within us (Jn 1:1-18). It is this wordless Word, this *Who,* that
we name "yes": "For the Son of God, Jesus Christ, whom we proclaimed among you . . . was not 'Yes and No'; but in him it is always
'Yes.' For in him every one of God's promises is a 'Yes.'" (2 Cor
1:19-20). That is why "*parole* must *first* pray, address itself to us: put
in us its trust, its confidence, depend on us, and even have *already*
done it" (*OS* 134). And this pledge, Derrida continues, this
"already," is essential because it reaches back to a moment of

already-having-trusted, an older event, part of a past that never returns and never "was."[87]

In this regard the fundamental movement of deconstruction is a celebration of commitments, pointing out the pledges and promises that ground discourse—and the academy. Thus the university, any university, is founded on faith: *before* the work of scholarship happens every scholar says a little prayer, whispers her pledge, commits and entrusts herself to language. The university, we might suggest, is quite religious, even if it has not been founded by priests, and it is this grounding commitment that deconstruction is sworn to celebrate.

We could say this otherwise, as Derrida does in *Memoirs of the Blind,* his running commentary on the exhibition he hosted at the Louvre. Here his hypothesis is that drawing proceeds from a certain structural blindness, begins where it cannot see and hence, where one cannot "know." Thus Derrida sketches a rather Augustinian structure that affirms one must believe in order to understand *(credum ut intelligam).* In contrast, a dominant Western tradition (which includes Aquinas) has come to suggest that to know is to have an "idea" *(eidon),* hence to "see" *(idein).* One who is blind, then, cannot know.

But Derrida, along with the New Testament, wants to problematize this, suggesting that knowing or seeing is predicated upon a certain blindness, upon what one does not see; knowing, as such, would proceed from a commitment to that which is beyond seeing, the "unbeseen" as absolute invisibility, to which one is entrusted.[88] In this blind economy of faith, to see, in a sense, is not to see, such that Jesus' opponents are blind precisely because they claim to see (Jn 9:40-41). On the other hand, those who are blind nevertheless see, walking by faith and not by sight. To see is not to believe, whereas blindness is a kind of faith such that one must rely on others for direction, often walking with arms outstretched, like in prayer. "Look at Coypel's blind men," Derrida suggests as an example. "They all hold their hands out in front of them, their gesture oscillating in the void between prehending, apprehending, praying, and imploring" (*MB* 5).

The movement of modern thought and technology is to probe beyond the limits of sight "with instruments—anoptic or blind—that sound out, that allow one to know *[savoir]* there where one no longer sees *[voir]*" (*MB* 32). To expand one's vision is to eliminate faith, to undo the commitment that blindness necessitates; but because of the *structural* invisibility of the absolutely other than sight, the probes can never sound deep enough, can never plumb the depths of blindness, or faith.

Derrida sees this structure outlined in the healing of Tobit's blindness by his son, behind whom stands an angel as the condition for the possibility of Tobit's healing, who also announces a commandment: "acknowledge God *[rendez grâce à Dieu]*" (*MB* 29). Thus the healing, and more precisely the story of the healing, begins *by* and *from* a debt: "What guides the graphic point, the quill, pencil, or scalpel is the respectful *observance* of a commandment, the acknowledgment before knowledge, the gratitude of the receiving before seeing, the blessing before knowledge" (*MB* 29-30). The angel, then, indicates the place of faith, acknowledgment, commitment and trust; but in Rembrandt's rendering of this scene, for example, the angel is withdrawn, and the human actors are now engaged in what appears to be simple surgery, such that the sketch was originally but mistakenly referred to by the title *Surgeon Bandaging a Wounded Man*—a recovery of sight by knowledge, by more seeing.

But such a construal, on Derrida's accounting, fails to give credit to the role of faith *(credo)* to the commitments that make such seeing possible. Writing, drawing and speaking are all indebted, committed; they all owe credit to that which is originarily other, such that "at the origin of the *graphein* there is debt or gift rather than representational fidelity. More precisely, the fidelity of faith matters more than the representation, whose movement fidelity commands and thus precedes. And faith, in the moment proper to it, is blind" (*MB* 30).

To translate this into a classical idiom, Derrida is offering another way to think of the relationship between faith and reason or trust and suspicion; however, he would see any disjunction or opposition between the two as untenable, precisely because reason is grounded, structurally, in commitments, trust, pledge. Before knowledge there is acknowledgment; before seeing there is blindness; before questioning there is a commitment; before knowing there is faith.

While blindness is the condition for the possibility of faith, there is also a sense in which faith is blinded because it sees too much, blinded by bedazzlement, "the very bedazzlement that, for example, knocks Paul to the ground on the road to Damascus" (*MB* 112). And if faith in linked to blindness, it is also associated with madness; or, as Derrida remarks, the "clairvoyance of the all-too-evident is Paul's madness" (*MB* 117). Paul is mad, Festus asserted (Acts 26:24), or as we sometimes say, he should be "committed," to Bellevue, perhaps. He is one who should be committed because of his mad commitments—because of his faith.

Thus deconstruction, if it is a celebration of commitments, is also a celebration of a certain madness—the madness of faith. Further, deconstruction is committed to pointing out the place of this madness within and before the academic community as that which is the very condition for its possibility—which often enough makes people a little mad. Such is Derrida's promise: to announce the promise that precedes us, the commitment that is older than us, the "yes" to which we always already have acquiesced. That is deconstruction's prayer and in-vocation; as such, it might seem appropriate to close with a prayer, but Derrida's request is precisely that we recognize it is with prayer that we begin.

Given this primordial trust, as the correlate of the goodness of creation, space is made for a plurality of interpretations, a multiplicity of tongues, which is also a very pneumatic-Pentecostal notion. When we recognize both the situationality of human be-ing and the fundamental trust of human be-ing, then we are able to

184 THE FALL OF INTERPRETATION

relinquish a mono-logical hermeneutics in favor of a creational and Pentecostal diversity, the plurality preceding Babel and following Pentecost.[89] Given the phenomenological constraint of the world (that which is interpreted) and the pneumatological criterion in the fundamental guidance of the Spirit as rooted in a primordial trust, a hermeneutical space is opened that invites our creation, that beckons us to heed the call and accept the gift and risk of human be-ing in its creatureliness, refusing both the metaphysical dream of immediacy and the differential narrative of violence. A creational-pneumatic hermeneutic is a hermeneutic that celebrates humanity, but it is one that also mourns its rupture and roots its lament precisely in its belief in a good creation. The heart of a creational-pneumatic hermeneutic is a space, a field of multiplicitous meeting in the wild spaces of love (James Olthuis) where there is room for a plurality of God's creatures to speak, sing and dance in a multivalent chorus of tongues.

Notes

Introduction: Interpretation & the Fall

[1]Dante Alighieri *Paradiso* 26.117 (in *Paradiso*, Temple Classics [London: J. M. Dent & Sons, 1899]).

[2]Or "mirror" *(speglio)*, likely an allusion to 1 Corinthians 13:12: "For now we see through a mirror *[esoptrou]* enigmatically, but then we shall see face to face." I turn my attention to "dim-mirror hermeneutics" in chapters one and two.

[3]Dante Alighieri *Paradiso* 26.104-8 (in *The Divine Comedy: The Inferno, Purgatorio, and Paradiso*, trans. Lawrence Grant White [New York: Pantheon, 1948]).

[4]These themes are masterfully traced by Kevin Hart, *The Trespass of the Sign: Deconstruction, Theology and Philosophy* (Cambridge: Cambridge University Press, 1989), pp. 3-39.

[5]Traditions, of course, are by no means monolithic, and so this should be qualified to say that *some aspects* of the Christian and continental traditions characterize hermeneutics as fallen. This is important since I will retrieve alternative aspects of both traditions for my critique and constructive proposal.

[6]See Jacques Derrida, *Writing and Difference*, trans. Alan Bass (Chicago: University of Chicago Press, 1978), p. 293, and OG 178-79. See also John D. Caputo, *Radical Hermeneutics: Deconstruction, Repetition and the Hermeneutic Project* (Bloomington: Indiana University Press, 1987), p. 95. This book owes an incalculable debt to Professor Caputo and to his *Radical Hermeneutics*.

[7]For instance, see Sallie McFague, *Metaphorical Theology: Models of God in Religious Language* (Philadelphia: Fortress, 1982); and her *Models of God: Theology for an Ecological, Nuclear Age* (Philadelphia: Fortress, 1987). Avery Dulles has employed models as a theological tool and in some senses is a pioneer in this regard: see his *Models of the Church* (Garden City, N.Y.: Doubleday, 1974); his *Models of Revelation* (Garden City, N.Y.: Doubleday, 1983); and more recently his *Assurance of Things Hoped For: A Theology of Christian Faith* (Oxford: Oxford University Press, 1994). I would also note Stephen Bevans's *Models of Contextual Theology* (New York: Orbis, 1992), which provides further references (see notes on pp. 120-21).

[8]David Kelsey, *The Use of Scripture in Recent Theology* (Philadelphia: Westminster Press, 1975); see also his addendum and update, "The Bible and Christian Theology," *Journal of the American Academy of Religion* 48 (1980): 385-402.

[9]John Goldingay, *Models for Scripture* (Grand Rapids, Mich.: Eerdmans, 1989). His focus here is actually a doctrine of Scripture and not hermeneutics *per se.*

[10]John Goldingay, *Models for the Interpretation of Scripture* (Grand Rapids, Mich.: Eerdmans, 1995).

[11]The neologism *be-ing* is employed for philosophical reasons (similar to Søren Kierkegaard) in attempts to avoid essentialist language such as human "nature." By *be-ing* I mean human life or existence, being human. It may be considered a rough translation of Martin Heidegger's *Dasein* (discussed in chapter three) as "being-there" or "being-in-the-world."

[12]Kevin Vanhoozer's prodigious and ground-breaking work *Is There a Meaning in This Text?* came into my hands too late for me to engage it extensively in this book.

186   THE FALL OF INTERPRETATION

However, it seems to me that Vanhoozer tends to *oppose* interpretation and knowledge, remarking, for instance, that "instead of making robust claims to absolute knowledge, even natural scientists now view their theories as interpretations" (*Is There a Meaning in This Text? The Bible, the Reader and the Morality of Literary Knowledge* [Grand Rapids, Mich.: Zondervan, 1998], p. 19). However, he also offers what he describes as a "more positive sense (call it *realist*)" of interpretation, which is a "mode of knowledge" (ibid., p. 11 n. 1). What remains for us to consider is whether this is in fact interpretation at all.

¹³For a helpful discussion of this point, see Hart, *Trespass of the Sign*, pp. 14-30.

¹⁴Like John Milbank, I too will return to Augustine as an important resource for our contemporary situation: viz., the articulation of a Christian philosophical hermeneutic in a postmodern context. However, I will not affirm what Milbank refers to as "Platonism/Christianity." Rather, I will seek to liberate the Christian Augustine both from a sedimented Platonism in his corpus as well as from the platonizing of his legacy up to Heidegger.

¹⁵By "demythologizing" I mean "deconstructing," not as a destructing or a leveling but as another reading of Augustine: a reading of Augustine against himself, a deconstruction of Augustine in the name of Augustine. More specifically, it is a deconstruction of Augustine's Neo-Platonism in the name of Augustine's Christianity. For a similar suggestion and project, see Paul Ricoeur, " 'Original Sin': A Study in Meaning," in *The Conflict of Interpretations*, ed. Don Ihde (Evanston, Ill.: Northwestern University Press, 1974), pp. 269-86, where he asserts that "to reflect on its meaning is in a certain way *to deconstruct the concept*" (p. 270). As Caputo suggests, the task of demythologizing, or deconstruction, is not simply negative; it also involves a moment of positive production: in this case, the production of another Augustine (*Demythologizing Heidegger* [Bloomington: Indiana University Press, 1993], pp. 7-8).

¹⁶I was surprised and encouraged to find that Vanhoozer also (independently) claims an Augustinian genealogy for his hermeneutical framework (Vanhoozer, *Is There a Meaning*, pp. 29-32). However, while I appreciate his reasons for doing so, it seems to me that his claim to be developing an "Augustinian hermeneutic" is, at worst, contrived (Augustine plays a rather minor role in the text); at best, it draws on themes tangential to the heart of an Augustinian philosophical or general hermeneutic. Further, as I will indicate in chapters five and six, he fails to appreciate the degree to which Derrida himself adopts an Augustinian understanding of faith-commitments as the necessary condition for knowledge (see the final section of chapter six, "Of Spirit: 'Yes' and Amen").

¹⁷I have reservations about such postal operations, which attempt to get everything and everyone in the proper *Brieffach* (post-office box, pigeonhole).

¹⁸Bevans provides a very helpful discussion on this in "The Notion and Use of Models" (*Models of Contextual Theology*, pp. 23-29). He understands models as notions related to "critical realism": "While the critical realist realizes that one can never fully know a reality as it is in itself, at the same time she or he realizes that what is known is *truly* known" (p. 25). While Bevans's relativization of models is welcomed, my sense is that even a "critical" realism claims too much inasmuch as it asserts that the thing is known partially "in itself." I would rather speak of a "hermeneutical realism" (Hubert Dreyfus's, not N. T. Wright's or Vanhoozer's) or a

"phenomenological connection" that never claims to know something "in itself"
but that does gain access to "the things themselves." However, such connection
with *die Sachen selbst* is always understood "as" something, "as" I construe it. On
"hermeneutical realism," see Hubert Dreyfus, *Being-in-the-World: A Commentary on
Heidegger's 'Being and Time,'* Division I (Cambridge, Mass.: MIT Press, 1991), pp.
253-65. This "hermeneutical realism," however, should not be confused with the
postliberal notion, which remains, on my account, a little too "realist" and not
"hermeneutical" enough.

[19]I think my project is akin to Caputo's "Three Interpretations of Interpretation,"
where he discusses "left" and "right" sides of the Heideggerian heritage. See his
Radical Hermeneutics, pp. 95-119.

[20]I owe this phrase to James Olthuis, "A Hermeneutics of Suffering Love," in *The
Very Idea of Radical Hermeneutics,* ed. Roy A. Martinez (Atlantic Highlands, N.J.:
Humanities Press, 1997).

[21]For discussion of these matters in a phenomenological context, see my "Alterity,
Transcendence and the Violence of the Concept: Kierkegaard and Heidegger,"
International Philosophical Quarterly 38 (1998): 369-81.

[22]Here I should make a methodological clarification: I understand this book to be a
philosophical exploration that analyzes phenomena from a Christian perspective,
or worldview. For me, just because philosophy engages religious or theological
motifs does not mean that it has lapsed into theology. As I understand it (and have
formulated elsewhere), theology is a special science *(eine positive Wissenschaft)*
that explores the experience, or modality, of faith. It investigates a particular
aspect of human existence, just as biology explores the biotic, mathematics the
numeric, etc. Philosophy is directed toward the foundations of these special sciences and the coherence and interconnection of the diverse aspects of human
experience. Given this distinction, the focus of this book is philosophical, not
(strictly speaking) theological. Nevertheless, it *is* an exercise in the scandalous
project of *Christian* philosophy. On the possibility of a Christian philosophy,
which rejects Heidegger's philosophical atheism, Plantinga's theistic philosophy
and Gilson's proposal, see my essay, "The Art of Christian Atheism: Faith and Phi
losophy in Early Heidegger," *Faith and Philosophy* 14 (1997): 71-81. I have discussed
the relationship between philosophy and theology further in "Fire from Heaven:
The Hermeneutics of Heresy," *Journal of Theta Alpha Kappa* 20 (1996): 13-31. My
work in this area is dependent on Martin Heidegger, *Phänomenologie und Theologie*
(Frankfurt: Vittorio Klostermann, 1970); and Herman Dooyeweerd, "Philosophy
and Theology," pt. 3 of *In the Twilight of Western Thought: Studies in the Pretended
Autonomy of Philosophical Thought,* series B, vol. 4 of *Collected Works,* ed. James K.
A. Smith (Lewiston, N.Y.: Edwin Mellen, 1999).

[23]Martin Heidegger, *History of the Concept of Time: Prolegomena,* trans. Theodore Kisiel
(Bloomington: Indiana University Press, 1985), p. 283. In *Being and Time,* Heidegger
is adamant that "falling" must not be construed as a "negative 'evaluation'" (*BT* 265).
These disclaimers are exactly what I will contest in chapter three.

[24]As I will suggest in chapter five, the central effect of the Fall with regards to interpretation is *domination*—the domination of texts and the domination of others by
the oppressive imposition of *one* interpretation. The plurality of interpretation, we
will suggest, is not a result of the Fall; rather it is shut down in a broken world that

tends toward hegemonic oppression. In short, we will be reading Babel rather differently.

25Caputo, *Radical Hermeneutics,* chap. 10.

26John D. Caputo, *Against Ethics: Contributions to a Poetics of Obligation with Constant Reference to Deconstruction* (Bloomington: Indiana University Press, 1993), p. 264 n. 80, citing *OG* 68. The note is a muted critique of Drucilla Cornell, *The Philosophy of the Limit* (New York: Routledge, 1992), esp. pp. 1-12, where she describes deconstruction as a philosophy of the limit, of finitude.

27Dennis J. Schmidt, *The Ubiquity of the Finite: Hegel, Heidegger and the Entitlements of Philosophy* (Cambridge, Mass.: MIT Press, 1988), p. 4.

28See P. Christopher Smith, *Hermeneutics and Human Finitude: Toward a Theory of Ethical Understanding* (Bronx, N.Y.: Fordham University Press, 1991), pp. 267-83. Another representative of this tradition is Stephen David Ross; see his trilogy *Inexhaustibility and Human Being: An Essay on Locality* (Bronx, N.Y.: Fordham University Press, 1989); *The Limits of Language* (Bronx, N.Y.: Fordham University Press, 1994); and *Locality and Practical Judgment: Charity and Sacrifice* (Bronx, N.Y.: Fordham University Press, 1994). I am not saying that there are no affinities between my proposals and that of this conservative Gadamerian tradition; however, there are some fundamental differences that will be addressed as they arise in the following chapters.

29For instance, Thomas McCarthy remarks that the challenge for philosophy today "is to rethink the idea of reason in line with our essential finitude" ("Introduction" to Jürgen Habermas, *The Philosophical Discourse of Modernity,* trans. Frederick Lawrence [Cambridge, Mass.: MIT Press, 1987], p. x).

30I would also agree with Jürgen Habermas that for Michel Foucault, "the experience of finiteness became a philosophical stimulus" ("Taking Aim at the Heart of the Present: On Foucault's Lecture on Kant's *What Is Enlightenment?*" in *Critique and Power: Recasting the Foucault/Habermas Debate,* ed. Michael Kelly [Cambridge, Mass.: MIT Press, 1994], p. 149). In addition, Ronald Kuipers suggests Richard Rorty as another philosopher of finitude, in a qualified sense. See Kuipers, *Solidarity and the Stranger: Themes in the Social Philosophy of Richard Rorty* (Lanham, Md.: University Press of America, 1998).

31Ronald Numbers's almost Foucauldian archaeology of creation science is perhaps the most trenchant critique to date. See Numbers, *The Creationists: The Evolution of Scientific Creationism* (Berkeley: University of California Press, 1992).

32In response to Joseph Stephen O'Leary's concerns. I disagree with him, however, that creation is a concept that must remain foreign to philosophy and that by the employment of creation in phenomenology "we override the plurality and opacity of the world as phenomenologically accessible" (O'Leary, *Questioning Back: The Overcoming of Metaphysics in Christian Tradition* [Minneapolis: Winston, 1985], pp. 15, 17). This is due to O'Leary's assumption regarding the exclusion of faith from philosophy, which I do not share and, further, think is impossible. See my "Art of Christian Atheism."

33Dooyeweerd describes creation as an analogical concept in *In the Twilight,* pp. 149-151.

34J. Richard Middleton, "The Liberating Image? Interpreting the *Imago Dei* in Context," *Christian Scholar's Review* 24 (1994): 8-25; and his "Is Creation Theology

Inherently Conservative? A Dialogue with Walter Brueggemann," *Harvard Theological Review* 87 (1994): 257-77.

[35]Caputo, *Against Ethics*, pp. 39-40.

[36]Ibid., p. 33.

[37]I am playing here with *OBBE* 121. See also *TI* 102-4, 293-96, 304-5.

[38]Even though I disagree with James Brownson at key points, I very much appreciate his emphasis on a plurality of interpretation in his essay "Speaking the Truth in Love: Elements of a Missional Hermeneutic," *International Review of Mission* 83 (July 1994): 479-504.

Chapter 1: Paradise Regained

[1]If we have learned anything in the past decade, it is that the term *evangelical* is incredibly amorphous and even ambiguous. However, such flexibility is also its strength. In this chapter, my description of "evangelical" theology remains confined to one of its dominant traditions, that of "Old Princeton" and Reformed theology, which has dominated evangelical theological structures in America for the last century (even in non-Reformed camps, such as dispensationalism). In a sense evangelicalism is, thankfully, much broader than this (I will draw on pietist alternatives within the tradition), however, it seems to me that much of evangelical theology remains fundamentally shaped by the legacy of early Princeton (the Hodges and Warfield). For further discussion of this point, see James K. A. Smith, "Closing the Book: Pentecostals, Evangelicals and the Sacred Writings," *Journal of Pentecostal Theology* 11 (1997): 49-71, esp. pp. 59-63.

[2]This notion of "clarity" is not unrelated to the roots of modern philosophy and Descartes's "clear and distinct ideas," which marked a new requirement of knowledge in modernity—a stipulation that evangelical theology inherited precisely because of its own modernity. Richard Lints's "clarity" and Descartes's "clear and distinct ideas" fall within a tradition of immediacy that claims to have unmediated access to the world and God. It is, as Lints offers, a clarity of "comprehension"—a knowing that is a definitive grasping *(comprehendere)*. It is this tradition of immediacy—of comprehension and definition—that Jean Luc Marion describes as the domain of the idol. Concepts, Marion argues, need not necessarily be idolatrous and violent (they may be "icons"), but when they make claims to comprehension and immediacy, they *become* idols. "The concept," Marion writes, "when it knows the divine in its hold, and hence names 'God,' defines it. It defines it, and therefore also measures it to the dimension of its hold. Thus the concept on its part can take up again the essential characteristics of the 'aesthetic' idol." See Marion, *God Without Being*, trans. Thomas A. Carlson (Chicago: University of Chicago Press, 1991), p. 29. For my sketch of alternative, "iconic" concepts, see "Alterity, Transcendence and the Violence of the Concept: Kierkegaard and Heidegger," *International Philosophical Quarterly* 38 (1998): 369-81.

[3]I am concerned by what appear to be echoes of such a notion in Kevin Vanhoozer's work. While admittedly offering an account of "general" hermeneutics, he argues that the interpretation "of texts in general" has "a theological dimension" (*Is There a Meaning in This Text? The Bible, the Reader and the Morality of Literary Knowledge* [Grand Rapids, Mich.: Zondervan, 1998], p. 30). More specifically, his

"thesis is that ethical interpretation is a spiritual exercise and that the spirit of
understanding is not a spirit of power, nor of play, but the Holy Spirit" (p. 29).
Does this mean that only Christians can read properly, or generously? When he
goes on to specify, however, he seems to confine the operation to the believing
community's reading of the Scriptures, in which case he speaks only of special
hermeneutics (and here I would not disagree). If the role of the Holy Spirit in *general* hermeneutics is to be viable, we will need to develop a parallel account of
hermeneutical *common* grace (as I attempt to develop in chapter six); otherwise
we fall back into the notion that only those who are indwelt with the Holy Spirit
can interpret "texts in general."
⁴It is my hope that the reader who endures to part three will recall this early qualification.
⁵Another example would be the recent controversy among the evangelical public
regarding Zondervan's projected publication of the New International "Inclusive
Language" Version.
⁶The work by Donald Bloesch (*A Theology of Word and Spirit: Authority and Method
in Theology* [Downers Grove, Ill.: InterVarsity Press, 1992]); and Lint's *The Fabric of
Theology* are two of the more significant contributions on theological method. I
would also mention Stanley Grenz's *Revisioning Evangelical Theology* (Downers
Grove, Ill.: InterVarsity Press, 1993), which I will not deal with extensively. However, of the recent evangelical projects, I find Grenz's to be the most promising.
For Pentecostal engagement with contemporary hermeneutical theory, see
Pneuma: The Journal of the Society for Pentecostal Studies 15.2 (fall 1993), a special
issue devoted to hermeneutics.
⁷Dennis J. Schmidt, *The Ubiquity of the Finite: Hegel, Heidegger and the Entitlements
of Philosophy* (Cambridge: MIT Press, 1988), p. 1. See also the epigraph to the
Introduction.
⁸As Kevin Hart notes, Jacques Derrida takes Edmund Husserl to be inhabiting this
same model, offering an account of meaning similar to Dante's Adam (Hart, *The
Trespass of the Sign: Deconstruction, Theology and Philosophy* [Cambridge: Cambridge University Press, 1989], p. 11). While I would admit that in some respects
Husserl remains very Cartesian, I also think that he is a transitional figure with
regard to questions of immediacy and mediation. John D. Caputo offers a helpful
rereading in his *Radical Hermeneutics: Deconstruction, Repetition and the Hermeneutic Project* (Bloomington: Indiana University Press, 1987), pp. 36-59. For a defense
of Husserl in this regard, see James K. A. Smith, "Respect and Donation: A Critique of Marion's Critique of Husserl," *American Catholic Philosophical Quarterly* 71
(1997): 523-38.
⁹I think it is important to note and emphasize this: "we" do not deconstruct texts;
texts deconstruct themselves. So Vanhoozer is mistaken to describe "deconstruc-
tors" as "Undoers" (*Is There a Meaning*, p. 38 and *passim*), since deconstruction happens, Derrida says, "in the middle voice." It is not something *we* "do" to texts but
an operation internal to texts. On this point, see Jacques Derrida, "Letter to a Japanese Friend," in *A Derrida Reader: Between the Blinds*, ed. Peggy Kamuf, trans.
David Wood and Andrew Benjamin (New York: Columbia University Press, 1991),
pp. 273-74.
¹⁰When Rex Koivisto speaks of "explicit" teaching, he means "objective" teaching,

doctrine delivered apart from interpretation. Interpretation happens in areas of "lesser Scriptural clarity" where the Bible is not "crystal clear" (*OLOF* 132). Again, the notion of "clarity" is inextricably linked to the notion of pure reading *sans interpretation.* While Koivisto is constantly (and justifiably) delimiting the status of denominational distinctives as traditioned interpretations based on "less clear" passages, behind the whole discussion is the assumption of a collection of readings that *are* crystal clear. He refers at this point to a note jotted in the flyleaf of his first Bible: "What is clear in this book is vital; what is not clear in this book is not vital" (*OLOF* 133). The question is, however, clear *to whom?*

¹¹John H. Fish III, "Brethren Tradition or New Testament Church Truth?" *Emmaus Journal* 2 (1993): 111.

¹²Ibid., p. 126.

¹³Ibid., p. 127, emphasis added. Here, the *traditionedness* of interpretation is linked to subjectivism and arbitrariness. If everything is interpretation, Fish worries, then everything is up for grabs. In chapter six I counter this all-too-common linking of hermeneutics and arbitrariness with a reconsideration of criteria in interpretation.

¹⁴Fish does, however, pay lip service to this conditioning: "We would not question the fact that we all may have prejudices, blindnesses, and a lack of knowledge which affect and even distort our interpretation of Scripture" (ibid., p. 126). But it is this "may" that reveals his interpretation of interpretation. I will argue below that we *always* bring prejudices and presuppositions to our reading and that these are inescapable conditions of human be-ing.

¹⁵This would include the doctrines of the Trinity, the atonement, justification by faith, etc. To describe these as interpretations is not necessarily to reject them; the point is to relativize their status *as* interpretations and not as divinely given "readings" (which is precisely what Koivisto emphasizes with regard to microtradition). I have pushed these points in relation to questions of heresy and orthodoxy in my "Fire from Heaven: The Hermeneutics of Heresy," *Journal of Theta Alpha Kappa* 20 (1996): 13-31.

¹⁶Donald Dayton, "Rejoinder to Historiography Discussion," *Christian Scholar's Review* 23 (1993): 70. For Koivisto's adherence to the traditional Calvinistic doctrine, see *OLOF* 203-4.

¹⁷Derrida uses the French word *facteur,* which means both "postman" and "factor," to describe Sigmund Freud in an essay on psychoanalytic interpretation in *The Post Card.* Freud's hermeneutic claims in *The Interpretation of Dreams* would place him within the same "immediacy model" as Koivisto. (For a discussion of this double sense of *facteur,* see the translator's note on *PC* 413.)

¹⁸For a discussion of the modernity of evangelical theology, see James K. A. Smith and Shane R. Cudney, "Postmodern Freedom and the Growth of Fundamentalism: Was the Grand Inquisitor Right?" *Studies in Religion/Sciences Religieuses* 25 (1996): 35-49.

¹⁹While I am agreeing with Derrida regarding the interpolation of the postal space of interpretation, it should be noted that the burden of my essay "How to Avoid Not Speaking" is precisely to contest his final remark that letters "necessarily go astray." This will be taken up once again in chapter four. See James K. A. Smith, "How to Avoid Not Speaking: Attestations," in *Knowing Other-wise: Philosophy on*

the Threshold of Spirituality, Perspectives in Continental Philosophy Series, ed. James H. Olthuis (Bronx, N.Y.: Fordham University Press: 1997), pp. 217-34.

[20]John D. Caputo, "The Good News About Alterity: Derrida and Theology," *Faith and Philosophy* 10 (1993): 454. Unfortunately, this is precisely how many evangelicals hear Derrida.

[21]Caputo, "Good News," p. 455.

[22]John D. Caputo, "How to Avoid Speaking of God: The Violence of Natural Theology," in *Prospects for Natural Theology,* ed. Eugene Thomas Long (Washington, D.C.: The Catholic University of America Press, 1992), pp. 129-30.

[23]As such, Lints's book is part of a recent spate of works on the theme, including Mark Noll, *The Scandal of the Evangelical Mind* (Grand Rapids, Mich.: Eerdmans, 1994); David Wells, *No Place For Truth, or What Ever Happened to Evangelical Theology?* (Grand Rapids, Mich.: Eerdmans, 1993); and Wells, *God in the Wasteland: The Reality of Truth in a World of Fading Dreams* (Grand Rapids, Mich.: Eerdmans, 1995). Lints, Noll and Wells are all party to what I would describe as a "theological elitism." For my response to this general project undertaken by Lints, Noll and Wells, see my "Scandalizing Theology: A Pentecostal Response to Noll's *Scandal,*" *Pneuma: Journal of the Society for Pentecostal Studies* 19 (1997): 225-38. Another welcome countermovement can be found in Richard J. Mouw, *Consulting the Faithful: What Christian Intellectuals Can Learn from Popular Religion* (Grand Rapids, Mich.: Eerdmans, 1994).

[24]This is why I have described this as a *present immediacy model:* immediacy is restored in the present, and thus the grievous effects of the Fall and the interpolation of an interpretive space is banished.

[25]See for instance the curious note on *FT* 87, where Lints describes Cardinal John Henry Newman as one who "experienced an evangelical conversion early in life *but* later in life moved toward a high Anglo-Catholic view of church tradition, converted to Roman Catholicism, and was appointed a cardinal" (emphasis added)—as though his move to the Catholic church were a denial of his "evangelical conversion."

[26]For instance, in discussing the "bias principle" and the "realism principle," Lints speaks of "employing" bias (*FT* 23). What does it mean to "employ" bias? Are we not rather caught by it, enveloped by it? Is it not rather a question of recognition—recognizing our biases and the impossibility of realism? This kind of language will signal that, for him, bias is *accidental.*

[27]On *FT* 291, he insists that the "authority of the Scriptures is integrally connected with a proper understanding of those Scriptures, and the final court of appeals in interpretive matters must be the Scriptures themselves." Scripture is "the final interpretive lens" (*FT* 292).

[28]As James Olthuis has observed, "our submission to the Scriptures as the Word of God never takes place apart from concrete embodiment in a view of biblical authority through which and in which we articulate our submission" (James H. Olthuis, "Proposal for a Hermeneutics of Ultimacy," in James H. Olthuis et al., *A Hermeneutics of Ultimacy: Peril or Promise?* [Lanham, Md.: University Press of America, 1987], p. 11). Not only do we submit ourselves to an interpretation of Scripture, we are also conditioned by an interpretation of Scriptural authority.

[29]F. F. Bruce has cogently demonstrated that in fact tradition precedes Scripture and

that the New Testament itself is an interpretive tradition. In this light, Lints's naive opposition between Scripture and tradition becomes problematic. See Bruce, "Scripture and Tradition in the New Testament," in *Holy Book and Holy Tradition,* ed. F. F. Bruce and E. G. Rupp (Manchester: Manchester University Press, 1968), pp. 68-93.

[30]The best formulations of the principle of *sola Scriptura* are sensitive to this. See, for example, the recent proposal of Donald Bloesch, *Holy Scripture: Revelation, Inspiration & Interpretation* (Downers Grove, Ill.: InterVarsity Press, 1994), pp. 192-96, where he retrieves the Reformational principle in a more nuanced sense. I would also note the development of these themes in Trevor Hart, *Faith Thinking: The Dynamics of Christian Theology* (Downers Grove, Ill.: InterVarsity Press, 1995), pp. 107-34, where he situates this in the context of what is now described as "canonical criticism." But it must be conceded that Lints's account as well as many other evangelical accounts (including Koivisto [*OLOF* 155]) do indeed make appeals to "the Scriptures themselves" and their "clarity" that mitigates, if not excludes, the necessity of interpretation.

[31]See also Richard Lints, "Two Theologies or One? Warfield and Vos on the Nature of Theology," *Westminster Theological Journal* 54 (1992): 235-53.

[32]This is why Gadamer suggests that there are not really "two" horizons, because the horizon is not closed; in other words, different times or cultures are not discrete. See *TM* 304.

[33]For an instructive discussion on this point, see Bloesch, *Holy Scripture,* chap. 6, "Scripture and the Church" (pp. 141-70).

[34]See a number of the contributions in the fruitful volume *The Nature of Confession: Evangelicals and Postliberals in Dialogue,* ed. Timothy R. Phillips and Dennis L. Okholm (Downers Grove, Ill.: InterVarsity Press, 1996).

[35]In a practical manner, this is seen in Lints's privileging of the Pauline interpretation of justification by faith (as reinterpreted by Luther) as uncovering the "essence" of Christianity. Unfortunately, no one told the apostle John. See Lints, "A Chasm of Difference: Understanding the Protestant and Roman Views of Salvation," *Tabletalk* 18 (December 1994): 9-10, 53.

[36]"The Chicago Statement on Biblical Hermeneutics (1982)," reprinted in J. I. Packer, *God Has Spoken* (Grand Rapids, Mich.: Baker, 1988), p. 161. My thanks to Phillip Smith for directing me to this document.

[37]However, this is not to say that the apostolic writings do not carry authority or primacy within the believing community. They are authoritative and primary because they are the original testimony of the believing community, what Francis Schüssler Fiorenza refers to as the "founding constitution" of the church.

[38]Mark C. Taylor, *Erring: A Postmodern A/Theology* (Chicago: University of Chicago Press, 1984), p. 175.

[39]Throughout his discussion of postmodern theology (chap. 6), Lints employs a mode of exposition that believes it condemns a position merely by stating it. He seems to assume too much from his reader, or at least he assumes to know who his readers are and their predispositions regarding postmodern theologies.

[40]Lints is particularly disappointed with liberation and feminist theologies (*FT* 194-96).

[41]For a standard evangelical gloss on the story, see John J. Davis, *From Paradise to*

Prison: Studies in Genesis (Grand Rapids. Mich.: Baker, 1975), pp. 144-51.

[42]"And the LORD said, 'Look, they are one people, and they have all one language; and this is only the beginning of what they will do; nothing that they purpose to do will be impossible for them. Come, let us go down, and confuse their language there, so that they will not understand one another's speech" (Gen 11:6-7).

[43]For a similar reading, see Miroslav Volf, *Exclusion and Embrace* (Nashville: Abingdon, 1996), pp. 226-31.

[44]In R. A. Brower, ed., *On Translation* (Cambridge, Mass.: Harvard University Press, 1959), pp. 232-39.

[45]Here a note of clarification is necessary: I am not denying the effects of a broken world on interpretation: that in a fallen creation there is distortion and deception and painful misunderstanding. My point here, however, is that if hermeneutics is constitutive of human creatureliness (i.e., is an aspect of God's creation) and if we believe in the primordial goodness of creation as coming from God (as I am sure Lints and Koivisto would), then the state of affairs that occasions both interpretation and misinterpretation must also be "good."

Chapter 2: Through a Mirror Darkly
[1]For the importance of Wilhelm Dilthey's thought to Heidegger's project, see Martin Heidegger, "Wilhelm Diltheys Forschungsarbeit und der gegenwärtige Kampf um eine historische Weltanschauung: 10 Vortrage," *Dilthey-Jahrbuch* 8 (1992-1993): 143-77. See also Theodore Kisiel's commentary in "A Philosophical Postscript: On the Genesis of 'Sein und Zeit,'" *Dilthey-Jahrbuch* 8 (1992-1993): 226-32, and his incisive observations on "The Dilthey Draft" in *The Genesis of Heidegger's Being and Time* (Berkeley: University of California Press, 1993), pp. 315-61.

[2]I would offer a different gloss on this passage. As I hear it, we now see darkly not because of our finitude but because of the Fall. Seeing "face to face" does not promise the elimination of hermeneutics, for even the face-to-face relation happens across the space of interpretation.

[3]John D. Caputo, "Gadamer's Closet Essentialism: A Derridean Critique," in *Dialogue and Deconstruction: The Gadamer-Derrida Encounter,* ed. Diane P. Michelfelder and Richard Palmer (Albany, N.Y.: SUNY Press, 1989), p. 259.

[4]Ibid., p. 258.

[5]Their category arises from the tradition of philosophical historiography identified with Dutch philosopher D. H. Th. Vollenhoven (formerly of the Vrije Universiteit in Amsterdam). The most programmatic description and development are found in James H. Olthuis, *Models of Humankind in Theology and Psychology,* rev. ed. (Toronto: Institute for Christian Studies, 1990), pp. 46-49. See also Brian J. Walsh, *Futurity and Creation: Explorations in the Eschatological Theology of Wolfhart Pannenberg* (Toronto: AACS, 1979); and his, "Pannenberg's Eschatological Ontology," *Christian Scholar's Review* 11 (1982): 229-49; and Olthuis's "God as True Infinite: Concerns About Wolfhart Pannenberg's *Systematic Theology, Vol. 1,*" *Calvin Theological Journal* 27 (1992): 318-25.

[6]Olthuis, "God as True Infinite," p. 321.

[7]Ibid., p. 320 (emphasis added).

[8]Compare Caputo, "Gadamer's Closet Essentialism," p. 259.

[9]Olthuis, "God as True Infinite," p. 321.

[10]My thanks to Jim Olthuis for several discussions that helped me to see this kairological future in Wolfhart Pannenberg.

[11]Pannenberg's favorite "proof-text" (which he never exegetes) in this regard is 1 Corinthians 15:45-58. Both Olthuis and Walsh critique Pannenberg's isolationist use of Scripture as ignoring the narrative of the story. See Brian J. Walsh, "Introduction to 'Pannenberg's *Systematic Theology, Vol. 1:* A Symposium,'" *Calvin Theological Journal* 27 (1992): 306.

[12]*ST* 1:222-27f., 408-10; 2:92-94; *MIG* 76-79.

[13]John van Buren, discussing the theme of fallenness in the young Heidegger (which is also rather Plotinian, as is Pannenberg), notes that similar notions of the "privation" of human be-ing can be found in Luther's *Lectures on Romans* and *Commentary on Genesis*. See van Buren, "Martin Heidegger, Martin Luther," in *Reading Heidegger from the Start: Essays in His Earliest Thought*, ed. Theodore Kisiel and John van Buren (Albany, N.Y.: SUNY Press, 1994), pp. 169-70. These themes will be further explored in chapter three.

[14]This devouring nature of Hegel's "SA," the *savoir absolu*, is pursued throughout Jacques Derrida, *Glas*, trans. John P. Leavey and Richard Rand (Lincoln: University of Nebraska Press, 1988).

[15]Pannenberg is very insistent in this regard. I think he is constantly making this qualification precisely because he senses where his position must lead. But, I am arguing, his disclaimers cannot halt that trajectory.

[16]"God's eternity needs no recollection or expectation, for it is itself simultaneous with all events in the strict sense" (*ST* 2:91). It is important for the following discussion to note that Pannenberg links this experience of time to omnipresence. There is an important connection between space and time, omnipresence and eternity.

[17]As in Edmund Husserl, *Ideas Pertaining to a Pure Phenomenology and to a Phenomenological Philosophy*, bk. 1 of *General Introduction to a Pure Phenomenology*, trans. F. Kersten (The Hague: Martinus Nijhoff, 1983), pp. 109-12.

[18]Even if he does not actually posit a future *historical* consummation but rather a kind of *kairological* eschaton (here and now), his theory still emphasizes the overcoming of finitude and the transcending of human be-ing

[19]Note the comparison alluded to in note 13, above. Interestingly, Heidegger did offer some (Plotinian) reflections on time to the Marburg Theological Society in July 1924. There Heidegger proposed that since time "finds its meaning in eternity," it is theologians, and not philosophers, who are really the experts on time. See Martin Heidegger, *The Concept of Time*, trans. William McNeill, German-English ed. (Oxford: Blackwell, 1992), p. 1.

[20]Olthuis correctly remarks that Pannenberg's system determines his exegesis, which issues in "a pick-and-choose method that seems to skew the biblical narrative at crucial points" (Olthius, "God as True Infinite," p. 323).

[21]Pannenberg fails to distinguish between "perfection" and "goodness." This leads to his rejection of "original perfection," which I am taking in this context to be basically equivalent to original goodness, where goodness may be understood as "sufficiency" or "completeness," being without lack. The failure to distinguish perfection and goodness also results in a serious misreading of the Reformed tradition on the image of God in humanity. See his discussion, *ST* 2:211-15.

[22]Pannenberg takes himself to be siding with the Irenean idea of imperfect human beginnings over against the Augustinian emphasis on the goodness of our original estate. See *ST* 2:168 n. 43.

[23]I pose further questions: If this is the case—if the possibility of sin and evil is due to the finitude and independence of creaturehood—then can that possibility ever be removed without one's becoming God? In the eschaton, if we still maintain our finitude and independence—if we are not gods—then are we not forever plagued by the possibility of sin and evil?

[24]James H. Olthuis, "Be(com)ing: Humankind as Gift and Call," *Philosophia Reformata* 58 (1993): 169. The heart of my reading of Pannenberg has germinated from the seeds planted and watered by Professor Olthuis.

[25]Pannenberg's language refers mainly to the incarnation and little to the passion and crucifixion. Nevertheless, inasmuch as God "shoulders the responsibility" for evil on the cross, this sending of the Son as part of creation also includes the crucifixion of the Son.

[26]The issues of time and epistemology are integrally connected, for knowledge is only provisional "so long as time and history endure" (*ST* 1:16). So just as Pannenberg was forced to conclude that temporality is not constitutive of human finitude (*ST* 2:95), so here he is forced to conclude that provisionality is not constitutive of human knowing, despite his many assertions that finitude and provisionality are riveted together.

[27]The impetus for this emphasis on restoration is found in the work of the Dutch neo-Calvinist theologian Herman Bavinck. For a discussion, see J. Veenhof, *Revelatie en Inspiratie* (Amsterdam: Buijten & Schipperheijn, 1968), pp. 345-65. See also Albert Wolters, *Creation Regained* (Grand Rapids, Mich.: Eerdmans, 1985), pp. 57-71.

[28]I offer this, recognizing Gadamer emphasizes that "we understand in a *different* way, *if we understand at all*" (*TM* 297). My goal is to attempt to show that behind such statements there lurks a deep unity that ties together all of the differences. These "different understandings," which Gadamer admits, are different ways of reading the Tradition, "the one great horizon" (*TM* 304). I'm not sure how much room he makes for the notion that truth itself is constituted by difference, for the Nietzschean insight that truth is plural, a woman who knows her duplicity (see Friedrich Nietzsche, *Beyond Good and Evil*, in *Basic Writings*, trans. and ed. Walter Kaufmann [New York: Random House, 1968], p. 192).

[29]I have engaged Mark C. Taylor by questioning his strong reading of Derrida in my "How to Avoid Not Speaking: Attestations," in *Knowing Other-wise: Philosophy on the Threshold of Spirituality*, Perspectives in Continental Philosophy Series, ed. James H. Olthuis (Bronx, N.Y.: Fordham University Press, 1997).

[30]Susan E. Shapiro, "Rhetoric as Ideology Critique: The Gadamer-Habermas Debate Reinvented," *Journal of the American Academy of Religion* 62 (1994): 127.

[31]John D. Caputo, *Radical Hermeneutics: Deconstruction, Repetition and the Hermeneutic Project* (Bloomington: Indiana University Press, 1987), p. 111.

[32]Ibid., p. 113. This would be an indicator of Gadamer's contradictory monism.

[33]Shapiro traces and reinvents this debate in a very helpful manner in her "Rhetoric as Ideology Critique."

³⁴See Shapiro, "Rhetoric as Ideology Critique," p. 128.

Chapter 3: Falling into the Garden

¹This comes to the fore later in Martin Heidegger's "A Dialogue on Language Between a Japanese and an Inquirer" (in *On the Way to Language*, trans. Peter D. Hertz [New York: Harper & Row, 1971], pp. 1-54), where "language is the fundamental trait in human nature's hermeneutic relation to the two-fold of presence and present beings" (p. 32).

²Again, I ask for the reader's patience in awaiting a full development of this in part three.

³Jacques Derrida, of course, is no Heideggerian and is in no way a board member of Heidegger, Inc. However, his thought owes an incalculable debt to Heidegger even though it may represent the radicalization of Heidegger: the left side of the Heideggerian heritage (John D. Caputo, *Radical Hermeneutics*, [Bloomington: Indiana University Press], p. 95).

⁴James Olthuis, "A Hermeneutics of Suffering Love," in *The Very Idea of Radical Hermeneutics*, ed. Roy A. Martinez (Atlantic Highlands, N.J.: Humanities Press, 1997).

⁵Heidegger's technical use of the German *Dasein* is generally left untranslated in English editions of his works, largely because the multivalency of the term does not permit a satisfactory translation. For a helpful discussion, see Albert Hofstadter's "Translator's Appendix: A Note on the Da and the Dasein," appended to Martin Heidegger, *Basic Problems of Phenomenology* (Bloomington: Indiana University Press, 1982), pp. 333-37.

⁶As Gadamer suggests in *TM* 257.

⁷John van Buren, *The Young Heidegger: Rumor of the Hidden King* (Bloomington: Indiana University Press, 1994), p. 177.

⁸I will not concern myself here with this story in detail. It has now been masterfully told by Theodore Kisiel in *The Genesis of Heidegger's Being and Time* (Berkeley: University of California Press, 1993); and by van Buren in *The Young Heidegger*. I will delve only into those historical details that are crucial for the thesis of this chapter.

⁹Heidegger emphasizes that it is an *existential* spatiality and not simply "spatial" (i.e., physical). See *BT* 94, 138-40.

¹⁰Derrida's notion of *differance* has a similar duality, as both spatial dif-fering and temporal de-ferring. This was developed in contrast to the bivalent idea of *presence* as a temporal present ("now") and a physico-spatial "present to." In my earliest notes on the way to this book (September 1993), I proposed a "hermeneutics of hesitation," which emphasized that every interpretation must be held tentatively and was rooted in a similar duality: (1) a *quantitative* limitation and (2) a *temporal* limitation. This arose from my experience of holding adamantly to a particular interpretation, only to have it shattered by a completely new text, either one I had not read or one that had not been written. We must always hold our interpretations tentatively because we cannot read everything—there will always be a book we have not read (quantitative limit)—and later discoveries may "disprove" our beliefs and interpretations (temporal limit). Every bibliography is a demonstration of this situationality: its length or brevity, the dates of publication, the languages read, all indicate one's "hermeneutical situation."

¹¹The early sections of *Being and Time* are devoted to this fundamental point. See esp. *BT* sec. 12-24.

¹²I would suggest that Heidegger's notion of "as-structures" is a "translation" of Edmund Husserl's "constitution" within the framework of a hermeneutic phenomenology. As such, it is rooted in "Being-in-the-world," which corresponds to Husserl's "intentionality." For Husserl, consciousness is always consciousness *of* something: there is no "world" without consciousness and no consciousness without a world. As such, this world is "given" in intuition, but this involves an act of "constitution" in perception, whereby the perceiver puts the pieces together—the partial perspectives—in the context of what Heidegger will later call "a totality of involvements." For example, when I see the front side of a house, I understand it as the front, connected to two sides and a back, even though I do not perceive these other sides. It is because I perceive that which is in front *as* the front *of* a house that I thereby constitute it as such. With regards to Husserl's doctrine of intuition as giving the given, Caputo notes that "the injunction to remain with the given includes the reminder that the given is given only *as* something" (*Radical Hermeneutics*, p. 43). In Heidegger then, the world is constitutive of Dasein as Being-in-the-world and is therefore understood *as* something against the horizon of a totality of involvements (what he describes as "significance").

¹³Circumspection *[Umsicht]* is related to Dasein's basic structure as one of "care" *[Sorge]*: a way of being-in-the-world in which the world is a concern for me, within which I have "dealings" with the world. This is the structure that underlies the discussion above regarding things as *pragmata*, as things "for" something, things that I use. The basic structure of care will be addressed more extensively later.

¹⁴Although as van Buren notes, "For Paul, as for the young Heidegger, philosophy is an expression of fallen life" (*Young Heidegger*, p. 178).

¹⁵As developed in the winter semester lecture course of 1921-1922 (PIA 131-55).

¹⁶I will maintain the older translation of *das Man* as "they" in accordance with the Macquarrie and Edwards translation (see the abbreviations section for a full citation). It has been emphasized in recent Heidegger scholarship, however, that "the 'One'" or "the 'Anyone'" gives a better sense.

¹⁷This bears a remarkable resemblance to John Stuart Mill's use of the "tyranny of majority" (which he borrowed from Alexis de Tocqueville) in his treatise on individualism, entitled *On Liberty* (ed. Gertrude Himmelfarb [New York: Penguin, 1985], p. 62). More directly, however, the notion is grounded in Kierkegaard's critique of "the present age" (see Kisiel, *Genesis*, p. 334.)

¹⁸In his rectoral address of 1933, Heidegger called the university (and the German *Volk*) to assert its authentic character and to will the essence of the German university through labor service, military service and knowledge service. Then and only then will the German people (as collective Dasein) realize its authenticity and spiritual-historical mission. See Martin Heidegger, "The Self-Assertion of the German University," in *Martin Heidegger and National Socialism: Questions and Answers,* ed. Gunther Neske and Emil Kettering (New York: Paragon House, 1990), pp. 5-13.

¹⁹Jürgen Habermas, *The Philosophical Discourse of Modernity*, trans. Frederick Lawrence (Cambridge, Mass.: MIT Press, 1987), p. 149. He goes on to say that "in *Being and Time,* Heidegger does not construct intersubjectivity any differently than

Husserl does in the *Cartesian Meditations*" (pp. 149-50).

[20]Robert J. Dostal, "The Public and the People: Heidegger's Illiberal Politics," *Review of Metaphysics* 47 (1994): 520.

[21]The point I am attempting to make here is that Heidegger, while pushing the limits of the modern project, failed to ask some crucial questions (questions that Derrida also fails to ask). I am not suggesting that one could completely step outside of the metaphysical tradition; however, Heidegger seems to either concede too much or not ask enough. This is analogous to Jean-Luc Marion's critique of Heidegger's critique of onto-theo-logy. While Heidegger pushes the question back beyond and behind metaphysics, his critique remains within the horizon of ontology, or the "screen of Being"; it is simply *"another* idolatry" inasmuch as it assumes the "essential anteriority of the ontological question over the so-called ontic question of 'God.'" Being still sets the rules, and whoever makes the rules wins the game. See Marion, *God Without Being*, trans. Thomas A. Carlson (Chicago: University of Chicago Press, 1991), pp. 37-52. See also Marion, "The Final Appeal of the Subject *[L'interloque],*" in *Deconstructive Subjectivities,* ed. Simon Critchley and Peter Dews, trans. Simon Critchley (Albany, N.Y.: SUNY Press, 1996), pp. 85-104. Unfortunately, even Marion, despite his wonderful emphasis on love, gives the game to Being with respect to humans, for "we fall—in the capacity of beings—under the government of Being." Thus, in the end, to be finite is to be sinful, to fall under "the (sinful) 'economy' of the creature" (*God Without Being*, pp. 108-9). For my own critique of Marion on related matters, see James K. A. Smith, "Respect and Donation: A Critique of Marion's Critique of Husserl," *American Catholic Philosophical Quarterly* 71 (1997): 523-38; and "How to Avoid Not Speaking: Attestations," in *Knowing Other-wise: Philosophy on the Threshold of Spirituality,* Perspectives in Continental Philosophy Series, ed. James H. Olthuis (Bronx, N.Y.: Fordham University Press, 1997), pp. 221-23. See also Graham Ward, "The Theological Project of Jean-Luc Marion," in *Post-Secular Philosophy: Between Philosophy and Theology,* ed. Phillip Blond (New York: Routledge, 1998), pp. 229-39.

[27]Compare R. J. Sheffler Manning, *Interpreting Otherwise Than Heidegger: Emmanuel Levinas's Ethics as First Philosophy* (Pittsburgh: Duquesne University Press, 1993). Manning proposes that Emmanuel Levinas offers another interpretation, one other than Heidegger's. But as I will suggest in chapter four, with regards to the violence of intersubjectivity, Levinas, Heidegger and Derrida are agreed.

[23]James H. Olthuis, "God-With-Us: Toward a Relational Psychotherapeutic Model," *Journal of Psychology and Christianity* 13 (1994): 37-49; his "Being-With: Toward a Relational Psychotherapy," *Journal of Psychology and Christianity* 13 (1994): 217-31; his "Be(com)ing: Humankind as Gift and Call," *Philosophia Reformata* 58 (1993); his "Crossing the Threshold: Sojourning Together in the Wild Spaces of Love," *Toronto Journal of Theology* 11 (1995): 39-57, esp. pp. 40-41; and his "A Hermeneutics of Suffering Love."

[24]Olthuis, "Be(com)ing," p. 161.

[25]Olthuis, "Being-With," p. 217.

[26]Olthuis, "Crossing the Threshold," p. 41. This will be further explored in connection with Levinas in the following chapter. Paul Ricoeur may also be included here, when he asserts that it is "difficult to imagine situations of interaction in which one individual does not exert power over another by the very fact of act-

200 THE FALL OF INTERPRETATION

ing." Thus "violence taints all the relations of interaction." (*Oneself as Another*, trans. Kathleen Blamey [Chicago: University of Chicago Press, 1992], pp. 220, 351.) But why is this so hard to imagine, unless one begins with an ontology of domination? Could it not be otherwise? Could we not imagine differently?

[27]Olthius, "Be(com)ing," p. 161.

[28]Olthuis, "Crossing the Threshold," pp. 49-50.

[29]This is the project that Caputo sets out to accomplish in his *Demythologizing Heidegger* (Bloomington: Indiana University Press, 1993), pp. 1-8.

[30]See Introduction, n. 33.

[31]Caputo, *Demythologizing Heidegger*, p. 7.

[32]Ibid., p. 3.

[33]John Milbank, *Theology and Social Theory: Beyond Secular Reason* (Oxford: Blackwell, 1990), p. 279. Milbank does a superb job of demonstrating the *religious* commitments that stand behind an ontology of violence (pp. 280-89).

[34]Ibid., p. 289.

[35]Ibid., p. 294.

[36]Martin Heidegger, *History of the Concept of Time: Prolegomena*, trans. Theodore Kisiel (Bloomington: Indiana University Press, 1985), p. 283.

[37]Rudolf Bultmann, "New Testament and Mythology," in Bultmann et al., *Kerygma and Myth*, ed. Hans Werner Bartsch, trans. Reginald H. Fuller (New York: Harper & Row, 1961), p. 5.

[38]Ibid., p. 11.

[39]Ibid., p. 16.

[40]"The real question is whether this understanding of existence is true" (ibid., p. 11).

[41]To press the analogy further, Bultmann also emphasizes that there is a point at which faith must cross the abyss where reason fails; that is, the New Testament interpretation of existence is not identical to Heidegger's "existentialism," for the New Testament asserts that one does not solve this riddle by resolution but by grace (ibid., pp. 28-33). So also for Thomas Aquinas, there is only so much that one can know about God by reason. A "saving" knowledge of God requires faith. For a very succinct discussion, see Aquinas's commentary on Boethius's *De Trinitate* in Aquinas, *Faith, Reason and Theology*, trans. Armand Maurer (Toronto: Pontifical Institute of Medieval Studies, 1987), Q1.A4; Q3.A1, 4.

[42]Bultmann, "New Testament and Mythology," p. 24.

[43]Ibid., p. 25, emphasis added.

[44]Martin Heidegger, *Introduction to Metaphysics*, trans. Ralph Manheim (New Haven, Conn.: Yale University Press, 1959), p. 7. Caputo sees a discontinuity between this critique and those of the early Freiburg lectures, but I would suggest that both critiques of a Christian philosophy are rooted in Heidegger's understanding of philosophy as radical questioning. See Caputo, *Demythologizing Heidegger*, pp. 43, 174-78. Incidentally, it is precisely the privileging of the "question" that is questioned in Derrida's *Of Spirit*, a line of questioning that leads him eventually to faith (OS 129-30).

[45]Martin Heidegger, *Phänomenologie und Theologie* (Frankfurt: Vittorio Klostermann, 1970), p. 32. This opposition is rooted in Paul's discourse on the foolishness of faith (1 Cor 1:18-25) as taken up by Martin Luther. For a discussion, see John van Buren, "Martin Heidegger, Martin Luther," in *Reading Heidegger from the Start:*

Essays in His Earliest Thought, ed. Theodore Kisiel and John van Buren (Albany, N.Y.: SUNY Press, 1994), pp. 167-68.

[46]Martin Heidegger, *The Concept of Time,* trans. William McNeill, German-English ed. (Oxford: Blackwell, 1992), p. 1.

[47]Heidegger, *Phänomenologie und Theologie,* p. 32, and *Introduction to Metaphysics,* p. 7.

[48]See the bibliography of Heidegger's reading list on the phenomenology of religion (1917-1919) in Kisiel, *Genesis,* pp. 525-26.

[49]Van Buren, "Martin Heidegger, Martin Luther," p. 170.

[50]These are included in one of the most recently published volumes of the *Gesamtausgabe,* Band 60, *Phänomenologie des Religiösen Lebens,* which includes Heidegger's lecture course from summer semester 1921, *Augustinus und der Neuplatonismus,* ed. Hg. Claudius Strube (Frankfurt: Vittorio Klostermann, 1995), pp. 157-299.

[51]Martin Heidegger, "A Dialogue on Language Between a Japanese and an Inquirer," in *On the Way to Language,* trans. Peter D. Hertz (New York: Harper & Row, 1971), pp. 9-10.

[52]Compare *BT* 151: "Perhaps when Dasein addresses itself in the way which is closest to itself, it always says 'I am this entity,' and in the long run says this loudest when it is 'not' this entity."

[53]Caputo, *Demythologizing Heidegger,* p. 173. Derrida makes a similar observation: "The same Heideggerian thinking often consists, notably in *Sein und Zeit,* in repeating on an ontological level Christian themes and texts that have been 'de-Christianized.' Such themes and texts are then presented as ontic, anthropological, or contrived attempts that come to a sudden halt on the way to an ontological recovery of their own originary possibility (whether that be, for example, the *status corruptionis,* the difference between the authentic and inauthentic or the fall *[Verfallen]* into the One, whether it be the *sollicitudo* and care, the pleasure of seeing and of curiosity, of the authentic or vulgar concept of time, of the texts of the Vulgate, of Saint Augustine or of Kierkegaard)" (Jacques Derrida, *The Gift of Death,* trans. David Wills [Chicago: University of Chicago Press, 1995], p. 20).

[54]For further development of this critique and an alternative constructive proposal, see my essay, "The Art of Christian Atheism: Faith and Philosophy in Early Heidegger," *Faith and Philosophy* 14 (1997): 71-81.

[55]Martin Luther, *Heidelberg Disputation,* in *Luther's Works,* ed. J. Pelikan (St. Louis: Concordia, 1955), 31:39.

[56]In this tracing of an alternative history I follow Michel Foucault, "Two Lectures," in *Critique and Power: Recasting the Foucault/Habermas Debate,* ed. Michael Kelly (Cambridge, Mass.: MIT Press, 1994), pp. 17-46. For an account of the marginalization of these voices by evangelical theology, see James K. A. Smith, "Closing the Book: Pentecostals, Evangelicals and the Sacred Writings," *Journal of Pentecostal Theology* 11 (1997): 49-71; and his "Scandalizing Theology: A Pentecostal Response to Noll's *Scandal,*" *Pneuma: Journal of the Society for Pentecostal Studies* 19 (1997): 225-38.

[57]Edith Wyschogrod also suggests a Neo-Platonic moment in Heidegger. See her *Saints and Postmodernism* (Chicago: University of Chicago Press, 1990), pp. 90-92.

[58]Jürgen Becker, *Paul: Apostle to the Gentiles,* trans. O. C. Dean Jr. (Louisville, Ky.: Westminster John Knox, 1993), p. 381.

[59]Milbank, *Theology and Social Theory*, p. 302.

Chapter 4: Edenic Violence

[1]Jacques Derrida, "Edmond Jabès and the Question of the Book," in *Writing and Difference*, trans: Alan Bass (Chicago: University of Chicago Press, 1978), p. 67.

[2]Aristotle *De Interpretatione* 16a3-8, in *The Basic Works of Aristotle*, ed. Richard McKeon (New York: Random House, 1941).

[3]I have been aided in my understanding of Ferdinand de Saussure by Kerryl Lynne Henderson, "Ferdinand de Saussure: Friend or Foe?" *Glass* 8 (1993): 12-29; and the first chapter of Stephen D. Moore, *Poststructuralism and the New Testament* (Philadelphia: Fortress, 1994), pp. 13-41. On structuralism, which provides the context of *Of Grammatology*, I was helped by Bill Stancil, "Structuralism," in *New Testament Criticism and Interpretation*, ed. David Alan Black and David S. Dockery (Grand Rapids, Mich.: Zondervan, 1991), pp. 319-44.

[4]This must be surrounded with a careful discourse. Admittedly, Derrida appropriates the language of fallenness from the logocentric tradition that construed writing as accidental, as fallen from a pure and originary full speech. However, Derrida retains such a category, only pushing it back to the "origin." The "fall" is "original"—again, something of a Plotinian moment as in Martin Heidegger. For a similar suggestion, see Edith Wyschogrod, *Saints and Postmodernism* (Chicago: University of Chicago Press, 1990), pp. 21-24, 90-92.

[5]Recall my discussion of "Envois" in chapter one, in the section "A Postcard from the Edge: Koivisto Meets Derrida."

[6]"The breaking of the Tables articulates, first of all, a rupture within God as the origin of history" (Derrida, "Edmond Jabès," p. 67).

[7]This is also why Derrida believes that negative theology—which attempts to honor God by not speaking about him—remains a violent discourse, for silence is an impossible ideal. See Jacques Derrida, "How to Avoid Speaking: Denials," in *Derrida and Negative Theology*, ed. Harold Coward and Toby Foshay (Albany, N.Y.: SUNY Press, 1992), pp. 73-142. I have criticized this valorization of silence in Derrida and Caputo in "How to Avoid Not Speaking: Attestations," in *Knowing Other-wise: Philosophy on the Threshold of Spirituality*, Perspectives in Continental Philosophy Series, ed. James H. Olthuis (Bronx, N.Y.: Fordham University Press, 1997), pp. 228-29.

[8]Since this early confession, Derrida has penned his own *Circumfessions*, which tells the story of this Algerian who was raised on rue Saint-Augustin, not far from Hippo. See Derrida, *Circumfession*, in Geoffrey Bennington and Jacques Derrida, *Jacques Derrida*, trans. Geoffrey Bennington (Chicago: University of Chicago Press, 1993).

[9]The influence of Emmanuel Levinas on Derrida's later "ethical" work is widely recognized. See Jacques Derrida, "Force of Law: The 'Mystical Foundation of Authority'" (see the abbreviations section for a full citation); and his *The Gift of Death*, trans. David Wills (Chicago: University of Chicago Press, 1995). In *Of Grammatology* Derrida attributes his notion of the "trace" to Levinas (*OG* 70).

[10]This is a critique of Heidegger's signification and "as-structure" in *Being and Time*. For a discussion, see the section titled "The Interpretedness of *Dasein*" in chapter three.

[11]This is a gloss of Derrida's comments on reading Jean-Jacques Rousseau. I have interpolated Derrida's name in the places of Rousseau's ("Jacques," as it were, in the place of "Jean-Jacques").

[12]He also accepts, without challenge, the traditional ascription of interpretation to writing. But because he thinks full presence and the absence of interpretation are a dream (as do I), he posits a more originary "writing," arche-writing. But by doing so, he maintains the traditional confinement of interpretation to writing. In contrast, I would emphasize the interpretedness of speech.

[13]We also have from Derrida a note that confesses his conjuring of Heidegger's ghost. Though he does not accept the call from Heidegger ("What will he do with the ghost or Geist of Martin?"), "all this must not lead you to believe that no telephonic communication links me to Heidegger's ghost, as to more than one other. Quite the contrary, the network of my hookups, you have the proof of it here, is on the burdensome side, and more than one switchboard is necessary in order to digest the overload" (PC 21, note). In chapter six I will consider yet another ghost—or rather, *pneuma*—that haunts Derrida's discourse, one to whom he has yet to pay his debts.

[14]Permit me to acknowledge here a debt to Jeffrey Dudiak, whose paper "Infinite Hauntings" was read as a response to an earlier version of this chapter presented to the Society of Christian Philosophers—Canada at Brock University, May 1996. Jeff's probing and constructive criticisms helped me to see just what is at stake in the debate between Levinas and Husserl/Heidegger. I only hope I have done justice to his remarks.

[15]John D. Caputo, *Against Ethics: Contributions to a Poetics of Obligation with Constant Reference to Deconstruction* (Bloomington: Indiana University Press, 1993), p. 264 n. 80.

[16]FL 24-26.

[17]It is precisely this question which I pursued in my dissertation, "How to Avoid Not Speaking: On the Phenomenological Possibility of Theology" (Ph.D. diss., University of Michigan, 1999).

[18]Ibid., p. 26.

[19]This is Derrida's argument "in defense" of Husserl in "Violence and Metaphysics: An Essay on the Thought of Emmanuel Levinas," *Writing and Difference*, trans. Alan Bass (Chicago: University of Chicago Press, 1978), pp. 120-22. To appropriate this framework would still mean a certain deconstruction of "violence and metaphysics," inasmuch as Derrida continues to maintain that the economy of violence is originary.

[20]I have in mind here the birth of our children. It is difficult to understand that the moment of naming them in the delivery room was a first act of violation against them. It was rather the moment of welcoming them, of granting an identity, of offering them a family and a home.

Chapter 5: Interpreting the Fall

[1]For instance, Martin Luther identifies humanity in its prelapsarian state as enjoying immediacy, as does Dante's Adam: "Whatever God wanted or said, man also wanted, believed, and understood the same thing. The knowledge of all the other creatures necessarily followed this knowledge; for where the knowledge of God is *perfect*, there also the knowledge of other things that are under God is necessarily

perfect" (Luther, *Lectures on Genesis*, Luther's Works, ed. J. Pelikan [St. Louis: Concordia, 1955], 1:141). For a discussion of Luther's logocentrism, see Stephen D. Moore, *Poststructuralism and the New Testament* (Philadelphia: Fortress, 1994), pp. 33-34.

[2]Dennis J. Schmidt provides a wonderful analysis of this theme in *The Ubiquity of the Finite: Hegel, Heidegger and the Entitlements of Philosophy* (Cambridge, Mass.: MIT Press, 1988), pp. 1-17.

[3]John Milbank, *Theology and Social Theory: Beyond Secular Reason* (Oxford: Blackwell, 1990), pp. 290, 295. Milbank dismisses "the Augustinian Platonizing rhetoric of spiritual essence over against bodily and symbolic integuments" as misleading (pp. 290-91). But I would suggest that such a dualism lies at the very heart of Milbank's "Platonism/Christianity" and, perhaps, the majority of Christian thought. Though Milbank hears in Heidegger "echoes of Valentinian gnosis" (p. 302), I think he is deaf to similar echoes in "Platonism/Christianity." My project in this chapter is to effect a marked distinction rather than a conjunction between these two trains of thought, particularly by considering their relationship within the thought of Augustine.

[4]Marcion's canon, the first of its kind, was structured around his Gnostic theology, which rejected the creator God in favor of Jesus Christ, thereby setting redemption against creation, spirit against flesh. This Gnostic canon was composed only of the Pauline epistles and Luke's Gospel (the most Pauline of the Synoptics). Why was that? What was it that the Gnostic Marcion saw in Paul? Though the dominant Christian tradition has constantly renounced gnosticism, there is a sense in which it has never freed itself from its shadow, precisely because it is possible—if one is looking through the gnostic lens of a Marcion or reading the New Testament through Platonist eyes, as Augustine did—to see seeds of Gnosticism implanted within the Pauline corpus. Gnosticism, Derrida might say, is inside/outside Christianity. While other examples could be cited, I would mention here Paul's notion of absence from the body (2 Cor 5:1-8), the inauthenticity of concern for the world (1 Cor 7:25-35) and the relegation of the "world" to depravity (Rom 1; 12:2). However, Neo-Platonic and gnostic movements within the Christian tradition read such passages *to the exclusion of* other aspects of the Pauline corpus and New Testament that point to a creation theology. Again, the project of this chapter is to read those biblical motifs *against* Neo-Platonic trajectories within the tradition.

[5]Erasmus, in his debate with Luther regarding free will (which is not wholly unrelated to this study), remarks that Luther and his followers (on this point, the Calvinists!) distort things because they "immeasurably exaggerate original sin." See Erasmus, *De Libero Arbitrio*, in *Luther and Erasmus: Free Will and Salvation*, ed. E. Gordon Rupp and Philip S. Watson (Philadelphia: Westminster Press, 1969), p. 93; see also the discussion of this point above with respect to Heidegger.

[6]John Burnaby, *Amor Dei: A Study of the Religion of Saint Augustine* (London: Hodder & Stoughton, 1938), p. 231. Jansenius was the founder of a reform movement in the sixteenth and seventeenth centuries known as "Jansenism." The Jansenists—often disparagingly linked with the Protestant Calvinists—considered themselves to be the defenders of the "true" Augustine and counted among their ranks Antoin Arnauld and Blaise Pascal. But as is the case with most "disciples," these "Augustinians" seemed to have taken Augustine beyond himself, such that

sin seems to become "natural," a fundamentally un-Augustinian notion. For an accessible discussion of these matters, see Marvin R. O'Connell, *Blaise Pascal: Reasons of the Heart* (Grand Rapids, Mich.: Eerdmans, 1997), pp. 30-70.

[7]Paul Ricoeur, " 'Original Sin': A Study in Meaning," in *The Conflict of Interpretations,* ed. Don Ihde (Evanston, Ill.: Northwestern University Press, 1974), pp. 269-86. Here he asserts that "to reflect on its meaning is in a certain way *to deconstruct the concept*" (p. 270).

[8]How can a theory that claims to be a retrieval of Augustine also align itself with this tradition? This is an expected question. To fully address it, one would need to reconsider the debate between Augustine and Pelagius (and not "Pelagians" such as Rufinus and Caelestius). Much modern research has pointed to exaggerations by "disciples" on both sides of this debate, as well as to the political interests at stake. For discussions, see especially Gerald Bonner, *Augustine and Modern Research on Pelagianism* (Villanova, Penn.: Villanova University Press, 1972); and "Pelagianism Reconsidered," in *Studia Patristica,* ed. Elizabeth A. Livingstone (Leuven: Peeters, 1993), 27:237-41. Such a reconsideration might point to a certain rapprochement between Augustine (not Augustinianism) and Pelagius (not Pelagianism). We might even suggest that the "recovery" of this alternative tradition, whose seeds we also find in Augustine, is more a Greek rather than a Latin account, elements of which are adopted by Wesley. Finally, we would also point to Kierkegaard's account as representative of this alternative tradition. See Søren Kierkegaard, *The Concept of Anxiety,* trans. Reidar Thomte (Princeton, N.J.: Princeton University Press, 1985), esp. pp. 25-51.

[9]This recovery of the Wesleyan impetus of Pentecostalism guides Steven J. Land's work *Pentecostal Spirituality: A Passion for the Kingdom,* JPTSup 1 (Sheffield: Sheffield Academic Press, 1993).

[10]Augustine *The Spirit and the Letter* 28.48 (in *Augustine: Later Works,* trans. John Burnaby [Philadelphia: Westminster Press, 1965]).

[11]Ibid., 27.47.

[12]The New Testament word *hygiaino* (to heal) means "to restore to original condition" and points to the reinstatement of original status. For a discussion, see D. Muller, "Heal," in *The New International Dictionary of New Testament Theology,* ed. Colin Brown (Grand Rapids, Mich.: Zondervan, 1986), 2:169-71.

[13]For example, John Calvin speaks of the freedom death provides "from the prison house of the body." Further, when it comes to questions regarding human nature, he concludes that Plato is the closest to a Christian understanding. (*Institutes* 1.15.2, 6). I cite this as an example of how Abraham Kuyper's retrieval of Calvin (and even more so the retrievals by Herman Dooyeweerd and the later Calvinian tradition) is at the same time a demythologizing of Calvin.

[14]For Kuyper's most accessible ideas on creation, fall, redemption and grace, see his *Calvinism: Six Stone Foundation Lectures* (Grand Rapids, Mich.: Eerdmans, 1943), esp. lecture four, "Calvinism and Science," pp. 110-41. For two helpful works from the tradition, see Albert Wolters, *Creation Regained* (Grand Rapids, Mich.: Eerdmans, 1985); and Brian J. Walsh and J. Richard Middleton, *The Transforming Vision: Shaping a Christian Worldview* (Downers Grove, Ill.: InterVarsity Press, 1984), esp. pp. 41-90.

[15]In order to keep this chapter focused I have generally limited my consideration to

Augustine's earlier work, up to and including the *Confessions* (though *De doctrina christiana* is a work that is both early and late). I hope in the future to pursue this line of research in a companion study that would consider this theme in his later work, particularly in *De trinitate* and *De civitate dei*. Despite some later shifts in his thinking, there seems to be a strong continuity in his position on the question of time, language and the Fall. For further discussion, see Robert J. O'Connell, S.J., *The Origin of the Soul in St. Augustine's Later Works* (Bronx, N.Y.: Fordham University Press, 1987). For an overview of the issues at stake, see Richard Penaskovic, "The Fall of the Soul in Saint Augustine: A *Quaestio Disputata*," *Augustinian Studies* 17 (1986): 135-45.

[16]It will be important for the contemporary reader to appreciate that for Augustine, the paradigm of interpretation is an *oral/aural* model primarily and a written model only derivatively. Brian Stock emphasizes the orality of interpretation for Augustine in *Augustine the Reader: Meditation, Self-Knowledge and the Ethics of Interpretation* (Cambridge: Belknap Press of Harvard University Press, 1996), pp. 26-27; on the "oral culture" of late antiquity and the early medieval period, see his *The Implications of Literacy: Written Language and Models of Interpretation in the Eleventh and Twelfth Centuries* (Princeton: Princeton University Press, 1983), pp. 12-87.

[17]As will be discussed further below, God and angels neither "read" nor "interpret," precisely because they are not conditioned by time (*CSA* 13.15.18).

[18]Roland J. Teske, S.J., *Paradoxes of Time in Saint Augustine*, The Aquinas Lecture 1996 (Milwaukee: Marquette University Press, 1996), p. 30.

[19]In Augustine's understanding of the mediated relation between "interior" selves, we see anticipations of Edmund Husserl's discussion of intersubjectivity in the fifth of his *Cartesian Meditations* (trans. Dorion Cairns [Dordrecht: Kluwer, 1993], pp. 89-151), where the other is "appresented" precisely because her or his experience or consciousness *(Erlebnisse)* is not accessible *originaliter*—it cannot be made present to another consciousness—and thus it must be mediated. Further consideration of this connection will appear elsewhere.

[20]"I was no longer a baby incapable of speech but already a boy with power to talk" (*CSA* 1.8.13). For Augustine, words are only one kind of sign or mode of signification; gestures, written letters and other things *(res)* can function as signs. For discussion, see his *De magistro* (CSEL 77), 4.8-10, and *De doctrina christiana* (CCSL 32), 2.1.1-2.5.6.

[21]Augustine *De magistro* 1.2 (in *Against the Academicians and the Teacher.* trans. Peter King [Indianapolis: Hackett, 1995]).

[22]Augustine *De magistro* 1.2. The same thematics of "prayer" is encountered when Augustine reflects on "confession," which is undertaken not to inform God but as a task for the benefit of oneself and others (*CSA* 10.2.2-10.3.4).

[23]"He who is making confession to you is not instructing you of that which is happening within him. The closed heart does not shut out your eye" (*CSA* 5.1.1). "Indeed, Lord, to your eyes, the abyss of human consciousness is naked" (*CSA* 10.2.2).

[24]There is, for Augustine, a fundamental analogy between the mediating function of words *(verbi)* and the mediating function of the Word Incarnate *(Verbum)*. For a discussion, see Mark D. Jordan, "Words and Word: Incarnation and Signification in Augustine's *De doctrina christiana*," *Augustinian Studies* 11 (1980): 177-96.

[25]Augustine *De doctrina christiana* 2.2.3 (in *Teaching Christianity*, The Works of Saint Augustine 1/11, trans. Edmund Hill, O.P. [New York: New City Press, 1996]), emphasis added.

[26]Brian Stock notes an important aspect of this, which we cannot pursue here: "If language, from which reading and writing derive, is definable through a community of speakers, then selves, souls, or minds, which depend on language for their human expression, have to have their communities too. . . . It is this intersubjective quality that makes Augustine's *Confessions* unique in the ancient literature of the soul, rather than the doctrine that the inner self is veiled, mysterious, or inaccessible. His story hovers between thought and the world before it enters the world in words that are intended to be interpreted by others" (Stock, *Augustine the Reader*, p. 16). See also note 30 below.

[27]Compare Jacques Derrida, "Edmond Jabès and the Question of the Book," in *Writing and Difference*, trans. Alan Bass (Chicago: University of Chicago Press, 1978), pp. 64-78; where Derrida explores the thesis (in Jabès) that "in its representation of itself [in language] the subject is shattered and opened" (p. 67). With the advent of writing, "we have ceased hearing the voice from within the immediate proximity of the garden" (p. 68). For Jabès, speech (orality) represents immediacy, whereas writing represents a fall and disruption of immediacy. For Augustine, however, spoken words already signal a loss of immediacy; for him, it is not writing but language itself—indeed, the very order of signification—that signals a fall from immediacy. Augustine, then, is not a "phonocentrist," on Derrida's terms; rather, his theory of language stands very close to Derrida's as developed in *Of Grammatology* (see the abbreviations section for a full citation), where Derrida emphasizes that speech/orality already constitutes mediation and thus demands interpretation (see chapter four of this book). The most significant difference between Derrida and Augustine is that Augustine, as we will see below, posits a pre-embodied soul that knows *im*-mediately.

[28]Augustine *De Genesi contra Manichaeos libri II* 2.4.5 (in *Saint Augustine on Genesis*, FOTC 84, trans. Roland J. Teske, S.J. [Washington: Catholic University of America Press, 1991]).

[29]Ibid.; see also ibid., 2.5.6. Augustine emphasizes that it is the *soul* that sinned; "man" *(homo)*—as an embodied, temporal being—is a postlapsarian being. This will be considered in our reading of *Confessions* 12 (below). For further discussion, see Roland J. Teske, S.J., "The World-Soul and Time in St. Augustine," *Augustinian Studies* 14 (1983): 75-92.

[30]This also raises a question about the "authenticity" of intersubjectivity for Augustine: if language, which makes intersubjective communication possible, is the result of the soul's fall into the external world, would there have been any "dialogue" between souls before this fall? In other words, is the soul "before sin" only in relation to God, in "the secret place of conscience" *(De Genesi 2.5.6)*? Is the soul's "going public" with language (which is necessarily public) always already a compromise of its "private" relationship with God? Is it by language, for Augustine, that the "subject is shattered and opened" (cf. Derrida, "Edmond Jabès", p. 65)?

For a similar tension and problem, cp. Søren Kierkegaard, *Fear and Trembling*, trans. Howard V. Hong and Edna H. Hong (Princeton, N.J.: Princeton University Press, 1983), pp. 82-120. Abraham's challenge is to communicate in language (which is public and universal) the call of Yahweh (which is private and singular). For Kierkegaard, this is true of each individual's relation to God: as a unique and private relation with the absolute, it cannot be communicated in language *simpliciter.* The "solution" to this challenge is his notion of an "indirect communication" (developed in his *Philosophical Fragments* and *Concluding Unscientific Postscript*), which is strategically very similar to Augustine's understanding of "confession" (see *CSA* 10.2.2-10.3.4). For a discussion of Kierkegaard's strategy of "indirect communication," see James K. A. Smith, "Alterity, Transcendence and the Violence of the Concept: Kierkegaard and Heidegger," *International Philosophical Quarterly* 38 (1998).

[31]Augustine *De Genesi* 2.5.6. This is "tasted" in the ecstatic experience at Ostia, where the souls of Augustine and Monica "were lifted up by an ardent affection towards eternal being itself. . . . We touched it in some small degree [only to then return] to the noise of our human speech" (*CSA* 9.10.24). Reflecting on the possibilities of communication without language, Augustine suggests that in silence "we would hear his word, not through the tongue of the flesh, nor through the voice of an angel, nor through the sound of thunder, nor through the obscurity of a symbolic utterance. Him who in these things we love we would hear in person *without their mediation.* That is how it was when at that moment we extended our reach and in a flash of mental energy attained the eternal wisdom which abides beyond all things" (*CSA* 9.10.25, emphasis added).

[32]The temporal aspect of language and signs is not considered in Augustine's *De magistro* and appears in *De doctrina christiana* in only one respect: "Because words immediately pass away once they have agitated the air waves, and last no longer than the sound they make, [written] letters were invented as signs of words" (2.4.5). Here it is simply a question of the endurance of signs.

[33]"God made all of time along with all temporal creatures" (Augustine *De Genesi* 2.3.4).

[34]Compare also Augustine *De vera religione* (CCSL 32) 29.72: "Do not go abroad. Return within yourself. In the inward man dwells truth. If you find that you are by nature mutable, *transcend yourself*" (in *Augustine: Earlier Writings,* trans. J. H. S. Burleigh [Philadelphia: Westminster Press, 1953], emphasis added). As Hannah Arendt notes, "Thus it is not only the world, but human nature as such, that is transcended" (*Love and Saint Augustine,* trans. Joanna Vecchiarelli Scott and Judith Chelius Stark [Chicago: University of Chicago Press, 1996], p. 30).

[35]For Augustine, the most "primordial" sin is that of pride; thus, it is precisely because "it swelled out into external things through pride, [that] the soul ceased to be watered by the inner spring," requiring external language as a result (*De Genesi* 2.5.6).

[36]In Augustine's more allegorical readings of Genesis 1–2, he understands the creation narrative as describing the creation of the *intelligible* world ("in comparison with the 'heaven of heaven,' even the heaven of our earth is earth" *CSA* 12.1.2). Thus in *De Genesi* "heaven and earth" represent the intelligible world, and the "green of the field" represents the intellect (2.3.4). For an argument that the intellect in the "heaven of heaven" is the "world-soul," see Teske, "World-Soul and Time," pp. 75-92.

[37]*CSA* 12.9.9; cf. also 12.15.22: "it transcends all distention between past and

future."

[38]*CSA* 12.13.16. Here the soul's knowledge is akin to that of angels, who "have no need to look up to this firmament and read so as to know your word. They 'ever see your face' and there, without syllables requiring time to pronounce, they 'read' what your eternal will intends" (13.15.18).

[39]*CSA* 4.11.17. Note once again the notion of a "world-soul" that seems to be operating behind this concept of the soul's restraint. Compare *De vera religione* 22.43: "We have become parts of the ages *[saeculorum]* as a result of our condemnation." *Saeculorum* here carries the sense of "history," the ages of time (rather than J. H. S. Burleigh's "secular order").

[40]Augustine *De Genesi* 2.5.6: "When the soul was being watered by such a spring, it had not yet thrust forth its inmost parts through pride." Compare also his *De vera religione* 46.89: "Our real selves are not bodies" (see Teske, *Paradoxes of Time,* pp. 29-30).

[41]See also Robert J. O'Connell, S.J., *Saint Augustine's Platonism* (Villanova, Penn.: Augustinian Institute/Villanova University Press, 1984), pp. 3, 15; where he notes that for Augustine "our very presence in this temporal and bodily world [is] the result of a 'fall.'"

[42]Teske, *Paradoxes of Time,* pp. 31-32. Paul J. Archambault also notes that "time and language are treated as if they were the *fallen* parts of a universal whole"; thus the soul is "condemned to the use of discursive language" ("Augustine, Time and Autobiography as Language," *Augustinian Studies* 15 [1984]: 8). Archambault goes on to suggest, however, that "Augustine seems to have worked himself out of the dualistic dilemma that seemed to have been forced upon him . . . by his use of Platonic or Plotinian conception of time and language" (p. 11). The means of escape, he argues, is an "interior" language of the soul that remains unified and simultaneous (pp. 11-12). But we must note in response that this does nothing to redeem *speech* or language in its temporal sense. We must distinguish between two "kinds" of language in Augustine: an "interior" language of immediacy and an external language, which employs signs and functions within the horizon of time. While the former is "pure," the redemption *of* the latter is precisely a redemption *from* it. I will argue that it is precisely the "goodness" of temporal signification that ought to be affirmed by Augustine.

[43]In a very perceptive commentary on an earlier version of this chapter, which was presented to the American Catholic Philosophical Association, Ann Pang-White carefully noted the difference between my definition of finitude as "location in space and time" and Augustine's understanding of finitude. As she correctly emphasized, for Augustine, any being that is not the Creator (i.e., all *creatures*) is finite. However, this does not mean that they are located in space (e.g., angels) nor even temporality, as he suggests of the human soul "before sin." Thus the human soul before its fall is finite, though it is located in neither space (Augustine points to a "spiritual body") nor time; what distinguishes it from the Creator is mutability.

However, I retain my definition of finitude as location in space and time for two reasons: (1) I cannot imagine the state of a being that is *neither* eternal (in which case it would be God) *nor* temporal (as noted above, for Augustine, if human souls had not sinned, they would not be located in time). But Augustine seems to think there is a third alternative, which seems to me nonsensical. In addition, I would suggest that this could not be a consistent Christian position, since it would see human embodiment as the result of sin. (2) My ultimate concern here, in the context of a hermeneutical discussion, is with Augustine's account of language and interpretation, which, he says, is only necessary for embodied, temporal beings. My special thanks to Dr. Pang-White for her insightful and constructive criticisms.

[44]Teske, "World-Soul and Time," p. 92. Teske later thinks that the "solution" to this problem is found in book 12 of the *Confessions:* "Though time may have come into being with the creation of the world, we rational souls were meant to remain in contemplation of God as partakers of his eternity" (*Paradoxes of Time*, p. 58). However, as with the "solution" pointed to by Archambault, this still means that we fall into time and *bodily* existence. In sum, finitude—in the sense of temporal, bodily, physical existence—remains fallen. In this final section I will argue that Augustine, on his own terms, ought to affirm the goodness of finitude.

[45]Etienne Gilson, *The Spirit of Medieval Philosophy*, trans. A. H. C. Downes (New York: Scribner's, 1936), p. 113.

[46]Augustine *Soliloquies* 1.1.2.

[47]Augustine *De vera religione* 11.21.

[48]"A life, therefore, which by voluntary defect falls away from him who made it, whose essence it enjoyed, and, contrary to the law of God, seeks to enjoy bodily objects which God made to be inferior to it, tends to nothingness" (Augustine *De vera religione* 11.21). I do not have the space here to develop this further, though it is central to my deconstruction of Augustine. What is crucial for the development of an Augustinian affirmation of the goodness of finitude is a phenomenological analysis of the central *uti/frui distinction* in Augustine's work. "Sin" for Augustine is a matter of *intentio*—when the intentional aim is "absorbed" in a world of things, which it comes to *enjoy* (as an end in itself), rather than *use* (for the sake of . . . being pointed to the Creator). Then the world becomes an "idol," which *absorbs* the gaze of the soul, rather than an "icon," which *deflects* the soul's aim to its Origin, the Creator. The most important text in this regard is *De doctrina christiana*, book 1, but see also the *Soliloquies* and *De vera religione*. For further discussion, see my "Between Prediction and Silence: Augustine on How (Not) to Speak of God," *Heythrop Journal* 41 (2000): 66-86.

[49]Derrida himself emphasizes that a deconstructive reading is essentially productive, seizing upon the "*surprising* resources" within a text or corpus that are able to "produce" another text, which is related to the first but which is also different, new, an invention (*OG* 157-58).

[50]This rereading of the status of hermeneutics is not simply a piece of theological speculation about humanity "before the Fall." Rather, the goal of appreciating the "creational" nature of hermeneutics is an *ethical* one: once we appreciate that interpretation is part and parcel of being human, we will also appreciate the *plurality* of interpretation as a creational good rather than as a post-Babelian evil to be overcome. The result will be space and respect for difference.

Chapter 6: Interpretation in Eden

[1]That is, beings located in space and time. For a discussion, see chapter five, note 43.

[2]This visual metaphor, which I have attempted to avoid, does however indicate that

what I am describing as an "interpretive tradition" is very close to, if not identical with, what has usually been identified as a "worldview." As "visions *of* life *for* life" (James Olthuis), worldviews constitute the primary commitments through which one "sees" the world. At the level of worldview the "as-structure" of interpretation (Martin Heidegger) unfolds. For discussions, see James H. Olthuis, "On World-views," *Christian Scholar's Review* 14 (1985): 153-64; Brian J. Walsh, "Worldviews, Modernity and Task of Christian College Education," *Faculty Dialogue* 18 (fall 1992): 13-35; and part two of James K. A. Smith and Shane R. Cudney, "Postmodern Freedom and the Growth of Fundamentalism: Was the Grand Inquisitor Right?" *Studies in Religion/Sciences Religieuses* 25 (1996): 41-44.

[3]I use the more generic term here so as not to restrict interpretation to humans. Inasmuch as animals communicate, there would also be a process of interpretation. For instance, the bear "understands" that the claw marks on the tree are the mark of another bear and that they represent a boundary of another's territory. Or perhaps in a more sophisticated fashion (I am only speculating), the auditory communication between dolphins could be misinterpreted if the sound waves were "heard" differently.

[4]It should also be emphasized that this "situationality," or uniqueness, cannot be reduced to temporal and/or spatial locality. I am not just my time and space; there is a mystery to the uniqueness of the self that persists outside of these conditions.

[5]For Aristotle, to "be" is to have boundaries *(perai)*, to be situated and located in a place. But in addition, the boundaries are also points of contact, signaling the fundamental relationality of being. See Aristotle *Physics* 4.1-5, 208a27-213a11.

[6]This was more fully developed in chapter three. Compare also *TM* 302.

[7]Brian Stock (in *The Implications of Literacy: Written Language and Models of Interpretation in the Eleventh and Twelfth Centuries* [Princeton, N.J.: Princeton University Press, 1983]) seems to suggest that a gestural mode of being, as found in the enactment of the Eucharist for example, is free of interpretive structures and that the necessity of interpretation comes on the scene with the advent of writing and "literate theology."

[8]I first came across the notion of traditionality in Carroll Guen's essay "Gadamer, Objectivity and the Ontology of Belonging," *Dialogue* 28 (1989): 589-608 (esp. p. 597).

[9]I resist the notion of finitude as "limiting" for the same reasons that I reject any conception of finitude as ipso facto violent. To speak of finitude as "limiting" entails that it prevents access in some way or that it is "lacking" in some sense, which can only be said if we are somehow "expecting more." Rather than understanding finitude as a limitation or even as violent, I want to step outside of that paradigm and see it as enabling. However, any attempt to speak about finitude always risks "falling back" into a more metaphysically determined paradigm. I have taken up this question of violence in a more properly phenomenological context in two recent essays: "Respect and Donation: A Critique of Marion's Critique of Husserl," *American Catholic Philosophical Quarterly* 71 (1997): 523-38; and "Alterity, Transcendence and the Violence of the Concept: Kierkegaard and Heidegger," *International Philosophical Quarterly* 38 (1998): 369-81.

[10]See Mark C. Taylor, *Erring: A Postmodern A/Theology* (Chicago: University of Chi-

cago Press, 1984), pp. 170-74; following Friedrich Nietzsche, *The Will to Power*, trans. R. J. Hollingdale and Walter Kaufmann (New York: Random House, 1967), sec. 600: "No limit to the ways in which the world can be interpreted; every interpretation a symptom of growth or of decline. Inertia needs unity (monism); plurality of interpretations a sign of strength. Not to desire to deprive the world of its disturbing and enigmatic character!"

[11]David Hume, *An Enquiry Concerning Human Understanding*, ed. L. A. Selby-Bigge and P. H. Nidditch, 3rd ed. (Oxford: Oxford University Press, 1975), pp. 18-19.

[12]See, for example, Paul Ricoeur, *Oneself as Another*, trans. Kathleen Blamey (Chicago: University of Chicago Press, 1992), p. 299.

[13]Claude Geffre, *The Risk of Interpretation: On Being Faithful to the Christian Tradition in a Non-Christian Age*, trans. David Smith (New York: Paulist Press, 1987), p. 169. Ricoeur also speaks of "traditionality as cultural heritage" in *Oneself as Another*, p. 272.

[14]Thomas S. Kuhn, *The Structure of Scientific Revolutions*, 2nd ed. (Chicago: University of Chicago Press, 1970), p. 7.

[15]Ibid., pp. 5, 23.

[16]Ibid., p. 10.

[17]The heart of Kuhn's book is to explore the status of these paradigms and to understand how shifts occur. Briefly, he argues that science experiences a "paradigm shift" when the existing paradigm fails to explain an aspect of "reality" that confronts research, precipitating a crisis, which then gives birth to a new paradigm.

[18]Ibid., p. 35.

[19]Richard Lints jumped into the fray with "A Chasm of Difference: Understanding the Protestant and Roman Views of Salvation," published in the December 1994 issue of the popular journal *Tabletalk*. For other responses, see the entire issue and the document "Resolutions for Roman Catholic and Evangelical Dialogue" from Christians United for Reformation (CURE), reprinted in *Christian Renewal*, November 7, 1994, p. 12. It warrants mention here that the matters at stake in this book, though tackled within an academic discourse, find their origin and most explicit forms in *popular* arenas. While it is more difficult to find such explicit examples in philosophical and theological works, any who have lived and breathed within the evangelical community will readily identify the "interpretation of interpretation" that I have been attempting to describe here.

[20]For a classic essay, see Ernst Käsemann, "The Canon of the New Testament and the Unity of the Church," in *Essays on New Testament Themes* (London: SCM Press, 1964), pp. 95-107. See also F. F. Bruce, "Scripture and Tradition in the New Testament," in *Holy Book and Holy Tradition*, ed. F. F. Bruce and E. G. Rupp [Manchester: Manchester University Press, 1968). Bruce argues that the New Testament itself constitutes an interpretive tradition.

[21]Recognizing and seizing upon the traditionedness of interpretation, Cheryl Bridges Johns (following Walter Brueggemann) calls for a "legitimate sectarian hermeneutic" that not only recognizes the impact of tradition on interpretation but celebrates it as a way of owning our humanity and our tradition as a gift. See Johns, "The Adolescence of Pentecostalism: In Search of a Legitimate Sectarian Identity," *Pneuma: Journal of the Society for Pentecostal Studies* 17 (1995): 3-17.

[22]For a provocative discussion along these lines, see Philip Kenneson, "There's No

Such Thing as Objective Truth (And It's a Good Thing, Too)," in *Christian Apologetics in a Postmodern World,* ed. Timothy R. Phillips and Dennis L. Okholm (Downers Grove, Ill.: InterVarsity Press, 1995).

[23]Compare Tremper Longman III, "What I Mean by Historical-Grammatical Exegesis—Why I Am Not a Literalist," *Grace Theological Journal* 11 (1990): 150; where he remarks, "I must admit, though, that in reading some writers, and they are most often of the literal [dispensational] school, they communicate the impression that they can control the text. . . . I also suspect such a sentiment when scientific or legal analogies are used to describe the hermeneutic certainty, a good example being Johnson. Yes, I believe there are controls on interpretation (genre analysis being a good example), but none which allows us to say that I have arrived at a definitive, exhaustive understanding of the text which we can then prove to everyone beyond a shadow of a doubt. The *lack of such hermeneutical certainty* invites us to be open to challenge in our exegetical conclusions" (emphasis added).

[24]In the section "The Ethics of Interpretation" of this chapter, we will see that the limits to the "many truths" are ethical, rooted in love.

[25]I have discussed this further in my essay "Between Athens and Jerusalem, Freiburg and Rome: John Caputo as Christian Philosopher," *Paradigms* 10 (1995): 19-23.

[26]Søren Kierkegaard, *Philosophical Fragments/Johannes Climacus,* ed. and trans. Howard V. Hong and Edna H. Hong (Princeton, N.J.: Princeton University Press, 1985), p. 108.

[27]Ibid., p. 256.

[28]I would also point to Ricoeur's discussion of attestation in *Oneself as Another,* pp. 21-23.

[29]At the heart of this book lies a concern for the unity of the church and the ecumenical project. Among other *teloi,* this book has an ecclesial destination, based on the project's ecclesial origin (see the preface). What motivates this entire book is a concern with how the ecclesial community deals with interpretive difference and the plurality of interpretation within its "boundaries." By emphasizing the structural undecidability of interpretation, I am seeking to make space for interpretive difference. I have addressed these issues in more detail in "Fire from Heaven: The Hermeneutics of Heresy," *Journal of Theta Alpha Kappa* 20 (1996): 13-31.

[30]Given certain trends in contemporary thought, I am assuming that violence is an evil. The notion of "good violence" is, on this account, a contradiction in terms.

[31]Here we ought to note a distinction between *structure* and *direction:* the structures of creation (including hermeneutical structures) are fundamentally good; however, in a fallen, broken world they can take an evil or sinful direction or intention. This allows us to account for the way in which hermeneutics remains essentially (i.e., structurally) good but also potentially violent.

[32]John D. Caputo, *Radical Hermeneutics: Deconstruction, Repetition and the Hermeneutic Project* (Bloomington: Indiana University Press, 1987), pp. 272-79.

[33]Ibid., p. 279.

[34]John D. Caputo, *Against Ethics: Contributions to a Poetics of Obligation with Constant Reference to Deconstruction* (Bloomington: Indiana University Press, 1993), p. 245.

[35]John D. Caputo, "Hermeneutics and Faith: A Response to Professor Olthuis," *Christian Scholar's Review* 20 (1991): 170.

[36]On "lament" as the biblical response to evil, see especially J. Richard Middleton, "Why the 'Greater Good' Isn't a Defense: Classical Theodicy in Light of the Biblical Genre of Lament," *Koinonia* (1997); Paul Ricoeur, "Evil: A Challenge for Philosophy and Theology," in *Figuring the Sacred,* ed. Mark Wallace (Minneapolis: Fortress, 1995).

[37]This will be taken up once again in this chapter's final section with regards to a hermeneutics of trust and a hermeneutics of suspicion.

[38]Stanley Fish, *Is There a Text in This Class?* (Cambridge, Mass.: Harvard University Press, 1980), p. 350.

[39]That is, Nietzsche offered, truth may be a woman (*Beyond Good and Evil,* trans. W. Kaufmann [New York: Random House, 1966], p. 2). "Because if woman *is* truth," Derrida continues, "*she* knows that there is no truth, that truth does not take place, and that no one has it, the truth. She is woman insofar as she, for her part, does not believe in truth, thus in what she is, in what she is believed to be, which therefore she is not." (*Spurs: Nietzsche's Styles,* trans. Barbara Harlow [Chicago: University of Chicago Press, 1979], p. 53.) And as Caputo has reminded us, even a Christian like Johannes Climacus confessed this truth (*Radical Hermeneutics,* p. 189).

[40]Jean-François Lyotard takes up the question in a similar way in *The Differend: Phrases in Dispute,* trans. Georges Van Den Abbeele (Minneapolis: University of Minnesota Press, 1988). In many ways, his project is analogous to mine here, insofar as he is attempting to account for both plurality but also limits, in particular, limiting the discourse of revisionist historians who would deny the Holocaust (see sec. 5, pp. 4-5).

[41]For heuristic purposes, I will retain the terminology of "language games," though Lyotard later rejects such (*The Differend,* sec. 188). In *The Differend* the structure of the problem of legitimation remains basically the same; however, there the incommensurability is found between "genres" (sec. 218). For my purposes, what is later described as a "genre" is functionally the same as that earlier described as a "language game."

[42]There is a chain of terms that, for our purposes here, could be understood to be interchangeable. What I will describe as "worldviews" are basically or operatively equivalent to Kuhn's "paradigms" or Lyotard's "language games." All are locally and historically determined "frameworks" of *commitments*—closely linked to "culture"—that determine how one perceives and interprets the world. In this book, I am assuming this rather than arguing the case. For a more extensive discussion that does give an account of this, see James K. A. Smith, "The Art of Christian Atheism: Faith and Philosophy in Early Heidegger," *Faith and Philosophy* 14 (1997): 71-81. There I argue that these paradigms have a structurally religious nature, as H. Tristam Engelhardt also suggests: "When there are numerous unmediateable [i.e., incommensurate] senses of morality, rationality, and justice, each will have *a status analogous to a religious vision of the world;* each will depend on special premises not open to general rational justification" (Engelhardt, *Bioethics and Secular Humanism: The Search for a Common Morality* [Philadelphia: Trinity Press, 1991], p. xiii, emphasis added).

[43]Lyotard has never been faulted for excessive attention to precision; as such, what is sometimes referred to as "postmodern" (as in the *Postmodern Condition*) is in

other places described as "modern" in contrast to "classical" (as in *Just Gaming*); he notes that "what I mean is that anytime that we lack criteria, we are in modernity, wherever we may be, whether it be at the time of Augustine, Aristotle, or Pascal. The date does not matter" (*JG* 15).

⁴⁴This point is contested by Richard Rorty, who claims that while language games are incommensurate, they are not "unlearnable"; or, in other words, Rorty's position (and hope) is that no *differend* is a priori untranslatable—that every differend could be turned into a litigation (see Rorty, *Essays on Heidegger and Others*, Philosophical Papers, vol. 2 [Cambridge: Cambridge University Press, 1991], pp. 215-17). Apart from an interpretive disagreement I have with Rorty regarding Wittgenstein, I think Rorty also misses Lyotard's careful distinction between "languages" and "language games"; throughout this discussion, Rorty uses the two interchangeably. Lyotard is emphasizing (in a better reading of Wittgenstein, I think) that to change games is to change rules and hence to change criteria for evidence, and so on.

⁴⁵Lyotard, *The Differend*, p. 151.

⁴⁶Ibid., pp. 8, xi.

⁴⁷Ibid., p. 157.

⁴⁸For Lyotard, the simple *imposition* of a law without legitimation is "terror."

⁴⁹In volume two of his *New Critique of Theoretical Thought*, Herman Dooyeweerd deconstructs the contrast between "a priori" and "empirical" and the accompanying rending of the world into noumena and phenomena. Thus Dooyeweerd speaks of a structural horizon of human experience that is a priori, but not "in the Kantian sense of *non-empirical*." The result is what I have here called *empirical transcendentals*. See Dooyeweerd, *A New Critique of Theoretical Thought*, trans. David H. Freeman and H. De Jongste (Amsterdam: H. J. Paris, 1955), 2:546-50. Dooyeweerd's framework will be discussed further below. A similar notion is found in Emmanuel Levinas, which will also be discussed below.

⁵⁰It would be helpful, I think, to think about "authorial intent" within this phenomenological framework (though I cannot do so here). I would only suggest that for Edmund Husserl, the "intentions" of an author can never be present to me, as the text can. Rather, intentions, as *cogitationes* (thought processes) of another subject, are transcendent in such a way that they can never be present but only "appresented."

⁵¹Edward Farley, *Ecclesial Reflection: An Anatomy of Theological Method* (Philadelphia: Fortress, 1982), p. 188. Edith Wyschogrod's "carnal generalities" may be seen as analogous to this (*Saints and Postmodernism* [Chicago: University of Chicago Press, 1990], p. 50).

⁵²In Levinas, it is the "face" of the Other that is "before" interpretation and can never be captured in construal because it resists articulation. This ethical limit to interpretation will be taken up in the next section, "The Ethics of Interpretation."

⁵³Edmund Husserl, "das ist gegen Heidegger," bk. 1, pp. 30ff., in Leuven Archives, cited in Hubert Dreyfus and John Haugeland, "Husserl and Heidegger: Philosophy's Last Stand," in *Heidegger and Modern Philosophy*, ed. Michael Murray (New Haven, Conn.: Yale University Press, 1978), p. 233.

⁵⁴Edmund Husserl, *Ideas Pertaining to a Pure Phenomenology and to a Phenomenological Philosophy*, bk. 1 of *General Introduction to a Pure Phenomenology*, trans. F. Ker-

sten (The Hague: Martinus Nijhoff, 1983), sec. 24, pp. 44-45.

[55]Ibid., p. 35.

[56]Ibid., p. 44.

[57]Ibid.

[58]Caputo, *Radical Hermeneutics,* p. 43.

[59]Dooyeweerd, *New Critique,* 2:548. (I have eliminated some of the text's excessive italicizing.)

[60]Ibid.

[61]Ibid., p. 551.

[62]Ibid., p. 554. Dooyeweerd, despite all of this emphasis on structure, also notes that this horizon is "plastic" and part of a "continuous dynamic-structural coherence" (p. 558).

[63]Thus ibid., part 2, chap. 4, sec. 3 (pp. 565ff.) is entitled "The Perspective Structure of Truth" and is constituted largely by a critique of a correspondence theory of truth (in a manner almost identical to sec. 44 of *Being and Time*).

[64]Ibid., pp. 577-78.

[65]Ibid., p. 577.

[66]"Reality is *resistance,* or, more exactly, the character of resisting" (*BT* 252). Dooyeweerd also points to this "resistance" of the structural order in "Philosophy and Theology," pt. 3 of *In the Twilight of Western Thought: Studies in the Pretended Autonomy of Philosophical Thought,* series B, vol. 4 of *Collected Works,* ed. James K. A. Smith (Lewiston, N.Y.: Edwin Mellen, 1999). As I will suggest in the next section, following Levinas, this resistance marks the *ethical* limit of interpretation.

[67]Dooyeweerd is right to note that "it remains possible for [subjective insight] to misinterpret the a priori horizon of experience. In other words, the law-conformable structure is no guarantee for the correctness of our a priori subjective insight" (*New Critique,* 2:574). However, I would want to underscore that different interpretations do not constitute misinterpretations. Subjective insight, while opening space for misinterpretation, also opens space for a plurality of "true" interpretations by deconstructing the mono-logic of both a notion of immediacy and a correspondence theory of truth.

[68]Any interpretation that infringes on this structure of the world as given will become entangled "in internal antinomies at every infringement." Thus Dooyeweerd's standard of truth is not the principle of noncontradiction but rather the principle of exclusion of antinomies (ibid., p. 579).

[69]In the midst of adopting Levinas's account of the "ethics" of interpretation, I am at the same time questioning his own account of the violence of interpretation (vis-à-vis Husserl and Heidegger). However, my critique of Levinas on this point will appear elsewhere. For a first sketch, see my "Alterity, Transcendence and the Violence of the Concept," esp. sec. 1 and 4 ("The Ethics of the Concept").

[70]Jeffrey Dudiak has (tentatively) suggested the same in "Metaphsyical Assymetry: Levinas' Ethical Transcendental," which is forthcoming in his dissertation at the Free University of Amsterdam. My thanks to Jeff for sharing this with me and for his general assistance in my reading of Levinas.

[71]On the Real/Irreal distinction, see Edmund Husserl, *Ideas Pertaining to a Pure Phenomenology,* p. xx. It may be helpful to suggest that Husserl's Irreal phenomena would be analogous to what Aristotle would describe as being *'en logō,'* or "in

thought," or to what Aquinas describes as concepts of "second intention."

[72]I would suggest that Lyotard's "differend" functions in an analogous manner, as the suffering other that places limits on every game (*The Differend*, p. 13).

[73]This is the heart of Levinas's critique of Husserl's phenomenology: by reducing all intentional objects to Irreal phenomena, Husserl thereby eliminates all resistance, which means that the object is "delivered over" to the intention of the subject and becomes entirely "immanent" to consciousness; and thereby "the object's resistance as an exterior being vanishes" (*TI* 123-25). The Face, on the other hand, is precisely that which cannot be immanent to thought because of its Infinity.

[74]*De doctrina christiana* is *not* about "Christian doctrine" (as commonly translated) but rather, as Edmund Hill, O.P., translates, "Teaching Christianity." It is a book written for pastors: the first three books are devoted to interpretation of the text, and the last book is concerned with communication of that which is discovered, or preaching (a "Christian rhetoric").

[75]Augustine *De doctrina christiana* 1.5.5; 1.22.20. The essence of sin, for Augustine, is a kind of idolatry by which we enjoy what we ought to use; that is, we substitute the creature for the Creator (1.12.12).

[76]Ibid., 1.22.20.

[77]For a discussion, see Hannah Arendt, *Love and Saint Augustine*, part 1.

[78]*De doctrina christiana* 1.33.37.

[79]Ibid., 1.35.39.

[80]Ibid., 1.36.40.

[81]Ibid., 1.36.40-1.36.41.

[82]Ibid., 3.15.23; cf. 3.10.14.

[83]Compare the discussion of "undecidability" in the section that begins this chapter, "Human Be-ing and the Conditions of Hermeneutics."

[84]Patricia A. Sayre gives a helpful overview of some of these currents, particularly the predominance of suspicion in postmodern discourse. Suspicion and trust, she argues, are two different attitudes that one can choose in the face of contingency. In the end, she argues, as do I, that a Christian philosophy will be characterized by a primordial trust, though not one without suspicion. See Sayre, "The Dialectics of Trust and Suspicion," *Faith and Philosophy* 10 (1993): 567-84.

[85]My goal is not to construct a Pentecostal *biblical* hermeneutic (as per Gordon Fee, McLean, Menzies et al.). Rather my goal is to develop a Pentecostal *general* or *philosophical* hermeneutic (as a project within the equally scandalous endeavor of Christian philosophy). As such, my work stands closer to the proposal of Howard M. Ervin, who offers, in the name of Pentecostal hermeneutics, a "Pentecostal epistemology" (see Ervin, "Hermeneutics: A Pentecostal Option," *Pneuma: Journal of the Society for Pentecostal Studies* 3.2 [fall 1981]: 11-25). However, as will be seen, this pneumatic general hermeneutic is not limited to the province of Pentecostals.

[86]Thus what Derrida observes regarding Heidegger's relation to Trakl could also be said of Derrida's relation to Heidegger: "Statements like those I have just cited and translated . . . are obviously statements *of* Heidegger. Not his own, productions of the subject Martin Heidegger, but statements to which he subscribes apparently without the slightest reluctance. On the one hand, he opposes them to everything which he is in the process of opposing, and which forms a sufficiently determining context. On the other hand, he supports them in a discourse of which the least

one can say is that it does not bear even the trace of a reservation. It would thus be completely irrelevant to reduce these statements in ontological form to 'commentaries.' Nothing is more foreign to Heidegger than commentary in its ordinary sense" (OS 85).

[87] I think this passage (and a similar discussion in FL 5) marks something of a *Kehre* in the Derridean corpus. Indeed, it seems to me that what Derrida here offers regarding a primordiality of trust is precisely what Gadamer was pushing him toward in their encounter, at which time Derrida consistently sided with the "question," with suspicion. But as Gadamer noted, "Whoever opens his mouth wants to be understood; otherwise, one would neither speak nor write. And finally, I have an exceptionally good piece of evidence for this: Derrida directs questions to me and therefore he must assume that I am willing to understand them" (Gadamer, "Reply to Jacques Derrida," in *Dialogue and Deconstruction: The Gadamer-Derrida Encounter*, ed. Diane P. Michelfelder and Richard Palmer [Albany, N.Y.: SUNY Press, 1989], p. 55).

[88] Derrida describes this unseen as the "unbeseen" and the "absolutely invisible" in order to emphasize it is that which is radically heterogeneous to sight, which can never be seen. "To be the other of the visible, *absolute* invisibility must neither take place elsewhere nor constitute another visible" (MB 51). Structurally it is *the* invisible, the *tout autre* of sight.

[89] At this juncture, Heidegger once again fails to avoid speaking of the spirit, but here it is not *Geist* but rather the *pneuma hagion*, with explicit reference to "the miracle of Pentecost" (Heidegger, "The Nature of Language," in *On the Way to Language*, trans. Peter D. Hertz [New York: Harper & Row, 1971], pp. 96-97).

Author Index

Subject Index